TRUST DRAFTING FOR PARALEGALS

TRUST DRAFTING FOR PARALEGALS

Stephen Haas

EDUCATION DIRECTOR,
NATIONAL PARALEGAL COLLEGE

CAROLINA ACADEMIC PRESS
Durham, North Carolina

Library of Congress Cataloging-in-Publication Data

Haas, Stephen.
Trust drafting for paralegals / Stephen Haas.
    p. cm.
Includes index.
ISBN 978-1-59460-925-1 (alk. paper)
1. Trusts and trustees--United States. 2. Legal assistants--United States--
Handbooks, manuals, etc. I. Title.

KF730.H33 2011
346.7305'9--dc23

2011031380

CAROLINA ACADEMIC PRESS
700 Kent Street
Durham, North Carolina 27701
Telephone (919) 489-7486
Fax (919) 493-5668
www.cap-press.com

Printed in the United States of America

CONTENTS

Foreword

Preparing and drafting a trust for a client is akin to juggling, except that the balls that you are juggling are anything but uniform in size and shape. Perhaps it is more akin to juggling an apple, a sword and a torch. Legal professionals working on trusts must juggle a wide variety of factors, some of which are known to the client and some of which the client will not fully understand.

A client may want a trust based on one single overriding factor. But the legal professional must have the vision and patience to explore all of the legal consequences of any trust strategy.

From a tax perspective, the practitioner must take into account the income tax, capital gains tax, estate tax, gift tax and property tax ramifications of any trust strategy. The practitioner must also take into account the impact of any strategy on the government benefits eligibility of the client and the trust beneficiaries. Potential creditor access to trust assets is another key concern. These must all be considered apart from ensuring that the client's assets are eventually distributed in accordance with the client's wishes.

The goal of this book is to make the student aware of the myriad of factors that must be considered in the course of drafting a trust. The book will also walk the student through the basis of the laws that govern these issues. It is understood, however, that additional research may be required before the student becomes competent to draft trusts for real world clients.

This book has been written to be as practical as possible. Except where required for an understanding of the issue, theory and the theoretical basis for rules has been left out. Wherever appropriate, the concepts discussed have been reinforced with detailed examples. Actual trust provisions that have been used by the author have been provided as well. These have been provided to illustrate the points presented, but also to build the student's skill in using laws and concepts to draft practical trust provisions.

It is the author's intent that this book be viewed as a synchronous whole rather than merely the sum of its parts. For example, although chapter 7 deals with Medicaid trusts, it must be understood that while drafting Medicaid trusts, gift tax issues discussed in chapter 3, estate tax issues discussed in chapter 4, income tax issues discussed in chapter 5 and creditor protection issues discussed in chapter 6 may also be applicable. If this book were an instruction manual, I'd include as instruction 1: "Read everything before doing anything."

It is the author's hope that students will find the area of trust preparation as interesting and challenging as the author has in almost ten years of elder law and estate planning practice.

I welcome any and all questions or feedback. I can be contacted at my National Paralegal College phone number (800-371-6105 x104) or email address (shaas@nationalparalegal.edu).

ACKNOWLEDGMENTS

Although I am the only person listed as the author of this book, it was hardly a solo effort. I have many people to be thankful to for allowing and pushing me to complete this project.

First, I owe an enormous thank you to Anne Lewis, who worked so hard to edit many parts of this book and for giving me so many helpful suggestions regarding citations, additional materials, etc. When Anne started this project, she was my student at National Paralegal College. Now she is a staff member. Throughout, she has been nothing but a remarkable help to me in this effort. Thank you also to Bill Brannon, another NPC student, for helping to edit and find citations for this work.

Second, I want to thank William Mulkeen from Thomas Edison State College for suggesting, during a DETC site visit to National Paralegal College, that I write this book. Without his suggestion and his putting me in contact with several book publishers, this book would not exist.

Third, I want to thank Beth Hall from Carolina Academic Press for being so friendly and easy to work with and for giving me the guidance and suggestions that I needed, especially in the early going.

I owe a tremendous debt of gratitude to my parents, Manny and Susan Haas that cannot be expressed by words. I have worked with my father in the fields of estate planning and elder law for many years and he taught me so much of what has gone into this book.

Next, a huge thank you to Avi Katz, my supervisor at National Paralegal College, for encouraging me to go through with this project even with the understanding that it had to borrow some of my focus from the school.

Last, but certainly not least, thank you from the bottom of my heart to my dear wife, Melissa, for her consistent support and understanding. And thank you as well to our three children, Naomi, Michelle and Daniel, for letting Daddy work in peace (sometimes). For being so understanding on all those boring weekends when Daddy was cooped up in his office and unable to do anything fun with you, thank you!

Trust Drafting for Paralegals

CHAPTER 1

WHAT IS A TRUST?

A trust, at its most basic form, is simply an arrangement whereby one party holds property for the benefit of another party. The complexities of different forms of trusts that exist are almost limitless, but all trusts boil down to this simple arrangement. Although most trusts are formed through the execution of a written agreement, a trust arrangement can sometimes be oral (or implied) as well.

Parties to a Trust

There are three parties involved in the formation of every trust. The person who establishes the trust (and usually, the person who funds it as well) is the *grantor* (or the "settlor"). The person to whom the trust property is entrusted is the *trustee*. The person for whose benefit the trust property is being held is the *trust beneficiary*.

A trust arrangement splits title (i.e., ownership) of the property. Legal title to the trust property belongs to the trustee. The trustee thus has the legal power to act with respect to the trust property. For example, if a trust transfers real property, the trustee would sign the deed as the seller.

The beneficial (or "equitable") ownership in a trust belongs to the beneficiary. Although the beneficiary has no direct control over the trust assets, the property is being held for his or her benefit. The beneficiary's interest in the trust is enforceable by law against the trustee or other parties. The beneficiary need not be (and generally is not) a party to the initial trust agreement.

> *Example: Bert gives Ernie $5,000 to hold for Bert's daughter, Sarah. Under the agreement between Bert and Ernie (called "The Sarah Trust," for example), Ernie is to spend the money for Sarah's education in the manner that he deems most beneficial to Sarah. In this case, Bert is the grantor, Ernie is the trustee and Sarah is the beneficiary. Ernie has legal title to the $5,000. If the money is held in a bank*

account, he would sign as the account holder. The account would likely be titled as "The Sarah Trust, Ernie, as trustee." Furthermore, if Ernie loses or wastes the $5,000 through his negligence or misconduct, Sarah could maintain an action against him for damages.[1]

These parties need not be individuals. There may be multiple grantors, trustees and/or beneficiaries to a trust. Entities such as partnerships, corporations and other trusts can also serve any of these roles. In addition, one party may serve a dual role as grantor and trustee, grantor and beneficiary or trustee and beneficiary. In fact it is possible for one party to partially assume all three roles in a trust arrangement.

> ***Example:*** *Claude and Claudette Walker (who are spouses) establish* The Walker Family Trust. *They name their daughter, Terri Walker, as trustee. Under the trust agreement, Claude and Claudette are to receive all of the interest and other income generated by the trust for the rest of their lives. After their deaths the trust assets are to be distributed to the Walkers' children, Terri, Shane and Molly, in equal shares. Claude and Claudette are both grantors and (lifetime) beneficiaries of the trust. Terri is both the trustee and a beneficiary (or a remainder interest). Shane and Molly are merely beneficiaries.*

The only exception to this principle is that the same person cannot be both sole trustee and sole beneficiary. If that occurs, the legal interest of the trustee in the trust property and the beneficial interest owned by the same person "merge." The trust is thus extinguished and the entire ownership interest in the trust vests in the trustee/beneficiary.[2]

> ***Example:*** *Doug establishes a trust with Donna as trustee. The trust terms dictate that Donna may spend trust assets on her own behalf to whatever extent she deems necessary. After Doug's death the trust assets will go to Donna. Donna has the sole legal interest (as trustee) and is the sole beneficiary. Therefore, those interests "merge" and the trust terminates. The complete ownership interest vests immediately in Donna outright.*

---

1. *See, e.g.,* Shriners' Hospitals for Crippled Children v. Gardiner, 733 P.2d 1110 (Ariz. 1987).

2. *See* In re A Successor Trustee of the Trust of Edward L'e, 1 A.D.2d 695 (2d Dept. 1955).

Trust Formation

Although oral trust arrangements are theoretically possible, it is difficult to imagine the circumstances under which a practitioner would advise a client to establish an oral trust agreement. Some states, in fact, require that trust agreements be in writing to be valid.[3] Thus, although we will briefly look at trusts that are established without a written agreement, we will generally confine our discussion to written trust agreements.

Trust agreements can often be long and complex documents with many complicated provisions. However, all trusts are required to have at a minimum, the following elements:[4]

Identification of All Three Parties to the Trust: The Grantor, Trustee and Beneficiary

The grantor(s) and the trustee(s) must be identified outright. However, the beneficiary or beneficiaries may be identified as a class of people (e.g., "the children of the grantor"). In fact, a trust can (and often does) list a class of beneficiaries whose membership may change.

> *Example:* The XYZ Trust *states "The trustee may make distributions of income or principal from XYZ trust to or on behalf of any child or grandchild of the grantor, for the health, education, maintenance or support of any such beneficiary." Even though this is a class of people that could be expanded if the grantor has more grandchildren, the beneficiary designation is valid.*

Identification of Trust Res

A trust cannot exist without owning any assets. A trust must therefore be funded with something at the time of its formation. In practice, however, this can be accomplished with a minimal initial contribution. The grantor can later contribute assets to the trust at his or her leisure. Absent any provision to the contrary, any other person may also contribute asset to the trust, subject to acceptance of such asset by the trustee.

---

3. *See, e.g.,* N.Y. E.P.T.L. §7-1.17.
4. *See* In re Estate of Fontanella, 33 A.D.2d 29 (N.Y. App. Div. 3d Dep't 1969).

Because many trusts are not actually funded until weeks or months after their formation, it is important to fund the trust with something at the outset. A typical trust funding provision may read something like this:

> The grantor hereby transfers to the trustee the sum of ten dollars ($10) in cash to the trustee to be held in accordance with the provisions hereunder. Any party may contribute assets to the trust, provided, however, that the trustee may reject any contribution to this trust in the event that the trustee deems it to be against the best interest of the trust to accept such contribution.

Signature of the Grantor and Trustee

In addition to the basic signature requirement, some states require that the signatures on trust agreements be notarized and/or witnessed by two witnesses.[5] It is important to know the requirements of your jurisdiction in this regard. People named in the agreement as successor (backup) trustees and trust beneficiaries need not sign the trust agreement. In fact, they need not necessarily even know of the trust's existence.

Trust without the Writing

As discussed above, in some jurisdictions, trust agreements can be made orally.[6] In addition, there are other ways in which trusts can be created and/or inferred by a court even in the absence of a trust agreement, written or oral. Various doctrines have been developed in the case law of various states under which courts can do such to prevent injustice. These include the doctrines of implied trusts, constructive trusts, resulting trusts, secret trusts, semi-secret trusts, etc.

Although a discussion of these doctrines and the nuances that separate them is beyond the scope of this text, it will suffice to note that these devices have all been developed to enable courts to remedy unfair situations that occur because of a defect in the structure of a trust or some similar problem.

> *Example: Mike and Carol wanted to purchase a residence in 1990 for $250,000. Because they did not have enough money to purchase the*

---

5. *See, e.g.,* N.Y. E.P.T.L. §7-1.17
6. *See* Hartkopf v. Hesse, 49 N.Y.S.2d 162 (N.Y. Sup. Ct. 1944).

house, their son, Bobby, agreed to pay $125,000 toward the purchase price in exchange for one-half ownership in the property. When the house was purchased, the deed stated that the buyers were "Mike and Carol, husband and wife as to a combined one-half interest, and Bobby, as to a one-half interest."

In 1995, Mike and Carol wanted to take out a mortgage loan, to be secured by the house. To allow Mike and Carol to receive favorable owner-occupied rates, Bobby conveyed his one-half interest in the house to Mike and Carol, with the understanding that one-half of the house "really" belonged to Bobby.

Mike died in 2008 and Carol died later, in 2011. During the administration of Carol's estate, Bobby claims that he should be entitled to one-half of the house, apart from whatever his share would be under Carol's Will. Although under the 1995 deed, the entire house belonged to Carol, a court may judicially create a "constructive trust" (or "implied trust" depending on the jurisdiction). The court may rule that even though no agreement was signed, Mike and Carol were really holding one-half of the property for Bobby. Thus, it may award one-half of the house to Bobby.

Practice Tip: Look into the possibility of arguing that an implied or constructive trust has been formed whenever a client complains that his or her parents/children/friend was "really" holding his or her assets and that the client now wants these assets back. Furthermore, this technique may sometimes be used to argue that the portion of the property so held should not be considered part of the taxable estate of the deceased parent.

Types of Trusts

Revocable Trusts

The most basic type of trust that exists is the revocable trust. That is not to say that revocable trusts cannot have complex provisions. Revocable trusts can be as or more complex than irrevocable trusts. However, the revocable trust is considered basic because the consequences of establishing and funding a revocable trust are generally, by definition, reversible. Aside from time, legal fees and related expenses, there is little risk in establishing and funding an revocable trust.

As the name implies, revocable trusts can be revoked by the grantor(s). They can also generally be altered or modified in any way by the grantor.

The key advantage of the revocable trust is its flexibility in that it can be modified or rescinded by the grantor at any time. On the other hand, revocable trusts do not achieve most of the estate planning goals that are the focus of trust practice. For example, transferring assets to a revocable trust does little or nothing to protect those assets from claims of creditors. In addition, assets in a revocable trust are treated as the grantor's for purposes of calculating the grantor's eligibility for government benefits and in calculating the grantor's taxable estate upon his or her death.[7]

> **Example:** *Marianne creates* The Marianne Family Revocable Trust. *Marianne transfers $100,000 to the trust. If Marianne is later sued, this $100,000 will be vulnerable to a judgment just as would be the rest of her assets. In addition, the $100,000 would be considered an "available resource" that may disqualify her from being eligible for certain government assistance programs (such as Medicaid). Furthermore, if Maryanne dies, the entire $100,000 is considered part of her taxable estate.*

The main function of a revocable trust is to act as a "will substitute." That is, the revocable trust allows the grantor to retain functional control over the trust assets during his or her lifetime. Upon the grantor's death, the trust assets are distributed in accordance with the trust's instructions. The trust can also create subtrusts upon the death of the grantor just as a will can create testamentary trusts (discussed later in this chapter).

The most common strategy is to have the grantor serve as initial trustee (or make both spouses the trustees of a revocable trust established by one spouse) during the grantor's lifetime, or as long as the grantor is competent. A different person, such as the grantor's child, friend or sibling, can be named as the successor trustee in the event that the grantor is unable to continue serving as trustee.

Advantages of a Revocable Trust over a Will

1) Probate Avoidance

Unlike assets that pass through a will, trust assets pass to the beneficiaries without the necessity for a probate proceeding.

---

7. *See* Lurie v. Comm'r, 425 F.3d 1021 (7th Cir. 2005).

When a person dies, a probate proceeding is usually required so that an administrator of the person's estate (often called an "executor" when designated by a will) can be appointed by a court (typically a "probate" court or "surrogate's" court) and vested with the authority to collect and distribute trust assets.

However, there is only a need for probate when assets are titled in the name of the deceased. Banks and brokerage firms will not allow an heir or administrator to access such assets without court approval. However, assets not held in the decedent's name, such as those already in a trust at the time of the decedent's death, need not be re-titled. The trustee can simply distribute or continue to hold the trust assets in accordance with the trust instrument. There is no need to obtain permission from a court to administer assets in an existing trust. Therefore, a probate proceeding can be avoided.

This is especially important where the client owns interests in real property in multiple states. Probate proceedings would be required in all states in which the property resides were the properties titled in the decedent's name alone. Placing such assets into a revocable trust would avoid this necessity.

2) Disability Planning

A comprehensive estate plan includes a mechanism whereby a person's assets can be administered in the event that the person is unable to manage his or her own affairs because of a temporary or permanent disability. The most common method by which to accomplish this is through a power of attorney. This document vests a person (usually a relative or friend) with the authority to manage the disabled person's assets immediately (a general "durable" power of attorney) or upon the principal becoming disabled (a "springing" power of attorney).[8]

However, even properly executed powers of attorney are not always sufficient to allow a designee to manage one's assets. First, some banks require their own power of attorney forms to allow access to a non-account holder, and will not accept a generic power of attorney form. Second, certain types of transactions, such as real estate sales, are much more difficult to do through power of attorney, as title companies are sometimes reluctant to issue title insurance for a sale being carried out through power of attorney.

Conversely, transactions regarding assets in a trust can usually be carried out with relative ease by the trustee of the trust. Consent of the disabled per-

---

8. *See* Geren v. Geren, 29 Kan. App. 2d 565 (Kan. Ct. App. 2001).

son and/or reliance on a power of attorney form is not required. The trustee has the authority to act on his or her own accord on behalf of the trust. The trustee has substantially more freedom and authority to act on behalf of the trust than he or she would have to act on behalf of the client under a power of attorney.

Revocable trusts often have provisions that allow a successor trustee to control trust assets in the event of a disability of the grantor. A sample trust provision directing such might read:

> In the event that, in the judgment of the successor trustee, the grantor is unable to manage his own affairs due to incapacity for whatever reason and for whatever duration, the successor trustee is empowered and authorized to assume management of the trust assets as trustee and to assume all authorities held by the grantor hereunder on behalf of the incapacitated grantor.

Disadvantage of a Revocable Trust as Compared to a Will

The disadvantage of the revocable trust strategy is the cost and inconvenience of establishing, funding and administering it. A will can simply be drafted, executed, filed away and forgotten about until the testator decides to amend it or dies. A trust, on the other hand, to be effective, requires that the grantor fund it with his or her assets.

For real estate, this is accomplished by deed. For accounts at banks, brokerage firms and other financial institutions, the accounts will have to be re-titled in the name of the trust. In many cases, financial institutions require that a new account be opened in the name of the trust and the assets transferred to the new account.

Obviously, this adds time, complexity and expense to the process of enacting an estate plan. It may also make future transactions more complex as banks may require opinions of counsel letters and/or similar documents to ensure that the right person is controlling the trust account. In fact, if a client has a wide variety of accounts at different financial institutions, that might make it impractical to use the revocable trust as an estate planning device.

Practice Tip: Practitioners must encourage clients to ensure that all of his or her assets and accounts are transferred to his or her revocable trust. Otherwise, if assets remain in the client's name, a probate proceeding may have to be brought after the client's death after all, thereby negating one of the key advantages of the trust. The responsibility of completing the funding of the trust needs to be discussed at the outset. The client may wish to take care of it himself or may agree to pay extra to have the law firm handle it. But it is the practitioner's responsibility to either complete the transfers or ensure that the client understands that he or she needs to do so.

It should be noted however, that assets with designated beneficiaries, such as life insurance policies, individual retirement accounts and 401(k) accounts, avoid probate by their nature and so need not be transferred to the revocable trust.

Irrevocable Living Trust

Most trusts that we will discuss in this text are irrevocable living trusts. These trusts, like revocable trusts, are created while the grantor is alive. The distinction is that irrevocable trusts cannot be revoked and generally cannot be modified by the grantor. Sole power over an irrevocable trust lies with the trustee.

It is, however, possible for the grantor to retain some control over the trust assets. Whether this is wise depends on the goals of the trust.

> *Example: Derek establishes the* DEF *Irrevocable Trust, with Erica as trustee. The trust names Frank, Fanny and Freddie as ultimate beneficiaries of the trust. However, the trust provides that Derek may decide to add any of his children and/or grandchildren as additional beneficiaries of the trust. Although Derek retains some control over the trust, the trust is still considered irrevocable.*

There are many types of provisions that can and should be used in irrevocable trusts. These provisions and their effects are the central focus of this text. As a threshold matter, however, the student should become familiar with certain trust archetypes and their basic functions.

Testamentary Trusts

A testamentary trust is a trust that is established by a will. Unlike a living trust, this trust is not established immediately. Rather, it comes into existence after the death of the grantor (or, more precisely, the "testator" since we are dealing with a will). The trust is not funded until after the death of the testator.

The types and functions of a testamentary trust are almost limitless. However, we will briefly discuss some of the most important types of testamentary trusts below and later in this text.

Marital Trust

A marital trust is a trust that benefits the grantor's spouse that seeks to take advantage of the rule that gifts to spouses pass free of gift or estate tax. Gifts to a marital trust are eligible for the estate tax martial deduction as long as the trust meets the criteria discussed in chapter 4. The main criterion is that the marital trust is for the exclusive benefit of the other spouse as long as he or she lives. Typically, a marital trust will be established by a will (though a living marital trust is certainly also possible). Such a will would provide that any amount that could not pass to other heirs (or other trusts) free of estate tax would be held for the benefit of a surviving spouse in a marital trust. In this way, that amount would pass free from federal and state estate tax.

Credit Shelter Trust

A credit shelter trust is a device that is often used to take advantage of both spouses' estate tax deductions. It is a trust that is set up in a will or living trust to take effect upon the death of the first spouse. The trust provision often provides at least some benefit to the surviving spouse during his or her lifetime and may be distributed to the client's children after the surviving spouse's death. This device is further discussed in chapter 4.

Minors' Trusts

For obvious reasons, it is usually impractical and unwise to leave large amounts of money to minor children. Therefore, many wills establish trusts for the benefit of minor beneficiaries. Instead of these minor beneficiaries receiving their shares outright, the shares are held in trust for their benefit. The executor or a separately named trustee may control the assets on behalf of the minor until adulthood or until the minor reaches a specific age.

These trusts often offer broad discretion to the trustee in terms of how to spend the trust resources on behalf of the minor. The main point is to ensure that a minor beneficiary will not be able to waste the assets earmarked for him or her.

A typical will provision for the creation of minors' trust may read something akin to as follows:

> If any of my Estate principal or income, or any Trust principal or income, shall vest in absolute ownership in a minor, my Executor and/or Trustee shall have the authority, in their discretion, and without court authorization, to hold and manage the property in a separate trust and to

defer payment or distribution of all or a part of the property to that minor until that minor reaches the age of twenty-one (21) years. During the time that this trust is in operation, the trustee may distribute part or all of the minor's property to a custodian for the minor under the Uniform Gifts To Minors Act or the Uniform Transfers To Minors Act of the jurisdiction where the minor resides. In addition, the trustee may distribute or pay part or all of the minor's property to the minor's legal guardian, to the adult person or persons with whom the minor resides, to the minor personally, to the trustee of any trust created for the sole benefit of the minor, or to the administrator or executor of the minor's estate. The trustee may also apply part or all of the minor's property in this trust for the minor's health, education, support or maintenance costs.

In fact, many clients do not wish their children to receive their distributions outright until they are significantly older than 21. In such event, a child's assets may be held in trust until the child reaches some other age dictated by the client. Distributions to the children may also be staggered so that the children receive their shares in stages, rather than all at once. Examples of such trusts for the benefit of minors are provided in chapter 2.

Trusts That Can Hold S Corporation Stock

Many clients of any estate planning firm will hold stock in one or more Subchapter S corporations. The "S Corp," as it is known, can be an excellent business form, especially for small businesses, because it combines limited liability for shareholders with "pass through" taxation status.[9] However, ownership of S Corp shares does pose potential challenges when it comes to estate planning.

Under federal tax law, among other limitations on S Corp shareholder, only individuals may hold stock in an S Corp. LLCs, other corporation and most trusts may not be shareholders of an S Corp.[10] Obviously, this makes it difficult for clients who wish to place substantially all of their assets into trust for estate planning purposes but who are shareholders of S corporations.

Example: Donna and her partner, Emma, started "DE Ice Cream Shoppes, Inc." in 1987. The company has been operating as an S Corp for 24 years. Donna, now 68 years old, comes to your office to do some estate planning. Your office would like to recommend that Donna place her assets into a trust. However, great care must be taken before plac-

---

9. *See* 26 U.S.C. § 1361.
10. 26 U.S.C. § 1361(b).

ing her S Corp shares into a trust; as placing the shares into the wrong type of trust may cause the corporation to lose its S Corp status and revert to being treated as a regular corporation.

There are three basic types of trusts that can safely hold S corporation shares:

1) Grantor Trusts

A "grantor trust" is a trust that is treated, for income tax purposes, as being owned entirely by the grantor. The provisions that determine whether a trust is a grantor trust and the pros and cons of grantor trusts are discussed in more detail in chapter 5. For our purposes, it is sufficient to note that grantor trusts may hold S corporation stock since the income tax rules consider grantor trust assets as being held by the grantor. Because the grantor trust income is treated as the grantor's personal income, the S corporation shares are considered as though they are owned by an individual.[11]

Since revocable trusts are, by definition, grantor trusts, revocable trusts may also hold S Corp stock.

However, it is important to note that, while grantor trusts can hold S Corp stock during the grantor's lifetime, after the grantor dies, the trust loses its status as a grantor trust. Therefore, if a grantor trust will hold S Corp, stock and the trust provisions do not call for the trust assets to be distributed immediately upon the death of the grantor, a provision should be put into the trust that allows the trustee to ensure that the trust fits into one of the other categories of trust that can hold S Corp stock (discussed below). A typical trust provision to this effect might read as follows:

> Upon the death of the grantor, the trustee is hereby authorized to set aside any Subchapter S corporation shares that are held by the trust and to hold such shares as separate subtrusts for the benefit of each beneficiary in a manner that would qualify such subtrusts as Qualified Subchapter S Trusts (QSST) under Section 1361(d)(3) of the Internal Revenue Code and/or any other applicable law.

2) Qualified Subchapter S Trusts

A Qualified Subchapter S Trust ("QSST") is a creation of the Internal Revenue Code as an exception to the rule that trusts may not hold S corporation shares. A QSST has only one income beneficiary, who must receive all of the

---

11. 26 U.S.C. §1361(c)(2)(A)(i).

income of the trust. Because there is a sole income beneficiary, the Code considers it as though the shareholder is an individual.

The formal requirements of a QSST are:

1. There can be only one beneficiary of the trust and he or she must be a US citizen or resident (US citizenship or residency is a requirement for all S Corp shareholders).

2. All income of the trust is required to be distributed at least annually to the one beneficiary.

3. If any principal is distributed from the trust (and the discretion as to whether to do so can be left to the trustee), the principal must go to the one beneficiary.

4. The beneficiary's income interest must terminate at the earlier of the beneficiary's death or trust's termination.

5. An election to be treated as an eligible S corporation shareholder must be filed by the trust.[12]

If a QSST, for whatever reason, loses its eligibility to be an S Corp shareholder (e.g., the beneficiary who is a non-US citizen leaves the US, thereby becoming no longer a US resident), the corporation could lose its status as an S Corp. However, if a person (or grantor trust) dies while holding S Corp stock, the executor or trustee who is administering the shares will have two years to establish a QSST to hold the S Corp shares belonging to the estate or trust.[13]

Practice Tip: If a client wishes to put S Corp shares into a trust, the simplest strategy is to simply cause the trust to be considered a grantor trust as long as the client is alive. A QSST requires a splitting of the trust into shares (or subtrusts) for each beneficiary. This increases complexity and decreases flexibility and is unlikely to appeal to most clients.

---

3) Electing Small Business Trusts

The Electing Small Business Trust ("ESBT") is another exception to the individual shareholder of an S Corp rule that is created by statute. The ESBT is similar to the QSST, but is much more flexible. While the QSST may have only one income beneficiary, the ESBT may have multiple beneficiaries. Furthermore,

---

12. 26 U.S.C. §1361(d)(3).
13. 26 U.S.C. §1361(c)(2)(A)(ii).

while all income of a QSST must be distributed to the lone beneficiary, the ESBT's income may be distributed to any combination of beneficiaries or may even be held by the trust from year to year.[14]

The bad news, as far as the ESBT is concerned, is that ESBT income is taxed at a very high rate. The ordinary income of an ESBT is taxed at the highest marginal income tax rate for individuals (35%, as of 2011).[15] In addition, the Code imposes other harsh tax rules on the ESBT, including the lack of any automatic income tax "exemptions" that other trusts enjoy and a higher long term capital gains rate.[16] These elevated tax rates apply even to income that is distributed to beneficiaries in lower marginal tax brackets.

Practice Tip: In spite of its flexibility, it is uncommon for the ESBT to be the best manner in which to hold S Corp shares that are expected to generate significant income. Clients are almost invariably nonplussed when confronted with the idea of paying the highest income tax rate for all trust income. The QSST is usually a better option from an income tax perspective. The ESBT may be a better option, however, for businesses that do not generate income, such as those that generate only enough cash flow to pay expenses and salaries.

Review Questions

1) Which three parties are required as part of any trust agreement?

2) When would the doctrine of "merger" apply to extinguish a trust?

3) When will courts typically seek to infer the existence of a trust absent a written document?

4) Why is a revocable trust an ineffective tool in protecting the client from potential creditors?

5) What is the major advantage of a revocable trust over a will?

6) Why would a client choose to opt for a will rather than to execute a revocable trust?

7) What is the difference between a living trust and a testamentary trust?

---

14. 26 U.S.C. §1361(e).
15. 26 U.S.C. §641(c)(2).
16. Id.

8) What aspect of the law are marital trusts and credit shelter trusts most focused on achieving?

9) What is the ultimate purpose of a minor's trust?

10) Why do S corporation shareholders present particular challenges to the estate planning process?

11) What is a "grantor trust"?

12) Why is a grantor trust eligible to hold shares of an S corporation?

13) Name one major disadvantage of establishing a "Qualified Subchapter S Trust" (QSST) to hold clients' S corporation stock.

14) Name one significant advantage of an "Electing Small Business Trust" (ESBT) over a QSST.

15) Name one significant disadvantage of an ESBT.

CHAPTER 2

Trust Administration and Distribution

Trust Administration Decisions

Trust agreements almost always dictate how the trust assets are to be maintained and distributed. Although default rules exist, they are hardly worth dwelling on as the author can hardly imagine a scenario in which a legal professional would draft a trust that does not dictate how the trust assets are to be distributed.

In addition, trusts may also (although often do not) specify how the trust assets are to be maintained during the trust's existence.

> *Example: David is 75 years old and wishes to establish a Medicaid planning trust for the benefit of his children. He appoints his daughter, Patricia, as trustee. However, as David has been a conservative investor all of his life and is intent on ensuring that his assets are not lost before they can be distributed to his children, he asks that a provision such as the following be drafted into the trust:*

> *During the lifetime of the grantor, the trustee shall maintain and administer all trust assets. During that time, the trustee may invest trust assets at her discretion. However, the trustee is instructed to invest trust assets in a manner that provides reasonable certainty that the trust corpus will be preserved for the eventual benefit of the beneficiaries. The trustee shall not unnecessarily risk trust corpus by investing in speculative or risky investments.*

The trust may even direct the specific types of investments that may be used by the trustee. For example, the trust may direct that the trust invest only in bank accounts, certificates of deposit and money market funds. The grantor may, in fact, maintain the power to direct trust investments without unduly risking the trust purposes, as long as the drafter of the trust is careful to avoid giving the grantor any pecuniary benefit from the trust.

However, as most grantors wish to allow the trustee flexibility to invest trust assets in a manner that would best serve the trust at any given time, such intense restriction of the trustee is uncommon.

The decision as to for what purposes the trustee may distribute assets must take into account, at a minimum, the following two key factors:

1) The wishes of the grantor as to how and when the trust assets should be distributed; and
2) The impact of this discretion on other important legal issues; such as estate tax, creditor protection and eligibility for government benefits.

The latter factor is an important thread throughout this book. The former, however, is largely based on the preferences and goals of the individual client.

There are a variety of factors that clients may consider when considering a distribution plan. Some clients' preferences are so common that little change will be required from your firm's standard trust templates. Some plans will require a considerable amount of creativity in drafting. As a general principle, law firms should try to accommodate any distribution plan desired by the client. However, it is also the job of a legal professional to ensure that the distribution plan does not interfere with other purposes of the trust.

> **Example:** *Mickey and Minnie, a married couple, come to your office seeking a Medicaid planning trust that would allow them to transfer their property so as to become eligible for Medicaid assistance. They are willing to give substantially all of the assets to a trust for the benefit of their children with Donald as trustee. However, they insist that Donald have the discretion to distribute assets to them in the event that they need to live off of them. As a knowledgeable elder law practitioner, you realize that such discretion would defeat the purpose of a Medicaid planning trust since this discretion on Donald's part would cause the entire trust to be considered an "available resource" to Mickey and Minnie for purposes of Medicaid eligibility. As much as you have a responsibility to fulfill the wishes of your client, you also have a responsibility to inform your clients that their strategy would be ineffective for its underlying purpose.*

Trust Distribution Provisions

Each trust should spell out its own rules for distributions during its existence. Although the possibilities for such allowable distributions are virtually limitless, some of the more common distribution plans will be discussed below.

One note on terminology: The term "grantor," as it appears in this book, generally refers to the person who established the trust. However, this is not the legally operative definition. If a person gifts assets to a trust, even if he or she did not establish the trust in the first place, that person is considered the grantor with regard to the assets that he or she contributed.

Example 1: Mom and Dad establish the Family Irrevocable Trust. *They initially fund the trust with a $100,000 gift. Two years later, Grandma gifts a vacation home to the trust. Grandma is considered the trust grantor with respect to the vacation home even though Grandma did not establish the trust.*

Example 2: Mom and Dad establish the Family Irrevocable Trust *for the benefit of their children. They initially fund the trust with a $100,000 gift. Two years later, Grandma gifts $50,000 to the trust. Grandma is considered the trust grantor with respect to the $50,000. Since money is fungible and cannot be properly traced, especially if all of the trust assets are invested together, it may be difficult to track and calculate the extent to which Mom, Dad and Grandma will be considered grantors of the trust. It is possible that all three will be subject to the disadvantages of being the grantor. Therefore, the best strategy would be for Grandma to instead create a separate trust to hold the proceeds she wishes to gift for the benefit of her grandchildren.*

Income to the Grantor

Typical of "income only Medicaid trusts" and revocable trusts, many trusts require that all of the income be distributed to the trust grantor (or grantors). A typical such trust provision in a trust established by a married couple might read something like this:

> As long as either grantor is living, the trustee shall collect all trust income and distribute such income to the grantors (or grantor, if only one is living, in quarterly or more frequent installments).

Provisions giving the grantor(s) such an income interest may be included because the grantor(s) require such income to live off of or to achieve certain specific tax or other estate planning advantages. However, there are pitfalls to be aware of. Most notably, keeping an income interest will cause all trust assets to be considered part of the taxable estate of the grantor[1] and will cause the income to be vulnerable in the event of a need for Medicaid assistance on the part of the grantor.[2]

Discretionary Distributions to the Grantor

Some trusts allow the trustee to distribute assets even beyond the income to the grantor. This is standard in a revocable trust but rare in an irrevocable trust. Allowing the trustee to distribute assets to the grantor, even at the trustee's discretion generally eviscerates the estate tax, Medicaid planning and creditor protection advantages that are the primary goals of most irrevocable trusts.[3] Therefore, few irrevocable trusts allow for principal to be distributed to the grantor.

One notable exception to this general rule is the "self-settled spendthrift trust" device. These trusts, which are only available and valid in some states, can actually allow the grantor to be a potential trust beneficiary and still maintain certain credit protection advantages. This device will be discussed in more detail in chapter 6.

Mandatory Income Distribution to Beneficiaries

Some trusts require that some or all of their income be distributed to or among certain beneficiaries. Trusts that require all income to be distributed to specific beneficiaries annually are referred to as "simple trusts." An example of such trust provision may read:

> As long as the trust operates, the trustee shall distribute to the trust beneficiaries, in equal shares, annually and in quarterly or more frequent installments, all of the net trust income.

---

1. 28 U.S.C. § 2036.
2. 42 USCS § 1396p(d)(3)(B)(i).
3. *See* the two statutes quoted in the two previous notes.

Discretionary Distributions to the Beneficiaries

Discretionary distributions to trust beneficiaries are a central feature of most trusts. Obviously, there is little point in a trust existing unless its assets are to benefit one or more people. Therefore, many trusts give the trustee the discretion to distribute assets among the trust beneficiaries. Such a provision is sometimes referred to as a "sprinkling" provision and a trust that allows discretionary distributions to trust beneficiaries is sometimes referred to as a "sprinkling trust." Such a trust provision might read something like this:

> As long as either grantor is living, the trustee shall continue to hold all trust assets. During this time, the trustee may distribute trust assets, including income and principal, to any beneficiary, or may spend such assets on behalf of such beneficiary, to the extent that the trustee, in his or her sole discretion, deems necessary and appropriate.

Vesting such a broad discretionary power in the trustee is not inherently problematic. However, there are pitfalls to be aware of. For example, if the trustee is herself a beneficiary, such a broad power may be considered a "general power of appointment" on the part of the trustee (since the trustee can, in effect, take as much of the trust assets for him or herself as he or she chooses).[4]

> *Example: Mom and Dad establish the* Family Irrevocable Trust *for the benefit of their children, Evan, Frank and Geena. They name Evan as sole trustee. The trust gives Evan the authority to distribute trust assets among "the children of the grantor, in any manner and amount that the trustee deems appropriate." Because Evan has a limitless power to distribute assets to himself, Evan's creditors can probably attach trust assets to satisfy Evan's debts. Furthermore, if Evan dies, the entire trust principal would be considered part of his taxable estate.*

Discretionary Distributions Subject to an Ascertainable Standard

To minimize the chance that any one trustee or beneficiary will be considered to have too much authority over the trust assets and to bolster the in-

---

4. *See* 26 U.S.C. §2041.

tegrity of the trust in general, trusts are often drafted so that the trustee is limited in the purposes for which he can distribute trust assets. Such limitation is often referred to as an "ascertainable standard," which means that the trustee is limited by a clearly definable set of rules under which he may make trust distributions.

The formula most often employed for this purpose is to allow the trustee to make distributions for the "health, education, maintenance and support" of the trust beneficiaries (sometimes referred to by their initials, "HEMS").[5] A provision that allows distributions subject to an ascertainable standard may be drafted as follows:

> Until the trust terminates pursuant to the provisions set forth hereinafter, the trustee may spend or apply trust assets on behalf of the trust beneficiaries to the extent he deems necessary and appropriate for their health, education, maintenance and support, after taking into account, to the extent the trustee deems advisable, other resources available to the beneficiaries.

Although this is the most common formula, it is by no means the only way to go in this regard. For example, the trustee can be given the authority to spend trust assets for the housing, wedding, sports equipment and summer camp expenses of the beneficiaries, just to name a few. As long as the purposes for which the trustee can use the trust assets are "reasonably definite," the tax and creditor protection advantages of limiting the trustee to an "ascertainable standard" are maintained.[6]

Discretionary Charitable Distributions

Another popular, helpful and generally harmless provision is one that allows the trustee to distribute trust assets to charities. This not only allows the trustee to keep up the charitable legacy of the grantors, but the trustee can also use this authority to save on income taxes. As will be discussed later, trust income is often taxed at very high rates. If undistributed trust income is going to be taxed at the highest tax rate in any case, the trustee may decide to distribute it to charity and take the income tax charitable deduction. It should be noted in this regard that, unlike individuals, a trust is not limited in the percentage of its income that it can give to charity and take a charitable deduction.[7]

---

5. 26 U.S.C. §2041(b)(1)(A).
6. *See, e.g.,* 26 U.S.C. §674(b)(5)(A).
7. 26 C.F.R. §1.642(c)-2.

It is important, however, to ensure that a charitable distribution clause limits the trustees' authority to distribute assets to only tax exempt charitable organizations. The provision might be more restrictive than this but it should not be less restrictive. An example of a broad but safe discretionary charitable provision might be:

> In addition to the authority of the trustee under the previous paragraph, the trustee shall also have the authority to distribute trust assets, including income and/or principal, to worthwhile charitable causes; provided, however that all distributions under this paragraph shall be made only to charitable organizations that are tax exempt under Section 501(c) of the Internal Revenue Code.

An example of a narrower discretionary provision might be:

> In addition to the authority of the trustee under the previous paragraph, the trustee shall also have the authority to distribute assets to charitable organizations whose purposes are to fund or advance medical or scientific research; provided, however, that all distributions under this paragraph shall be made only to charitable organizations that are tax exempt under Section 501(c) of the Internal Revenue Code.

Trust Termination

The next set of key provisions in a trust deal with:

1) The duration that the trust will be in existence; and
2) The disposition of the trust assets upon termination.

Neither of these requires certainty at the time of the trust's creation. They can be contingent on events as they occur later on. Many trusts, for example, end upon the death of the grantor(s) or upon the trust beneficiaries reaching a certain age.

The class of people to whom the trust assets will be distributed upon termination of the trust is also often subject to circumstances. For example, if a trust is to be distributed to the "issue"[8] of the grantor(s), the ultimate beneficiaries of the trust will be the children and/or grandchildren of the grantors who

---

8. Simply put, "issue" means to the children, in equal shares. If one or more children are deceased, their children would receive the assets in their place.

are alive at the time of the trust termination. Furthermore, the trust may provide its own contingencies for distribution.

> **Example:** *Mom and Dad establish the* Family Irrevocable Trust *for the benefit of their children. They want their children to share equally in the trust proceeds after their deaths. However, they also want to make sure that their children all have the benefit of having their college educations funded from the trust, apart from their other general inheritances. Therefore, the trust provides that, upon termination, the trust assets are distributed to the grantors' children, in equal shares "provided, however, that if any child of the grantors' have not yet completed their undergraduate college education, then the trustee shall, prior to distribution, set aside for each such child an adequate sum to pay the reasonable educational expenses of the remainder of such child's college education."*

We will now segue to a discussion of some of the most common types of distribution patterns, their advantages and how to draft their provisions.

Outright Distribution on Termination

A common provision for clients with adult competent children is to simply have all of the trust assets divided equally amongst the children upon termination of the trust. This has the advantage of simplicity. It also allows the beneficiaries to have maximum flexibility in handling these assets that are there for their benefit. In addition, this is generally the cheapest option, since all expenses associated with maintaining the trust (accountant's fees, trustee fees, attorney fees, etc.) will end once the trust assets are distributed.

This solution is not always advisable however. First, minor children (or even young adult children) may not be responsible enough to handle large sums of money. Second, trust beneficiaries may be receiving government assistance benefits that are asset-tested, meaning that an infusion of cash would disqualify the beneficiary from continuing to receive benefits. Alternatively, a beneficiary may have creditors that would be able to access outright distributions, thereby depriving the recipient of their benefit. Clients generally do not want their assets to be distributed to the government or their children's creditors upon their deaths.

To avoid this, a trust can restrict a distribution based on the circumstances. Distributions can be limited or altered based on the advisability of the distribution at the time. For example, the following trust provision may be used:

> Upon the death of the second grantor, the trust assets shall be distrib-
> uted to the grantor's children, in equal shares, per stirpes; provided,
> however, that if any child of the grantors certified to the trustee that, at
> the time of the death of the second grantor, he or she is receiving gov-
> ernment assistance benefits that are asset-tested, such child's share shall
> not be distributed to such child outright, but shall instead be held for the
> benefit of such child in accordance with the terms of ARTICLE VI, here-
> inafter.

Note that this provision also maintains maximum flexibility for the decision to be made at the time of the distribution. By deciding whether to certify
to the trustee that he or she is receiving government assistance, the beneficiary can, in effect, decide whether to receive the distribution outright or allow
it to be held in trust for his or her benefit.

Designation of Trust Assets to Subtrusts

Many trusts, especially more complex ones, routinely establish subtrusts
upon distribution for the benefit of each beneficiary's family. This is especially
popular for exceedingly wealthy clients where each generation is likely to have
a taxable estate. In such cases, it is common for the trust to establish "generation skipping" trusts for the benefit of the grantor's grandchildren upon the
grantor's death. This device and how it operates will be covered in chapter 4.

Many grantors unaffected by the estate tax still like the creditor protection
advantages that subtrusts afford. By establishing subtrusts upon distribution,
the grantors can ensure that these subtrusts provide a measure of protection
from the creditors of the children. These substrusts typically benefit the entire family of the child of the grantors for whom the share is allocated.

As with all trusts, the grantor has broad discretion to determine how these
subtrusts operate. Some common features of these trusts may include:

- The trustee can be the child for whose family the trust benefits or the
  grantor can choose someone else, as the client may be inclined to do if
  the grantor has doubts about the child's responsibility or competence. If
  the grantor's child is a trustee, it is often important to name a co-trustee
  to ensure that the child does not have complete discretion over the trust
  assets.
- The trustee will generally have the authority to distribute assets to the
  child, the child's children and maybe the child's spouse as well, for their
  health, education, maintenance and support (or some other ascertainable standard).

- Upon the death of the child, the trust assets are distributed to the child's children.

Family Trusts Established on Trust Termination

The next device is frequently used when the client has young children or children who have yet to complete their education. Rather than distributing the assets upon the death of the grantor or dividing them into subtrusts, the trust assets are held upon the death of the grantor(s) for the benefit of their children until the *youngest* child reaches a given age.

> **Example:** *Mike and Carol establish* The Brady Family Revocable Trust. *They know they want their children (Greg, Marsha, Peter, Jan, Bobby and Cindy) to share the assets after the death of the grantors. However, they want to ensure that all children's needs are provided for, in terms of support and education, until they reach age 25. Therefore, they decide that, upon the second death, the trust assets will remain in trust until the youngest child reaches age 25. Until the youngest child reaches age 25, the trustee will have the discretion to distribute trust assets for the health, education, maintenance and support (including college education) of any child. When the youngest child reaches age 25, the trust assets will be distributed equally among the children.*

This type of trust can be established by an existing trust or as a testamentary trust established by a will. An example of such a testamentary family trust is as follows:

> Upon my death, if there is at least one living child of mine who is under the age of twenty-five (25) years, then my Trustee shall distribute the proceeds of this Trust to my Trustee, hereinafter named, of THE FAMILY TRUST, the terms and conditions for which are set forth hereinafter in ITEM FOUR.
>
> ITEM FOUR:
>
> THE FAMILY TRUST shall be held, administered and distributed as follows:
>
> (1) Prior to division into shares pursuant to Paragraph (3), my Trustee may pay to or apply for the benefit of any one or more of my said children as much of the net income and/or principal of the trust in such shares and proportions as in his sole discretion shall be necessary or advisable from time to time for the health, education, support (in their accustomed

manner of living) or maintenance of my said child or children, taking into consideration to the extent my Trustee deems advisable, any other income or resources of my said child or children known to my Trustee. Any payment or application of benefits for any child of mine who is under the age of twenty-two (22) years that is made pursuant to this Paragraph shall be charged against this Trust as a whole rather than against the ultimate distributive share of a beneficiary to whom or for whose benefit the payment is made. Any payment or application of benefits for any child of mine who is age of twenty-two (22) years or older shall be charged against the ultimate distributive share of the beneficiary to whom or for whose benefit the payment is made (but without interest).

(2) At the time of the marriage of any child of mine, my Trustee may pay to or for the benefit of such child as much of the net income and/or principal of the trust as in his sole discretion shall be necessary or advisable for the expenses of marriage. Any payment or application of benefits for any child of mine that is made pursuant to this Paragraph (regardless of the age of the beneficiary) shall be charged against this Trust as a whole rather than against the ultimate distributive share of a beneficiary to whom or for whose benefit the payment is made.

(3) Upon such time when every child of mine who is living is over the age of twenty-five (25) years, my Trustee shall divide and distribute the trust assets as then constituted to my issue, in equal shares, per stirpes.

Individual Single Beneficiary Trusts

Another strategy that is popular among clients with young children is to stagger the distributions to the children so that the children of the client receive their shares outright in stages. This prevents the children from wasting their inheritance or trust share on a single unwise investment or other unfortunate incident. For example, a client may wish to provide that a child receives half of his or her share at age 25 and the remainder at age 30. A typical provision for this type of trust (sometimes referred to as an "individual single beneficiary trust," might read as follows:

Upon my death, if my wife does not survive me, I give, devise and bequeath all of my residuary estate to my children, in equal shares; provided, however, that the share of any child of mine who is younger than thirty (30) years shall be held for the benefit of such child in an individual single beneficiary Trust, in accordance with the terms hereinafter set forth in the next item.

. . .

An individual Trust that is maintained for the benefit of a single Beneficiary shall be held, administered and distributed as follows:

(1) My Trustee shall pay to or apply for the benefit of said Beneficiary, until distribution pursuant to Paragraph (2), as much of the net income and/or principal from the Trust as my Trustee in his sole discretion shall determine, for the health, education, support (in his/her accustomed manner of living) or maintenance of said Beneficiary, taking into consideration to the extent my Trustee deems advisable, any other income or resources of said Beneficiary known to my Trustee.

(2) Upon the Beneficiary's attainment of age twenty-five (25) years or if the Beneficiary has already attained the age of 25 prior to the Trust's creation, my trustee shall distribute to the beneficiary, one-half (½) of the trust assets. Upon the Beneficiary's attainment of age thirty (30) or if the Beneficiary has already attained the age of 30 prior to the Trust's creation, my Trustee shall terminate the Trust and shall distribute outright to the Beneficiary all of the remaining principal of the trust.

(3) In the event that the Beneficiary should die prior to the termination of the trust, the trust principal and income shall be distributed to the Beneficiary's children, per stirpes, or if the Beneficiary leaves no issue, to the Testator's other issue, per stirpes.

Powers of Appointment Upon Trust Termination

It is possible (and often advisable) to allow the grantor to retain some control over the ultimate distribution of the trust assets upon the grantor's death. This is referred to as a "power of appointment."

> *Example:* XYZ trust states: "*Upon John's death, the trust assets shall be distributed to whomever among his issue that John shall appoint by a will that specifically references this power of appointment. In default of appointment, the trust assets shall be distributed to John's children, in equal shares.*" *John has a power of appointment over the trust assets. Even if he does not exercise this power, his having the ability to exercise this power can have legal significance.*

A power of appointment can be established in a trust for practical reasons or for legal reasons. A power of appointment may simply be used to allow the grantor to retain some flexibility and control over his or her assets. For example, even if a parent wishes to leave his or her assets to his or her children, the parent may wish to retain the option of adjusting the percentages among his or her children for various reasons, including the needs and behavior of his or her children.

There are two types of powers of appointment that are similar in function but have enormous legal differences. The "limited" power of appointment (or "special" power of appointment) gives the holder the power to direct the distribution of trust assets to any group of people that does not include his or her self, his or her estate, his or her creditors or the creditors of the estate. A general power of appointment gives the holder the power to direct the distribution of trust assets to his or her self, estate, creditors or the creditors of the estate.[9]

> *Example 1: XYZ trust states: "Upon John's death, the trust assets shall be distributed to whomever among his issue and their spouses that John shall appoint by a will that specifically references this power of appointment." This is a limited (or "special") power of appointment.*

> *Example 2: XYZ trust states: "Upon John's death, the trust assets shall be distributed to whomever John shall appoint said assets by a will that specifically references this power of appointment." This is a general power of appointment.*

> *Example 3: XYZ trust states: "Upon John's death, the trust assets shall be distributed to whomever among his issue or among John's creditors that John shall appoint by a will that specifically references this power of appointment." This is a general power of appointment.*

For most legal purposes, holding a general power of appointment over an asset effectively renders that asset to be your asset. For example, any asset over which one holds a general power of appointment is automatically considered part of his or her taxable estate.[10] A person's creditors can also collect assets over which a person had a general power of appointment after his death. The consequences of holding a limited power of appointment are much more complex and will be referred to several times later in this book.

Practice tip: For most purposes other than inclusion in one's taxable estate (when retained by the grantor), assets over which one holds a limited power of appointment are not considered one's assets. Therefore, limited

---

9. 26 U.S.C. § 2041(b)(1).
10. 26 U.S.C. § 2041(a)(1).

powers of appointment are generally safe methods to achieve flexibility in determining the disposition of trust assets while not subjecting the client to increased risk from creditors or government agencies seeking recovery of benefits.

Review Questions

1) Name two potential drawbacks to allowing a trust to distribute its income to the grantor.

2) What is the difference between a "simple" trust and a "complex" trust, in terms of how their incomes are to be handled?

3) What is the difference between a "simple" trust and a "complex" trust, in terms of how they handle their income tax returns?

4) What is the difference between a discretionary distribution power and a distribution power that is limited by an ascertainable standard?

5) Why would a trust drafter limit a trustee's distribution authority by subjecting it to an ascertainable standard limitation?

6) State one reason why a client would be reluctant to allow an outright distribution of assets to his or her children upon his or her death.

7) In what way does a family trust provision operate differently that an individual single beneficiary trust provision?

8) How does the individual single beneficiary trust protect trust assets from the potential mistakes of the beneficiary?

9) What is the difference between a limited power of appointment and a general power of appointment, in terms of how it is set up?

10) What is the difference between a limited power of appointment and a general power of appointment, in terms of at least one legal consequence?

CHAPTER 3

GIFT TAX IMPLICATIONS OF GIFTS TO TRUSTS

Overview of Gift Tax Rules

The good tax news regarding gifts is that a gift is not a taxable event, as income from gifts is specifically excluded from the definition of "income" under the Internal Revenue Code.[1] Unfortunately, what the Code gives, the Code also takes away. While gifts are not subject to income tax, they can be subject to gift tax.[2] The further bad news with regard to gift tax is that, depending on the amount of the gifts a person has given in his lifetime, the gift tax rate can be in excess of 50%. The current gift tax rates appear in section 2502 of the Internal Revenue Code.[3]

A central component of any gifting strategy is to avoid the imposition of gift tax.

Gift tax is not assessed from the first dollar of the gift. Rather, two major exemption rules apply to allow many gifts to pass to the recipient free of gift tax.

Gift Tax Annual Exclusion

The annual gift tax exclusion allows a certain amount to be gifted by each person to each recipient each year free of any gift tax consequences. This amount was $13,000 as of 2011[4] and is elevated in periodic increments of $1,000 to compensate for inflation.[5]

---

1. 26 U.S.C. § 102(a).
2. *See* 26 U.S.C. § 2501, *et seq.*
3. 26 U.S.C. § 2501(a)(2).
4. http://www.irs.gov/publications/p950/ar02.html.
5. 26 U.S.C. § 2503(b)(2).

Example: Christine, who has five children and seventeen grand-children, is starting to advance in age and has several million dol-lars in assets. She is cognizant that her estate might be subject to estate tax upon her death and she wishes to reduce her estate to min-imize the estate tax that her estate will be subject to. If she were to simply gift all of her assets away at one time, she would be subject to a gift tax. However, because of the gift tax annual exclusion, she can gift $13,000 to each of her 22 beneficiaries if she so chooses. Therefore, by simply gifting the maximum amount allowed under the annual exclusion, she can gift up to $286,000 each year without any adverse tax consequences.

A married couple can give twice the amount of the annual exclusion each year without being subject to gift tax. This is true even if one spouse gives the entire gift. In such a case, where one spouse gives the entire gift, the Internal Revenue Code allows the spouses to "gift split" so that it is considered as though each spouse made one-half of the gift. The other spouse must consent to this gift splitting maneuver on a gift tax return that is filed for the year.[6]

Example: Christine and James are married. Christine has an account in her own name with $1,000,000 in cash in it. She wants to give this money to their 22 children and grandchildren as quickly as possible. Assuming that James consents and that James does not give other gifts to their children and grandchildren, Christine can give up to $572,000 to the children and grandchildren each year ($26,000 times 22). Each year, Christie should file a federal gift tax return (Form 709). James should indicate his acceptance of the gift split on the front page of the Form 709, as shown below.

---

6. 26 U.S.C. § 2513.

Form **709**	United States Gift (and Generation-Skipping Transfer) Tax Return		OMB No. 1545-0020
Department of the Treasury Internal Revenue Service	(For gifts made during calendar year 2009) ▶ See separate instructions.		20**09**

	1 Donor's first name and middle initial		2 Donor's last name	3 Donor's social security number
	Christine Smith			
	4 Address (number, street, and apartment number)			5 Legal residence (domicile)
	6 City, state, and ZIP code			7 Citizenship (see instructions)

			Yes	No
Part 1—General Information	8	If the donor died during the year, check here ▶ ☐ and enter date of death		
	9	If you extended the time to file this Form 709, check here ▶ ☐		
	10	Enter the total number of donees listed on Schedule A. Count each person only once. ▶		
	11a	Have you (the donor) previously filed a Form 709 (or 709-A) for any other year? If "No," skip line 11b		
	b	If the answer to line 11a is "Yes," has your address changed since you last filed Form 709 (or 709-A)?		
	12	**Gifts by husband or wife to third parties.** Do you consent to have the gifts (including generation-skipping transfers) made by you and by your spouse to third parties during the calendar year considered as made one-half by each of you? (See instructions.) (If the answer is "Yes," the following information must be furnished and your spouse must sign the consent shown below. **If the answer is "No," skip lines 13–18 and go to Schedule A.)**	✓	
	13	Name of consenting spouse James Smith 14 SSN 123-45-6789		
	15	Were you married to one another during the entire calendar year? (see instructions)	✓	
	16	If 15 is "No," check whether ☐ married ☐ divorced or ☐ widowed/deceased, and give date (see instructions) ▶		
	17	Will a gift tax return for this year be filed by your spouse? (If "Yes," mail both returns in the same envelope.)		✓

For a variety of reasons, many clients are reluctant or unable to liquidate their estates simply by giving away their cash to their beneficiaries in the increments allowed under the gift tax annual exclusion. First, the client's assets may be tied down in investments, including stocks, real estate, business interests, etc., that cannot easily be gifted. Second, some of the beneficiaries may be minors or otherwise incapable of handling large sums of money. Third, the client may want to retain some control over the assets while he or she is living, or at least allow someone that he or she trusts to maintain such control.

Fourth, the client may want to maintain the investment power that is inherent in a large pool of assets. Large sums of capital can be used to invest in a wider variety of investments than can small sums. Even assuming the same investment strategy, accounts with larger sums may garner higher interest rates or more favorable treatment from financial institutions than smaller accounts. Dividing up large sums by distributing them to many beneficiaries can greatly decrease the investing power of the family unit as a whole.

Therefore, many clients may wish to take advantage of devices that allow gifts to be made to beneficiaries that are effective for gift tax purposes, but that do not allow the beneficiaries immediate control over their gifts. Instead, these devices can allow centralized management of all of the family's assets while completing the transfer for gift and estate tax purposes.

Frequently used devices that accomplish these goals include family limited partnerships and limited liability companies. When using these devices, the client establishes a limited partnership or LLC and transfers assets (such as a brokerage account containing significant value) to the entity. The entity is initially owned by the client or the client and spouse. The client then transfers shares of the entity to the beneficiaries each year in amounts that are low enough to be covered by the annual exclusion.

> *Example: Jake and Linda McCoy are in their mid 60s and have three children and seven grandchildren. They own more than $5,000,000 in assets. To reduce their estate, they decide to use the "family limited partnership" device. They establish a limited partnership called "McCoy Family Limited Partnership." Jake and Linda are each 50% owners of the partnership and they are named as the general partners of the partnership. They then transfer stocks, bonds and cash with a value of $1,300,000 to the partnership.*
>
> *Because 1% of $1,300,000 is $13,000, they can each transfer 1% of the partnership interest to each beneficiary each year and stay within the annual exclusion.[7] By following this strategy each year, in five years Jake and Linda will have completely removed the $1,300,000 in assets from their estates while keeping their gifts entirely within the gift tax annual exclusion.*

Another common strategy that may be used to gift assets within the gift tax annual exclusion is the irrevocable trust. The trust strategy operates in a similar manner to the partnership device in that it seeks to take advantage of the annual exclusion. The trust lists all of the beneficiaries and limits annual contributions to the trust to the amount that is covered by the annual exclusion.

> *Example: Jake and Linda McCoy are in their mid 60s and have three children and seven grandchildren. They own more than $5,000,000 in assets. To reduce their estate, they decide to use the irrevocable trust device. They establish a trust for the benefit of all three children and seven grandchildren. With the help of some provisions that will be discussed below, Jake and Linda can each transfer up to $130,000 per year to the trust and stay within the gift tax annual exclusion.*

---

7. They can actually transfer more than 1% of the partnership each year to each beneficiary. Since shares of a limited partnership cannot easily be sold and because the other partners will have little control over the entity, a "valuation discount" in determining the value of the shares is appropriate. A full discussion of valuation discounts, however, is beyond the scope of this text.

Lifetime Gift Tax Exemption

A gift that is not completely covered by the annual exclusion is nevertheless not automatically subject to gift tax. Instead, each person has a lifetime "exemption" amount that he or she can gift tax-free beyond the annual exclusion amount. This amount is currently $1,000,000.[8] Any gift that is not covered by the annual exclusion is deducted from the lifetime exemption amount.

Gift tax returns (Form 709) must be filed during each year in which a person makes gifts that are not covered by the annual exclusion.[9] As long as a person has not used up his or her lifetime exemption, there will be no gift tax. Instead, the returns will be used to calculate and keep track of the amount of exemption remaining to the client. Once the exemption is used up, all further gifts during a person's lifetime that are not within the annual exclusion will be subject to gift tax.

> *Example:* Debbie, who is not married, transfers $100,000 in 2011 to her son, Mike. Since the annual exclusion is $13,000, the other $87,000 is deducted from Debbie's lifetime exemption amount. She now has $913,000 remaining on her lifetime exemption amount for gifts in future years. (This assumes that Debbie has made no previous gifts that were beyond the annual exclusion.)

> *Another Example:* Debbie, who is not married, transfers $1,000,000 in 2011 to her son, Mike. Since the annual exclusion is $13,000, the other $987,000 is deducted from Debbie's lifetime exemption amount. She now has $13,000 remaining on her lifetime exemption amount for gifts in future years. In 2010, Debbie gives $100,000 to her daughter, Cathy. The first $13,000 is covered by the annual exclusion. The next $13,000 uses the remainder of Debbie's lifetime exemption amount. The remaining $74,000 of the gift to Cathy is subject to gift tax.

There are some transfers that are exempt from gift tax regardless of the amount. The two major exemptions are the gift tax marital deduction and the gift tax charitable deduction.

---

8. 26 U.S.C. § 2505.
9. *See* http://www.irs.gov/pub/irs-pdf/i709.pdf (page 1).

Marital Deduction

Gifts that are made from one spouse to another spouse who is a United States citizen are exempt from gift tax implications.[10] Gifts to a non-citizen spouse are subject to a limit. For 2010, that limit was $134,000 and this limit rises periodically with inflation.[11] Beyond that, gifts are treated as though made to a non-spouse.[12]

Gifts to a trust or similar entity for the benefit of a spouse can qualify for the marital deduction, as long as the spouse's interest qualifies as a "qualified terminable interest in property" ("QTIP").[13] To qualify as a QTIP, a trust (or similar entity) must conform to the following requirements:

1) All of the income from the trust must be payable to the spouse, at least annually;

2) The spouse must have the right to demand that trust property be used in a manner that will allow it to produce income;

3) There can be no beneficiary other than the surviving spouse during his or her lifetime;

4) When the spouse dies, any remaining trust income must be payable to the estate of the surviving spouse.[14]

Example: Paul wants to establish a trust that will be held for his wife, Paula (a U.S. citizen), during her lifetime, and which will be distributed to his children after her death. He establishes a trust with his sister, Jane, as the trustee. The trust requires that Jane distribute the trust income to Paula on a quarterly or more frequent basis. It also allows Jane to distribute additional principal to Paula if Jane deems it necessary and appropriate. The trust allows Paula to demand that the trust assets be used to produce income for her. The trust states that upon Paula's death, the trust assets are to be distributed to Paul's children, in equal shares. Since Paul's interest in this trust is a qualified terminable interest in property ("QTIP"), all gifts that Paul gives to this trust are covered by the marital deduction and are not subject to gift tax.

---

10. 26 U.S.C. §2523.
11. *See* I.R.S. Publication 950.
12. 26 U.S.C. §2523(i).
13. 26 U.S.C. §2523(f)(2).
14. 26 U.S.C. §2056.

A "QTIP" trust can be established as a lifetime trust or as a testamentary trust. A typical QTIP provision in a lifetime trust may read as follows:

Marital Deduction Trust Provisions

1. In establishing and administering the trust created hereunder, the trustee shall be vested with all of the powers and authority hereinafter set out. However, it is expressly provided that the grant of rights, powers, privileges and authority to the trustee in connection with the imposition of duties upon the trustee by any provision of this Marital Trust or by any statute relating thereto, shall not be effective if it would disqualify the marital deduction as it is established in the Marital Trust hereof.

2. The trustee shall pay the entire net income in quarterly or more frequent installments to the grantor's wife, or apply it for her benefit, so long as she shall live.

3. In addition to the payment of income, the trustee may pay to the grantor's wife such amounts (including some or all) of the corpus of the trust property held for her benefit as may from time to time be deemed required to enable the grantor's wife to maintain substantially the standard of living to which she is accustomed. In making such payments the trustee may, but need not, take into account other financial resources available to her.

4. If non-income producing property is held, the grantor's wife shall have the right to direct that such property be exchanged for income-producing property.

5. At the death of the grantor's wife, any accumulated and accrued income shall be paid to the grantor's wife's estate, and all of the remaining trust assets shall be distributed to the children, in equal shares, per stirpes.

6. On the death of the grantor's wife, the trustee shall be authorized to withhold distribution of an amount of property sufficient to cover any liability that may be imposed on the trustee for estate or other taxes until such liability is finally determined and paid.

Similarly, gifts to a spouse who is not a U.S. citizen can be made eligible for the full marital deduction if the trust assets are transferred to a "qualified domestic trust" ("QDOT") for the benefit of the non-citizen spouse.[15] The rules of the QDOT are a bit more complex than for the QTIP. The key point of a QDOT

---

15. *See* 26 U.S.C. §2056A.

is that the trust must be subject to United States jurisdiction and the statute provides several requirements to ensure such.

Charitable Deduction

Assets gifted to charities that are tax exempt under Section 501(c) of the Internal Revenue Code are also exempt from gift taxes.[16] Most germane to our discussion are charitable trusts. If a trust qualifies as a completely charitable trust, then all gifts to it are exempt from gift tax. A trust can be a "split interest" trust as well, with charitable and non-charitable interests. However, crafting a proper split interest trust is a complex maneuver. Highlights of the rules regarding charitable trusts and split interest trusts are the subject of chapter 12.

Gift Tax on Transfers to Trusts

We will now turn our attention to how transfers to trusts are treated from a gift tax perspective. Whenever a transfer is made to a trust, there are three possibilities regarding the status of that transfer:

- The gift can be considered an "incomplete gift," thereby not incurring any gift tax ramifications. However, the assets transferred in this manner remain in the taxable estate of the grantor.
- The gift can be considered a completed gift of a *future* interest to the beneficiaries of the trust, removing the assets from the taxable estate of the grantor.
- The gift can be considered a completed gift of a *present* interest to the beneficiaries of the trust, removing the assets from the taxable estate of the grantor.

Completed Gifts vs. Incomplete Gifts

Depending on the trust provisions, a gift to a trust may not remove the assets gifted from the taxable estate of the grantor. Generally, if assets in a trust are considered outside the taxable gross estate of the grantor, then by defini-

---

16. 26 U.S.C. §2522.

tion, gifts to the trust are completed gifts.[17] However, the converse is not necessarily the case. Just because the gift to a trust is a completed gift it does not mean that the trust assets are necessarily outside the estate of the grantor.[18]

An advantage of a gift being considered incomplete is that these gifts are not subject to gift taxation. In addition, keeping assets in the taxable estate of the grantor can have significant capital gains tax advantages (discussed later in this text). Whether it is best to have a gift to a trust be considered a completed gift depends on the situation of the individual client.

Fortunately, the practitioner can control, relatively easily, whether gifts to a trust will be considered completed gifts.

The simplest manner in which to draft a trust so that gifts to the trust are not considered completed for gift tax purposes is to give the grantor the power to change the trust's ultimate disposition. In other words, the grantor can be given a power of appointment over the trust assets.

Because irrevocable trusts generally have certain Medicaid eligibility and/or creditor protection purposes, there are two important points to remember regarding this power to change the trust's ultimate disposition:

1) This power should be a limited (special) power of appointment and not a general power of appointment; and
2) The power should be exercisable only at the death of the grantor, not during his or her lifetime.

If the grantor holds a general testamentary power of appointment (i.e., a general power that can be exercised only upon his death), then upon his death, for most intents and purposes, the trust assets will be considered his money.[19] If the trust is a Medicaid planning trust, the government would be able to attach assets in a trust that are subject to a general power of appointment on the part

---

17. In this context and as discussed hereafter, the term "completed" gift refers to a gift that is subject to gift tax because it is removed from the ownership of the grantor. If the grantor retains enough control over the trust, the gift may be considered "incomplete" and it is not subject to gift tax because the grantor is not really giving away the asset.

18. Trust assets can be considered part of the taxable estate of the grantor, even if the transfers to the trust are completed gifts, if the grantor retains too much power over the trust assets or if the grantor retains too much benefit from the trust. Therefore, if it is important to remove assets from the estate of the grantor, care must be taken to avoid giving the grantor these powers or benefits. The specific rules in this regard are discussed in chapter 4.

19. See 26 U.S.C. § 2041.

of the grantor.[20] Creditors of the grantor would also be able to posthumously pursue and collect assets over which the grantor has a general power of appointment.[21]

The second suggestion (limiting the exercise of the power to the time of the death of the grantor) is necessary only in some cases. For example, many Medicaid planning trusts are intended to be non-grantor trusts for income tax purposes (see chapter 5). However, giving the grantor the authority to determine who received the assets during his or her lifetime will generally cause the trust to be considered a grantor trust.[22]

> *Example:* Martha establishes The Martha Irrevocable Trust. *The trust provides:*
>
> *Upon Martha's death, the trust assets shall be distributed to whomever other than Martha, Martha's creditors, Martha's estate and the creditors of Martha's estate, that Martha shall appoint by a will that specifically references this special power of appointment. In default of appointment, the trust assets shall be distributed to Martha's children, in equal shares, per stirpes.*
>
> *Although not functionally changing the trust in any other regard, this provision makes any transfer to this trust an "incomplete" gift. No gift tax return need be filed when assets are transferred to the trust and no annual exclusion or lifetime exemption need be used. Of course, conversely, assets in the trust remain part of Martha's taxable estate.*
>
> *Another Example:* Martha establishes The Martha Irrevocable Trust. *The trust provides:*
>
> *Upon Martha's death, the trust assets shall be distributed to whomever Martha shall appoint by a will that specifically references this power of appointment. In default of appointment, the trust assets shall be distributed to Martha's children, in equal shares, per stirpes.*
>
> *This provision makes any transfer to the trust an incomplete gift. However, it also gives Martha a general power of appointment of the trust assets. As such, the trust has limited or no asset protection or Medicaid planning benefits.*

---

20. *See* 42 U.S.C. § 1396p.
21. Braunstein v. Grassa (In re Grassa), 363 B.R. 650, 659 (Bankr. D. Mass. 2007).
22. 26 U.S.C. § 674.

Yet Another Example: Martha establishes The Martha Irrevocable Trust. *The trust provides:*

During Martha's lifetime, Martha may add or remove trust beneficiaries hereunder, provided that only people who are children, grandchildren, great grandchildren and/or their spouses may be added by Martha as trust beneficiaries.

This provision gives Martha a lifetime limited power of appointment over the trust assets. It makes any transfer to the trust an incomplete gift. The trust probably also can achieve many asset protection and Medicaid planning objectives. However, it also may have some unintended consequences, such as causing the trust to be considered a grantor trust.

The converse, i.e., ensuring that a transfer **is** a completed gift, is a bit more complex. The only reason to ensure that transfers to a trust are considered completed gifts is to remove the trust assets from the taxable estate of the grantor. Therefore, in drafting a trust whose assets will be outside the estate of the grantor (and thus the transfers to which will be considered completed gifts), one must be careful to avoid allowing the grantor any power or benefit that would bring the trust assets back into his or her taxable estate. The pitfalls to watch out for in this regard are discussed in chapter 4.

Maintaining the Annual Exclusion

When the transfer to a trust is to be a completed gift, it is important to ensure that gifts to the trust are eligible for the gift tax annual exclusion. The problem on that front is that, to be eligible for the gift tax annual exclusion, gifts must be of present interests.[23] A gift to a trust, on the other hand, is generally a gift of a future interest, since the beneficiary will not receive access to the trust benefits immediately. This factor appears initially to render gifts to trusts disadvantageous.

Example: Marlon has 5 children. If he were to give them outright gifts, he could give them each $13,000 in 2011 ($65,000 total) within the annual exclusion. However, Marlon does not want his children to have access to the funds immediately (he is afraid they will waste the gifts on unwise investments or recreational expenditures). Therefore, he

---

23. 26 U.S.C. §2503(b)(1).

instead establishes a trust with his children as trust beneficiaries. Because his children will not be able to access the trust funds immediately, this is considered a gift of a future interest. Therefore, if Marlon wants to give $65,000 to the trust, all of it would come off of his lifetime exemption amount (or, if he has none remaining, be subject to gift tax).

"Crummey" Rights of Withdrawal

Fortunately for the trust as a transfer tax planning device, an enterprising California attorney and a sympathetic federal circuit court helped craft a device that allows transfers to trusts to be eligible for the gift tax annual exclusion.

This device allows the beneficiaries a limited time following any contribution to withdraw his or her share of the contribution. Even if the beneficiary doesn't exercise this right, the fact that he or she could have done so is sufficient to convert the interest of the beneficiary into a present interest. This device was first allowed by a federal court in the seminal appellate of *Crummey v. Commissioner*.[24] Therefore, these withdrawal rights are sometimes referred to as "Crummey rights of withdrawal." and trusts that contain such withdrawal rights are sometimes called "Crummey trusts."

> *Example: Marlon, from our previous example, wants to give $65,000 to a trust for the benefit of his five children. He would like to do so without having to use any of his lifetime gift tax exemption. Therefore, the trust provides that upon any contribution to the trust, each trust beneficiary (his children) may, at any time during the 30 days that follows the contribution, withdraw up to 1/5 of the contribution. Even though Marlon may assume that his children will not exercise this right (and even if, in fact, they never do), the gift is of a present interest and is thus eligible for the annual exclusion.*

An example of a basic Crummey right of withdrawal provision is as follows:

> Immediately following any contribution to the trust, each of the grantor's children shall have the right to withdraw an amount equal to a pro rata share of each contribution to the trust. Such pro rata portion will be the amount of the contribution, divided by the number of the beneficiaries of this right of withdrawal at the time of the contribution. If any such

---

24. 397 F2d 82 (9th Cir. 1968).

beneficiary demands and receives a distribution in excess of the amount authorized under this article, the Trustee shall immediately notify him or her in writing, requiring the prompt repayment of such excess amount. This demand power takes precedence over any other power or discretion granted the Trustee or any other person.

A right of withdrawal can be exercised by the beneficiary who holds the right (usually by writing to the trustee) or by a parent or guardian of the beneficiary. The trust should establish clear procedures by which this can be done and the procedures for notifying the beneficiaries of their withdrawal rights. An example of a series of procedural rules as they may appear in a Crummey trust is as follows:

1. This demand power can be exercised by a written request delivered to the Trustee. If a beneficiary is unable to exercise such demand power because of a legal disability, any legally authorized personal representative, including (but not limited to) a parent, guardian, committee, or conservator, may make the demand on such beneficiary's behalf. In the event that no such legally authorized personal representative is available, then the Trustee may, acting as a fiduciary for the legally disabled beneficiary, exercise the demand power on the beneficiary's behalf. However, in no event can the Grantor make the demand for any beneficiary.

2. The Trustee must reasonably notify the person who would exercise the demand power granted under this Article of its existence and of any contributions made to the trust that are subject to the power.

3. The maximum amount that any beneficiary may withdraw with respect to all contributions made by the same donor during a single calendar year shall be the lesser of the total amount of such contributions and the amount of the federal gift tax annual exclusion in effect on the date of the earliest of such contributions. If requested by a married donor at the time of a contribution, the alternative limitation based on the gift tax annual exclusion shall be two (2) times the amount of the gift tax annual exclusion.

4. Each beneficiary's unexercised right to withdraw a contribution shall lapse after thirty (30) days following notification to the beneficiary of the contribution.

5. The Trustee may satisfy a demand for a distribution by distributing cash, other assets, or fractional interests in other assets, as the Trustee deems appropriate. Without limiting the Trustee's power to select assets to satisfy a demand, the Grantor prefers that cash or tangible assets

be distributed before life insurance policies and intangible assets, unless the Trustee decides that another selection is warranted.

6. "Contribution" means any cash or other assets transferred to the Trustee to be held as part of the trust funds and the payment of any premiums on life insurance policies owned (in whole or in part) by the trust. The amount of any contribution is its federal gift tax value, as determined by the Trustee at the time of the contribution.

7. After the calendar year in which the trust is created, a person who makes a contribution to any trust created under this instrument may, by a written instrument delivered to the Trustee at the time of such contribution and with respect solely to the contribution then being made, do one (1) or more of the following: (a) increase or decrease the amount subject to any person's demand power as to such new contribution; and (b) change the period during which any person's demand power as to such new contribution may be exercised. No such direction may in any way alter, amend or change such person's demand power with respect to any prior contributions.

Who Can Be a Beneficiary of a Right of Withdrawal?

The theory behind the Crummey withdrawal power is that the person with the right of withdrawal has a present interest in the trust because he or she could withdraw the contribution.[25] However, this does not mean that anyone can have such withdrawal power. Although the law on this issue is not completely clear, the general consensus is that withdrawal power must be held by a trust beneficiary. A Crummey power held by a person who is not a trust beneficiary (i.e., a "naked" Crummey power) will most likely be ineffective.

Any person who is currently a trust beneficiary may be a holder of a right of withdrawal, even if the person is only a discretionary beneficiary (a beneficiary whom the trustee may choose whether to allocate assets to). It is less clear whether a withdrawal power can be held by someone who is only a remainder or contingent trust beneficiary (i.e., someone who is not currently a trust beneficiary but will or may become one in the future). Although some courts have allowed this,[26] it is a risky maneuver and should not be done absent a compelling reason.[27]

---

25. I.R.S. Rev. Rul. 80-261.

26. *See* Estate of Cristofani v. Commissioner, 97 TC 74 (1991).

27. *See* Gregory M. McCoskey, *Why Relying on Cristofani to Draft Trust Withdrawal Powers Is a "Crummey" Idea,* http://findarticles.com/p/articles/mi_hb6367/is_n7_71/ai_n28687905.

Example: Doug established The Doug Irrevocable Trust. *Under its terms, the trustee may pay income or principal for the benefit of Doug's three children, Don, Donna and Dana. Upon Doug's death, the trust assets are to be distributed to Don, Donna and Dana, in equal shares. The trust provides that if Don is not alive at the time, his share will be distributed to his children, Eva and Evan. In this example, Don, Donna and Dana can definitely be named as holders of rights of withdrawal. Eva and Evan should probably not be named as withdrawal power holders. Doug's neighbor, Mike, should definitely not be granted a right of withdrawal, even if Doug trusts Mike not to exercise it.*

Right of Withdrawal Notifications

A right of withdrawal is meaningless unless the holders of the rights of withdrawal are notified of this right in a timely manner.[28] The best practice is for the trustee to mail (or fax or email) notifications of the right of withdrawal each time a contribution is made to the trust. If not done following each contribution, such notification should be sent to each beneficiary at least once per year. If the trustee cannot (or won't) send the notifications, the office of the attorney who drafted the trust may do so. The recipients of the notifications (the holders of the withdrawal powers) should countersign the notification to acknowledge receipt of the notification (this is good practice, but is not an absolute requirement). The signed notifications should be kept by the attorney's office in the client's file. This is important, as, in the event of a future IRS audit, the signed notifications provide evidence that the notifications were sent and received.

The notifications should briefly describe the contribution and the amount that the holder is allowed to withdraw. Equally important, the notice should give the beneficiary instructions as to how to exercise the withdrawal power.

Example: Your client, John Smith, established a trust on October 2, 2010 and immediately contributed $26,000 to the trust. His daughters, Sue and Lisa, each hold a right of withdrawal. John's neighbor, Sandra, is trustee of the trust. You therefore send out the following letter to both Sue and Lisa:

---

28. I.R.S. Rev. Rul. 81-7.

Dear Lisa:

On October 2, 2010, JOHN SMITH (the Grantor) created an irrevocable trust for the benefit of various beneficiaries.

On October 2, 2010, a contribution was made to the trust in the amount of $26,000. As a trust beneficiary and holder of a right of withdrawal under ARTICLE III of the trust, you may withdraw up to $13,000 of this contribution. This withdrawal right will lapse if the right(s) are not exercised within 30 days from the date of the contribution, provided, however, that the extent of the lapse of the right of withdrawal in any single calendar year shall not exceed the greater of Five Thousand Dollars ($5,000) or five percent (5%) of the trust assets. (If a contribution is made in December, the withdrawal right will extend into the next year, for the full 30 day period.)[29]

If you decide to exercise the right of withdrawal, please notify the trustee in writing that you seek to withdraw any amount of the contribution up to $13,000 within the time frame listed above.

To help facilitate the administration of this trust, please sign the acknowledgment below and return it to me at your earliest convenience.

Sincerely,

Sandra, *Trustee*

―――――――――――――――――

I acknowledge that I have received notice of the above referenced right of withdrawal.

―――――――――――――   ―――――――――――――

Lisa   *Date*

Lapse of Withdrawal Power

As referenced in the examples above, it is typical to keep the withdrawal right open for thirty days. This is a reasonable period of time to give the beneficiary the chance to decide whether to exercise the withdrawal. The period

―――――――――――――

29. See below for a discussion of the latter part of this paragraph.

in which the withdrawal rights can be exercised can certainly be longer than thirty days, although it's not clear that it should be shorter than that.

The major problem arises when the withdrawal power lapses. When the holder of the withdrawal power fails to exercise the right of withdrawal (i.e., allows it to expire), technically, the beneficiary is "gifting" that amount back to the trust. Therefore, the beneficiary would have to use some of his or her lifetime gift tax exemption amount every time a withdrawal power is allowed to lapse. Worse still, this lapse is not eligible for the annual exclusion since a "gift" back to the trust is not a gift of a present interest.

Fortunately, the Internal Revenue Code provides[30] that failure to exercise a withdrawal right from a trust is *not* considered a taxable gift as long as the value of such withdrawal power is not more than the greater of 5% of the total trust principal or $5,000. Therefore, the lapse of a Crummey withdrawal right in most trusts is subject to this limitation. In other words, the withdrawal power should not "lapse" (i.e., expire) to a greater extent than 5% of the trust's value (or $5,000) each year. The limitation is indicated by the sample provision below:

> In any calendar year the extent of the lapse of a right of withdrawal shall not exceed the greater of Five Thousand Dollars ($5,000.00) or five percent (5%) of the value of the trust assets from which such withdrawal could be satisfied. To the extent that a withdrawal power does not lapse on a particular December 31, the withdrawal power continues to be exercisable (whether or not a contribution was made in that year), in all later years, subject to the same lapse provisions.

> *Example: Melanie established a trust for the benefit of her son, Daniel. Daniel has a standard Crummey withdrawal power subject to the lapse limitations described above. In 2010, Melanie contributed $13,000 to the trust. Daniel had the right to withdraw the $13,000, but let this power lapse. Because of the limitation, only $5,000 lapsed in 2010. Daniel retained the right to withdraw $8,000. The right to withdraw $8,000 carried over to 2011.*

> *In 2011, Melanie contributed another $13,000. Now, Daniel had the right to withdraw up to $21,000 ($8,000 carried over from 2010 and $13,000 from the new contribution). If he allows this power to lapse, once again, only $5,000 will lapse. Going into 2012, Daniel will have the authority to withdraw up to $16,000.*

---

30. 26 U.S.C. §2514(e).

Fast forward to 2025 …

The value of the trust assets is now $250,000. The withdrawal powers that Daniel accumulates each year depend on the value of the contributions and on the annual exclusion (remember, it is modified for inflation). Assume that Daniel has the right to withdraw up to $50,000 from the trust because of carryover withdrawal rights from pervious years and contributions made in 2025. If Daniel does not exercise this power, $12,500 of his withdrawal power will lapse, because that is 5% of the trust's value. If Daniel fails to exercise his withdrawal right, he will carry over the right to withdraw up to $37,500 in 2026.

Review Questions

1) Why are most small gifts that are given to one's children or friends unlikely to be subject to gift tax?

2) Why does the amount of the gift tax annual exclusion change from time to time?

3) How can a client take advantage of the gift tax marital exclusion and still ensure that the gifted assets will be distributed to his own children at his spouse's death?

4) What are the statutory requirements of a "qualified terminable interest" regarding gifts to marital trusts?

5) How can a client pass assets to a non-U.S. citizen spouse and still take advantage of the gift tax marital deduction?

6) What specific types of charitable recipients should be beneficiaries of a charitable trust? Why?

7) Why would a client want a gift to a trust to be considered an "incomplete" gift for gift tax purposes?

8) Why would a client want a gift to a trust to be considered a "completed" gift for gift tax purposes?

9) Name one effective way to ensure that a gift to a trust is considered "incomplete" for gift tax purposes.

10) Why is a gift to a trust sometimes not eligible for the gift tax annual deduction?

11) How does a "Crummey" provision ensure that a gift to a trust qualifies for the gift tax annual deduction?

12) Who should hold a "Crummey" withdrawal power in a typical Crummey trust?

13) Who should be notified of a right of withdrawal power in the case of a minor beneficiary?

14) What are the essential elements of the notification that must be given to a trust beneficiary who is the holder of a right of withdrawal?

15) What is the problem with allowing a right of withdrawal to expire as soon as the 30 day window expires each year?

16) What can be done to offset the problem raised in your answer to question 15?

CHAPTER 4

ESTATE TAXATION ON
TRUST ASSETS

Connection Between the Gift and Estate Taxes

The gift tax and the estate tax should not be viewed as independent entities, but rather must be analyzed as two sides of the same coin. This is especially true in regard to trusts. There are multiple reasons for this:

- Either without the other would be largely ineffective. An estate tax without a gift tax would merely prompt wealthy people to give away all of their assets while terminally ill. A gift tax without an estate tax would merely discourage gifting during their lifetime. Either way, the government would get little in the way of transfer tax.

- The taxes are assessed at largely the same rates. In addition, most ancillary rules that affect one (e.g., the marital and charitable deductions, the generation skipping transfer tax rules) affect the other as well.

- The lifetime gift tax exclusion dovetails with the estate tax exemption amount. Any amount used against one's lifetime gift tax exemption amount also counts against his or her estate tax exemption amount.[1]

Example: Frank makes sure that all gifts to his children are generally within the annual exclusion amount. However, in 2006 (when the annual exclusion amount was $12,000), his daughter, Patricia, needed $112,000 for a down payment on her house. Frank gave Patricia the money. Because the gift was in excess of the annual exclusion, $100,000 came off of Frank's gift tax lifetime exemption amount. In addition, when Frank dies, that same $100,000 will come off Frank's estate tax exemption amount (to be discussed later in this chapter).

---

1. *See* IRS Publication 950 (http://www.irs.gov/pub/irs-pdf/p950.pdf).

To understand how various estate tax issues should be handled during the process of trust preparation, it is first necessary to have a basic understanding of the estate tax rules.

Estate Tax Introduction

When a person dies, a new legal "person" is born in the form of that person's estate. An estate is managed in a very similar manner to a trust. Until the estate assets are distributed and the estate is "closed," the estate exists as a separate legal entity and can invest money, conduct business, manage assets, sue or be sued. The person charged with managing an estate and distributing its assets is called an executor or administrator and his or her role is very similar to that of a trustee. The process by which this is done is called the "probate" or "administration" process. A detailed discussion of that process is beyond the scope of this text.

The federal government and most state governments assess an estate tax on the estate of a decedent. This tax is levied against the estate, not the individual beneficiaries. It is the estate that is responsible to file an estate tax return within nine months of the decedent's death (though extensions can be obtained if necessary) and it is the estate that is responsible to pay the tax. Some states levy additional "inheritance" taxes on the beneficiaries in some cases.[2] We will confine our focus to the federal and state estate taxes.

Estate tax law is some of the most complex tax law in the Internal Revenue Code. For purposes related to trusts, the salient aspects of estate tax law include:

- What is counted as part of the estate, for estate tax purposes
- The applicable exemption amount
- Applicable estate tax deductions

The Gross Estate

The "gross estate" is the total assets held by a decedent that are subject to estate tax. The Internal Revenue Code's definition of gross estate is quite broad.[3] The gross estate includes more than property held in the decedent's name. It also includes annuities and retirement accounts with named beneficiaries, the

---

2. *See, e.g.,* http://www.state.nj.us/treasury/taxation/pdf/other_forms/inheritance/o10c.pdf.
3. *See* 26 U.S.C. §§ 2031–2046.

decedent's share in a joint account[4] life insurance policies over which the decedent had control[5] and many others.

Most salient for our discussion, however, is that the following are also included in a decedent's taxable estate:

- **Revocable Transfers.** Under § 2038, this includes the transfer of any interest in property (including a trust) over which the decedent maintained the power to "alter, amend, revoke, or terminate."
- **Transfers with a retained life interest.** Under § 2036, this includes any transfer of assets over which the decedent maintained the right to possession, enjoyment or the income from property or the right to designate who shall enjoy the enjoyment from the property.
- Property over which the decedent relinquished his or her authority within three years of death, if such power would have caused the property to be included in the decedent's estate under various other provisions.[6]

Let us now examine the impact of these provisions on trusts.

Revocable Trusts

It is clear that all revocable trusts are part of the taxable estate of the grantor. This is hardly a surprise, as revocable trust assets are considered the property of the grantor for virtually all purposes. However, the converse is not necessarily true. Just because a trust is "irrevocable," does not mean that it is outside the gross estate of the grantor. A trust may, for example, not allow the grantor to revoke the trust, but allow the grantor to change or terminate the trust. Any such power will cause the trust to be considered part of the taxable estate of the grantor although the trust is irrevocable.

> *Example: Jane establishes the* Jane Irrevocable Trust. *Jane's children are the beneficiaries of the trust. The trust states that it is irrevocable. However, Jane retains the authority to declare at any time that the trust shall terminate and the trust proceeds be distributed to her children. Even though Jane cannot be a beneficiary of the trust and even though she cannot change the trust beneficiaries, all of the trust assets*

---

4. Which includes, at a minimum, the entire amount originally contributed by the decedent, even if another person now has a partial interest in the account. *See* 26 U.S.C. § 2040.
5. 26 U.S.C. § 2042.
6. 26 U.S.C. § 2035.

are part of her taxable estate because she has the power to terminate the trust.

Example: *Jake establishes the* Jake Irrevocable Trust. *The trust document gives Jake the power to "amend the trust, so long as he does not change or impair the interests of any beneficiary or remainder beneficiary hereunder." In spite of this restriction on Jake's ability to amend the trust, because he can amend the trust, its assets are part of his taxable estate.*

Practice Tip: In many states, the default rule is that a trust is revocable. Therefore a trust draftsman should state specifically that a trust is irrevocable, especially when the trust is meant to be outside the taxable estate of the grantor. This is good practice even in states in which trusts are, by default, irrevocable. A typical irrevocability provision can be as simple as:

This trust and all interests in it are irrevocable and the Grantor has no power to alter, amend, revoke, or terminate any trust provision or interest, whether under this trust or under any statute or other rule of law.

Trusts with Retained Life Interests

§ 2036 dictates that assets over which the grantor retains certain beneficial interests are part of his or her taxable estate. Although § 2036 is entitled "Transfers with Retained Life Estate," its provisions are quite a bit broader than the title suggests. In fact, the section brings back into the estate of the grantor any trust property over which the grantor has:

1) The possession or enjoyment of, or the right to the income from, the property, or
2) The right, either alone or in conjunction with any person, to designate the persons who shall possess or enjoy the property or the income therefrom.

Any trust that gives the grantor the right to receive the income (or even a portion of the income) earned by the trust assets for the remainder of his or her life (or for any undetermined period) will likely see its assets included in the grantor's estate. Furthermore, the right to determine which beneficiaries receive benefit from the trust is covered by § 2036. The right to use trust property, even without the right to receive income, would also likely bring the property back into the estate of the grantor.

Example: Alan B. Cairns established the ABC Trust *for the benefit of his children. The trust states, "During the lifetime of the grantor, the trust assets shall be invested in an interest bearing account. The interest shall be distributed annually to the grantor. Upon the death of the grantor, the trust assets shall be distributed to the children of the grantor, in equal shares, per stirpes." Because the trust granted Alan an income interest for the remainder of his life, the entire trust will be included in Alan's taxable estate upon his death.*

Example: Donna created The Donna Family Trust *in which she places her residence for the eventual benefit of her children. The trust gives Donna the right to "live in the residence owned by the trust until the earlier of the death of Donna or her requiring care in a nursing home residence or similar facility." The entire value of the residence will be included in Donna's taxable estate upon her death. The fact that she had the right to live in the house for a period that may not end until her death, brings the entire value of the house back into Donna's gross estate.*

Example: Jack created The Jack Irrevocable Trust. *Jack is named as trustee of the trust. Under the trust terms, the trustees have the authority to determine how much of the trust monies are distributed annually to the trust beneficiaries (who do not include Jack). Because he kept the power to determine the beneficial interests in the trust, the entire value of the trust assets is included in Jack's taxable estate.*

Example: Jack created The Jack Irrevocable Trust. *Jack is not named as trustee. However, the trustee provides that, "Each year, the trust income shall be distributed to Jack's children, in equal shares. In addition, with Jack's approval, the trustee may distribute additional trust principal to any of Jack's children, for their health, education, maintenance and support." Because Jack retained the authority to designate who shall receive enjoyment from the trust property, the trust assets are likely part of his taxable estate.*

As discussed in chapter 3, under §2041, the grantor's maintenance of a testamentary power of appointment over the trust assets will also cause the trust assets to be included in the grantor's estate.[7]

---

7. 26 U.S.C. §2041(a)(2).

Example: Jill creates The Jill Irrevocable Trust. *The trust gives Jill no authority over the trust assets during her lifetime. However, the trust states "Upon Jill's death, the trust assets shall be distributed to whomever among Jill's children and grandchildren that she shall appoint such assets by a will that specifically references this power of appointment. In default of appointment, the trust assets shall be distributed to Jill's children, in equal shares, per stirpes." Although this power of appointment is a limited (or "special") power of appointment and even if it is not exercised by Jill, the entire trust value is included in her taxable estate.*[8]

It is true that there is some level of benefit or control the grantor may have over the trust assets without the assets being included in his or her taxable estate. However, to be on the safe side, most trusts that are designed to be outside the estate of the grantor should remove all control of the trust assets from the grantor. In addition, the grantor should be afforded no potential benefit from the trust assets. The grantor should also not be named as a trustee, co-trustee or successor trustee.[9]

It should be noted, however, that the grantor's spouse (unless he or she is also a grantor of the trust) is not subject to these restrictions. Therefore, in general, the grantor's spouse can be named as trustee and/or beneficiary of a trust without adverse estate tax consequences. Of course, it is important to avoid giving the grantor's spouse (or any other trustee or beneficiary) a general power of appointment over the trust assets, as discussed later in this chapter.

Practice Tip: Clients are usually more comfortable with their spouses serving as trustee than their children or other parties. Therefore, it's better to try and determine whether a spouse can serve as trustee without adverse tax consequences rather than to always "err on the side of caution" and recommend that a child serve as trustee.

---

8. *See* 26 U.S.C. § 2038(a)(1).

9. *See, e.g.,* http://estateplanning.wealthcounsel.com/legalblog/bid/37929/Grantor-as-trustee-of-irrevocable-trust.

Property Over Which the Decedent Relinquished Authority within Three Years of Death

Under § 2035, any gift made within three years of death is brought back into the taxable estate of the grantor. This includes gift transfers to trusts. In addition, if the grantor of a trust relinquished any power that would have caused the trust assets to be included in the person's estate within three years of death, this is also considered a gift—and the value of the property is included in the taxable estate.[10]

> *Example: Teri establishes* The Teri Revocable Trust, *which is revocable by Teri. On June 15, 2011, Teri disclaimed all interest in the trust, removing all of her beneficial interest in the trust and her control over the trust. Teri dies on January 1, 2014. The entire amount of this trust will be included in her taxable estate because the revocable trust would have been included in her taxable estate. That she relinquished her control over the trust does not help in this regard because she did so within three years of her death.*

Practice Tip: While it's not a great idea to belabor the "three year" rule with clients (clients, in general, are not very comfortable contemplating their own death within three years), the practitioner should make his or her own assessment of the client's likelihood of living three years. For example, establishing and funding an irrevocable life insurance trust for the purpose of removing the death benefit from the taxable estate of the client[11] may not be appropriate for a client suffering from terminal cancer.

Completed Gifts That Are Part of the Grantor's Taxable Estate

Last chapter, we discussed the types of transfers to trusts that are considered completed gifts for gift tax purposes. This chapter we have discussed the types of transfers to trusts that remove the transferred assets from the person's taxable estate. In most cases, the two concepts are interrelated. In most cases,

---

10. *See* 26 U.S.C. § 2035.
11. Discussed in more detail in chapter 10.

transfers that are considered completed gifts for gift tax purposes also remove the transferred assets from the transferor's estate. Conversely, transfers that are incomplete gifts generally leave the transferred asset in the taxable estate of the transferor.

> *Example: Jill creates* The Jill Irrevocable Trust. *The trust gives Jill no authority over the trust assets during her lifetime. However, the trust states "Upon Jill's death, the trust assets shall be distributed to whomever among Jill's children and grandchildren that she shall appoint such assets by a Will that specifically references this power of appointment." This transfer is an incomplete gift, thus not requiring the filing of a gift tax return and it is not subject to gift tax consequences of any sort. However, when Jill dies, the full value of the trust assets will be included in her taxable estate.*[12]

However, it is possible for a gift to a trust to be a completed gift for gift tax purposes and nevertheless *not* be removed from the grantor's taxable estate.

> *Example: John owns a life insurance policy on his life. The policy is a whole life policy and has a cash value of $200,000, with a death benefit of $1,000,000.*[13] *On January 10, 2011, John transfers the policy to an irrevocable life insurance trust in which he retains no interest or control. Because this transfer is a completed gift, he must file a gift tax return. If he has already used up his lifetime gift tax exemption, he must pay gift tax.*
>
> *On May 1, 2012, John dies of a heart attack. Because he made this transfer within three years of death, the entire value of the death benefit will be part of John's taxable estate even though at the time it was given, the transfer to the trust was a completed gift for gift tax purposes. On the positive side, any gift tax paid at the time of the transfer can be deducted from the estate tax that will be paid at death.*[14] *In addition, the amount applied against the estate tax exemption will be the death benefit, not the value of the initial gift. In other words, for estate tax purposes, it will be as if the policy was never transferred to the trust.*

---

12. *See* 26 U.S.C. §2038.

13. See chapter 10 for a discussion of these terms and concepts.

14. See Line 7 of the United States Estate Tax Return (Form 706) (http://www.irs.gov/pub/irs-pdf/f706.pdf).

When Trust Assets Can Be Considered Part of the Estate of a Beneficiary or Trustee

Trust assets can also be included in the taxable estate of the trustee or beneficiary of a trust (or anyone else, for that matter) if the person has a general power of appointment over those assets.[15] Under Section 2041 of the Internal Revenue Code, a person has a "general power of appointment" over assets when he or she has a power to direct the disposition of the asset "which is exercisable in favor of the decedent, his estate, his creditors, or the creditors of his estate."[16] In other words, the person has the authority to direct that the assets be distributed to those parties. This power can be exercisable during the lifetime of the person or upon his or her death (the latter is also referred to as a "testamentary power of appointment").

> *Example:* Derek Jones established the Jones Family Trust. *The trust states, "During the lifetime of the Grantor's daughter, Maria Jones, Maria may distribute trust assets to whomever she deems appropriate." Maria has a lifetime general power of appointment over these assets because she has the power to direct them to herself, her creditors, etc. When Maria dies, the entire value of the trust will be included in her taxable estate. This is true whether or not Maria is the trustee of the trust.*

> *Example:* Derek Jones established the Jones Family Trust. *The trust states, "Upon the death of the Grantor's wife, Susan Jones, the trust assets shall be distributed to whomever Susan Jones shall appoint these assets by a Will that specifically referenced this power of appointment." Susan has a testamentary general power of appointment over the trust assets. Therefore, the entire value of the trust will be included in her taxable estate upon her death.*

> *Example:* Derek Jones establishes the Jones Family Trust. *The trust states, "Upon the death of the Grantor's wife, Susan Jones, the trust assets shall be distributed to whomever among a class of people that includes everyone except for Susan Jones, her estate, her creditors, and the creditors of her estate that she shall appoint these assets by a Will that specifically referenced this power of appointment." As this*

---

15. 26 U.S.C. § 2041.
16. 26 U.S.C. § 2041(b)(1).

does not meet the definition of a general power of appointment under §2041, it is only a limited power of appointment. Therefore, the value of the trust will not necessarily be included in her taxable estate upon her death (unless something else about the trust causes it to be considered part of her taxable estate).

Specific Types of Estate Tax Planning Trusts

There are many different forms of trusts that are designed to hold assets outside of the taxable estate of the grantor. A common thread through most of them is that the grantor may not retain any beneficial interest in the trust. This is usually necessary to ensure that the trust does not run afoul of §2036, which dictates that assets over which the grantor retains a "life" interest are part of his or her estate.[17]

However, there are several types of trusts that can be removed from the grantor's estate even though the grantor maintains *some* interest in them. Because of the complexity and uncertainty behind §2036, the best policy is to avoid making the grantor the beneficiary of any interest in a trust that is meant to be outside of the grantor's estate except for those interests that are specified in the Internal Revenue Code or applicable regulations or case law as being "safe" under §2036.

Below are some examples of trusts where the grantor holds some interests that are still considered outside the estate of the grantor.[18]

Grantor Retained Annuity Trust (GRAT)

A Grantor Retained Annuity Trust ("GRAT"), on its face, is quite a simple device. The grantor transfers assets to a trust and, in exchange, the trust guarantees the grantor an annual payment (an "annuity") of a given amount. The specifics of the GRAT requirements are complex and are set forth in the Treasury Regulations.[19]

---

17. 26 U.S.C. §2036.

18. It is beyond the scope of this text to discuss the complex rules that govern these instruments. It is the purpose of this text merely to make the student aware of these devices. The usage of any of these complex devices should not be attempted without considerable further research and study.

19. Treas. Reg. §25.2702-3.

Example: Mark creates a GRAT. He transfers $1,000,000 worth of assets to the trust. In exchange, the trust gives him a promissory note that guarantees that it will pay him $50,000 per year for the next 25 years.

Because Mark's interest in the GRAT is limited by a criterion that does not reference Mark's life, §2036 does not bring the value of the GRAT back into his taxable estate.[20] Instead, the trust will remain outside of his estate. Of course, the $50,000 per year that he receives from the GRAT will be part of his estate because he is entitled to receive it.

A contribution to a GRAT will be subject to gift tax. That is, the value of the property transferred minus the value of the annuity received is considered a gift to the trust. The value of the annuity depends on current interest rates, as calculated under Section 7520 of the Internal Revenue Code. The actual applicable rates are published in the IRS website.[21] There are many websites that will allow you to calculate the value of annuities relatively easily once you know the applicable interest rate.[22]

Example: Going back to Mark's GRAT, assuming an applicable interest rate of 4%, the value of Mark's annuity is $781,104.00. Since the assets transferred to the trust were worth $1,000,000, he would have to file a gift tax return and report a taxable gift of $218,896.00. If he still has any lifetime gift tax exemption remaining, this amount will use some or all of his exemption. Otherwise, it will be subject to gift tax.

It is also possible to ensure that the annuity that the grantor receives is worth as much as the initial investment. In such case, there are no gift tax implications upon the transfer since the grantor is being fully compensated for his transferred assets. This type of trust is sometimes referred to as a "zeroed out" GRAT.

Example: Let's change the facts of Mark's GRAT. Assuming the same applicable interest rate of 4%, assume that Mark's annuity was for a period of 30 years and the annual payment is $58,000. Using the website referenced above, we calculate that annuity is worth slightly more than $1,000,000. Therefore, this is a "zeroed out" GRAT and no gift tax will be due upon the initial transfer of the $1,000,000 to the trust.

---

20. 26 U.S.C. §2036(a).
21. http://www.irs.gov/businesses/small/article/0,,id=112482,00.html.
22. E.g., http://www.investopedia.com/calculator/AnnuityPV.aspx.

The GRAT is best used to hold assets that, in the opinion of the grantor, will outperform the applicable federal interest rate. While the value of the annuity interest coming back to the grantor is "frozen" by the terms of the promissory note, the asset can appreciate outside of the estate of the grantor.

> *Example: Mark contributes an investment portfolio worth $1,000,000 to a GRAT in exchange for a promissory note with an annual payment of $58,000 over 30 years. Under the applicable interest rates, the value of the annuity is $1,000,000. Therefore, this qualifies as a zeroed out GRAT. This is based on an applicable interest rate of 4%. Mark believes that his investment portfolio will earn an annual return of at least 6%. Because the annuity that is returned to him (and thus brought back into his estate) is locked in at a 4% interest rate, this extra growth will inure to the benefit of his beneficiaries free of estate or gift tax.*

The biggest downside to the GRAT is the somewhat peculiar and harsh rule that the grantor must survive the term of the GRAT for the GRAT assets to be removed from his or her taxable estate.[23] If the grantor dies within the annuity term, the entire value of the GRAT is brought back into his or her taxable estate.[24]

> *Example: Mark contributes $1,000,000 to a GRAT in exchange for a promissory note for an annual payment of $58,000 over the course of 30 years. Under the applicable interest rates, the value of the annuity is $1,000,000. In year 27, Mark dies. Everything remaining in the GRAT is considered part of Mark's taxable estate. In effect, the GRAT had no transfer tax benefit because Mark did not survive the term.*

Intentionally Defective Grantor Trust ("IDGT")

In spite of its unwieldy and misleading trade name, an IDGT is really nothing more than a standard irrevocable trust that is outside of the estate of the grantor. This trust mechanism works in a manner that is very similar to a "zeroed out" GRAT discussed in the previous section. The grantor transfers property or investments to the IDGT in exchange for the promissory note that promises, in return, an annuity that is of the same present value of the initial contribution. The asset can then grow outside of the taxable estate of the grantor.

---

23. 26 U.S.C. §2036(a) (including in the taxable estate an interest "which does not in fact end before his death").
24. Treas. Reg. §25.2702-3.

The trust is generally established as a "grantor" trust, so that the income earned by the assets in the trust are taxable to the grantor personally, thus avoiding high trust taxation.[25] Although this is not an essential element in the estate tax features of the trust, it is so common that the name of the device reflects this common feature. The term "intentionally defective" in the title of the device refers to the fact that, for income tax purposes, the trust is disregarded (as with all grantor trusts) and is thus "defective" for income tax purposes.

There are several advantages of the IDGT over the zeroed out GRAT strategy. The most important is that unlike the GRAT, the grantor need not survive the term of the promissory note for the trust assets to be considered outside the estate of the grantor.

> **Example:** *Marsha establishes an IDGT. She funds it with cash and investments worth $5,000,000. In exchange the IDGT promises to pay her $250,000 per year for 25 years. At an applicable interest rate of 3%, the value of this annuity is $4,353,286.92. Therefore, the initial gift to the trust is $646,713.08. Assuming that Marsha has not used her gift tax exemption, this amount would be within her $1,000,000 lifetime exemption amount. If Marsha dies when the trust investments have ballooned to $6,000,000, none of it will be in her taxable estate. Furthermore, if she dies 10 years into the note's payout period, only the remaining value of the note will be included in her taxable estate.*

One caveat, however, is that the IDGT must be funded with a substantial amount of "seed money" that is beyond the value of the promissory note. Otherwise, the IRS could take the position that it is unrealistic to expect that the IDGT would have the ability to generate the capital necessary to pay off the promissory note in a timely manner throughout its term. The exact amount of necessary seed money is unclear, but the general principle is that it should be more than 10% of the total value of the contribution. The contribution of the seed money is a gift and thus causes the grantor to use some of his or her available lifetime gift tax exemption amount.[26]

There are several other types of retained interest trusts that work in a manner similar to those described above. One of these, the Qualified Personal Residence Trust (QPRT) will be discussed later, in chapter 9.

---

25. See chapter 5 for more discussion on grantor trusts and income taxation of trusts.
26. See generally, http://www.cpa2biz.com/Content/media/PRODUCER_CONTENT/Newsletters/Articles_2007/CPA/Dec/Sales.jsp.

Practice Tip: Zeroed out GRATs and IDGTs are complex strategies and are generally only necessary for clients with excessive wealth (perhaps $5,000,000 more than the exemption amount). For clients with smaller estate tax issues, lifetime gifting, credit shelter trusts and similar simpler strategies will usually suffice.

Advantages to Keeping Trust Assets in the Grantor's Estate

Throughout this chapter, we have focused on ensuring that trust assets are maintained outside of the taxable estate of the grantor. However, in many trusts, it is important that the trust assets remain *within* the taxable estate of the grantor. There are two principle possible reasons for this. The first is that transfers to trusts that are in the estate of the grantor are generally not subject to gift tax. The second, often more important reason, is that property within the taxable estate allows a "step up" in cost basis for assets that have appreciated in value since they were acquired.[27]

Even when it is necessary to ensure that trust assets be kept in the estate of the grantor, it is still important that the grantor not be given a general power of appointment over the trust assets, as that may cause the trust assets to needlessly become vulnerable to the creditors of the grantor.

Practice Tip: The simplest and most benign way to keep trust property in the estate of the grantor is to give the grantor a limited testamentary power of appointment over the trust assets, as discussed earlier in this chapter. The grantor should be given the authority to appoint the trust assets upon death to whomever among a class of people that includes everyone except for the grantor, her estate, her creditors, and the creditors of her estate that she shall appoint these assets by a Will that specifically referenced this limited power of appointment." This keeps the trust property in the grantor's estate with no adverse consequences in other areas. In addition, it can be useful to the grantor, as it allows her the flexibility to change beneficiaries within her family (or even to appoint the assets to a trust upon her death).

---

27. *See* 26 U.S.C. §1014 (also explained in chapter 5).

Using the Estate Tax Marital Deduction

Current federal estate tax law allows an unlimited marital deduction for gifts (during lifetime and upon death) to a surviving spouse.[28] However, if not properly taken advantage of, the marital deduction can be easily wasted.

> *Example: George and Martha have $7,000,000 in their estate. Most of the assets are in joint accounts, but some assets are in each spouse's name. George and Martha each execute wills whereby they each leave their entire estate to the surviving spouse and, if there is no spouse, to their children, in equal shares. When George dies first, there is no estate tax because of the marital deduction. However, when Martha dies, all $7,000,000 is subject to estate tax. In effect, only Martha's estate tax exemption amount is used. George's estate tax exemption has been wasted. As we will see, much of this estate tax could have been avoided. If an attorney recommended these simple wills to George and Martha, then he committed gross malpractice.*

Credit Shelter Trust

The good news is that, using a rather simple device sometimes referred to as a "credit shelter trust" or "credit share" in a will or any trust that is within the taxable estate of the grantor, the estate tax exemption amount of both spouses can be used. Upon the death of the first spouse, the first spouse's estate is split into two components: one that will effectively pass to the other heirs (children, etc.) directly from the estate of the first spouse and the other that will be counted as part of the surviving spouse's taxable estate.

The first share is generally limited to the amount that can pass free of estate tax. Although this amount can be distributed directly to the client's children, clients are usually reluctant to do this. First, clients often want the surviving spouse to be able to receive some benefit from this money during his or her lifetime. Second, clients may believe that their children may not be ready to receive all of the assets upon the first death. Therefore, at the first death the amount that can pass free of estate tax is usually set aside into a trust (the

---

28. 26 U.S.C. § 2056.

"credit share" or "credit shelter trust"). The exact amount that will be set aside for the credit share depends on two factors:

1) The applicable estate tax exemption amount at the time; and
2) The amount of gift/estate tax exemption the grantor already used during his or her lifetime.

> *Example:* Janet Scott creates The Janet Scott Revocable Trust *and puts all of her $5,000,000 in assets into the trust. The trust states that if upon her death Janet's husband is living, the amount that can pass free of estate tax shall be held in a credit shelter trust. When Janet dies, the applicable estate tax exemption amount is $2,000,000, but Janet has already used $400,000 in gift tax lifetime exclusion. Since taxable gifts also count against the estate tax exemption, the credit shelter trust will be funded with $1,600,000 in assets. This amount will pass to the credit shelter trust free of estate tax.*

Prior to 2001, the federal estate tax exemption amount was the same as the exemption for all states. However, because of the major changes to estate tax law that were made in 2001, the federal and state estate tax exemptions amounts often are different from each other (some states, in fact, have no state estate tax). Thus, it is often necessary to specify that the amount that goes to the credit shelter trust has to be the *lesser* of the state estate tax exemption amount and the federal exemption amount. More can always be allocated to the credit shelter trust if necessary after the death of the first spouse by using a "disclaimer," a device which will be discussed later in this chapter.

> *Example:* Xavier lives in New Jersey, where the state estate tax exemption amount is only $675,000. If the federal exemption amount is $2,000,000, Xavier's will or trust may still be tailored to set aside $675,000 automatically for the credit shelter trust upon Xavier's death. A disclaimer provision (discussed below) may be used to allow more to be set aside in the credit shelter trust if the circumstances warrant such action.

Although the funds in the credit shelter trust will not be part of the surviving spouse's estate that does not mean that the surviving spouse cannot have any benefit from the trust. Because the surviving spouse is not the grantor, the following benefits can be maintained for the surviving spouse from the credit shelter trust without the credit shelter trust assets being considered part of the surviving spouse's taxable estate:

• The right to receive all income from the trust;

- The right to withdraw up to the greater of 5% of the trust principal and $5,000 each year;[29] and
- The right to receive additional principal at the discretion of the trustee.

Practice Tip: Although the surviving spouse can be the trustee of the credit shelter trust as long as this power to withdraw is limited by an ascertainable standard (e.g., "health, education, maintenance and support"), the best practice, if the client wants to allow the spouse these discretionary distributions, is to appoint a co-trustee with the spouse, or at least require the consent of a backup trustee before the spouse can make discretionary distributions to herself. Of course, the client can choose to give his or her spouse less benefit from the credit shelter trust, but, by and large, these are the guidelines used to maximize the surviving spouse's interest.

Upon the death of the surviving spouse, the trust assets are typically distributed among the children of the client (or held in further trust for their benefit if the client prefers). Of course, the client can direct pretty much any disposition of these assets at the time that the will or trust is executed. The surviving spouse may also be given a limited testamentary power of appointment over the trust assets upon the second spouse's death (but should not be given a general power of appointment).

A typical credit shelter trust provision (in a revocable trust) may read as follows:

> Upon the grantor's death, if the grantor's wife is living, the trustee shall set aside the largest amount that can pass free of federal and state estate tax; provided, however, that the sum disposed of by this Article shall be reduced by the value of property which passes outside the terms of this trust or which passes under other Articles of this trust and which does not qualify for the estate tax charitable or marital deductions. The trustee shall hold, administer and distribute these assets (known as the "credit shelter trust") as follows:
>
> A. During the lifetime of the grantor's wife, the trustee shall pay to or for the benefit of the grantor's wife, in quarterly or more frequent installments, all of the net income of the trust.
>
> B. During the lifetime of the grantor's wife, the trustee may also pay to or apply for the benefit of the grantor's wife such portions of the prin-

---

29. 26 U.S.C. § 2041(b)(2).

cipal of the trust as the trustee deems advisable to provide for the grantor's wife's health, education, support and maintenance after taking into account her other resources. If the grantor's wife is serving as trustee or co-trustee of this trust, however, she shall take no part in the decision to make a distribution under this Paragraph. Only the successor trustee or other co-trustee may make a distribution from this trust under this Paragraph to the grantor's wife.

C. In addition to the above provisions, during the month of December of any calendar year, the grantor's wife shall have the power to direct my trustee to pay to her out of the trust's principal in each year, an amount not in excess of the greater of five thousand dollars ($5,000) or five percent (5%) of the aggregate value of the trust principal as determined at the end of each taxable year of the trust. This power is noncumulative and can be exercised only by an instrument in writing signed by the grantor's wife during the month of December and delivered that month to my trustee in any calendar year of withdrawal.

D. Upon the death of the grantor's wife, the trust assets shall be distributed to whomever among the children of the grantor (including trusts for the exclusive benefit of the children of the grantor) that the grantor's wife shall appoint said assets by a Will that specifically referenced this limited power of appointment. In default of appointment, the trust assets shall be distributed to the children of the grantor, in equal shares, per stirpes.

Practice Tip: In many cases, clients are going to want to give their spouses the maximum allowable benefit from the credit shelter trust. However, in cases where the spouses have children from previous marriages or where there's some level of discord between the spouses, giving the surviving spouse less than maximum benefit may be appropriate. This issue, although requiring tact, must be raised in the estate planning process.

Marital Deduction Share

The remainder of the estate (i.e., that cannot pass free of estate tax) is typically either given outright to the surviving spouse or held for the surviving spouse's benefit. The primary goal is to ensure that this share of the estate is exempt from the estate tax due to the marital deduction. Distributing the assets to the surviving spouse outright, of course, qualifies for the marital deduction.

However, even a gift to a trust for the benefit of the surviving spouse can qualify for the marital deduction as long as the spouse's interest qualifies as a "qualified terminable interest property" ("QTIP") trust.[30] To so qualify, the following conditions must be met:

- The spouse must be entitled to all income earned by the trust.
- The spouse must have the right to demand that property be invested in a manner that allows it to earn income.
- No one other than the surviving spouse may have a beneficial interest in the trust. (The trustee may, but need not, be authorized to distribute additional funds to the spouse at the trustee's discretion.)
- Upon the spouse's death, all accrued trust income must be distributed to the surviving spouse's estate. (The remaining trust principal may be distributed in any manner the trust provides.)
- The QTIP assets are counted as part of the surviving spouse's estate upon her death.[31]

A QTIP is typically chosen over an outright distribution to the surviving spouse for any of several reasons including:

- A QTIP may help ensure that the ultimate beneficiaries of the trust, after the spouse's death, are the beneficiaries of the grantor. If the surviving spouse received the assets outright, he or she would be able to direct the assets in any manner he or she chooses, potentially being able to disinherit children of the grantor.
- Holding assets in a QTIP may allow the surviving spouse to qualify for government assistance programs such as Medicaid.
- If the surviving spouse is elderly or incompetent, the QTIP provides a convenient vehicle in which a trustee can hold trust assets for the surviving spouse while allowing the assets to be eligible for the marital deduction upon the first death.

Example: Gerald has $5,000,000 in assets. He has a wife, Shirley, and three children. Upon his death, he would like his estate plan to reflect the most favorable estate tax treatment for the family. However, he is afraid that if Shirley gets a large share of his assets outright, she might get re-married and give those assets to her new husband and/or step children. So, you suggest that Gerald execute a will or revocable trust

---

30. 26 U.S.C. § 2056 (b).
31. 26 U.S.C. § 2056 (b)(7)(B).

that divides his estate into credit shelter and marital trust shares. Shirley will have the right to income from both trusts and the QTIP requirements will be satisfied in the marital trust component.

A typical QTIP provision (this time from a will establishing a testamentary QTIP) may read as follows:

The Marital trust shall be held and administered as follows:

1. In establishing and administering the trust created hereunder, the Executor and Trustee shall be vested with all of the powers and authority hereinafter set out. However, it is expressly provided that the grant of rights, powers, privileges and authority to the Executor and Trustee in connection with the imposition of duties upon the Executor and Trustee by any provision of the Marital Trust or by any statute relating thereto, shall not be effective if it would disqualify the marital deduction as it is established in the Marital Trust hereof.

2. The Trustee shall pay the entire net income in quarterly or more frequent installments to my wife, or apply it for her benefit, so long as she shall live.

3. In addition to the payment of income, the Trustee may pay to my wife such amounts (including some or all) of the corpus of the trust property held for her benefit as may from time to time be deemed required to enable my wife to maintain substantially the standard of living to which my wife was accustomed at the time of my death, and in making such payments the Trustee may, but need not, take into account other financial resources available to her.

4. If non-income producing property is held, my wife shall have the right to direct that such property be exchanged for income-producing property.

5. At the death of my wife, any accumulated and accrued income shall be paid to my wife's estate, and all of the remaining trust assets shall be distributed to my Trustee, hereinafter named, to be held in trust for the benefit of my issue, to be held and administered in accordance with the instructions set forth below.

6. On the death of my wife, the Trustee shall be authorized to withhold distribution of an amount of property sufficient to cover any liability that may be imposed on the Trustee for estate or other taxes until such liability is finally determined and paid.

7. My Executor shall have the right to elect to qualify or not to qualify all or any fractional or percentile share of this trust for the marital de-

duction. Generally, I anticipate that my Executor will elect to minimize the estate tax payable by my estate. However, I would expect that some consideration be given to the estate tax payable by my wife's estate upon her death, especially if she should die prior to the time the election is made. Upon distribution of my residuary estate to the Trustee, my Executor shall certify to the Trustee the fraction of the trust which has qualified for the marital deduction. The Trustee shall divide the trust into a marital deduction share and a non-marital deduction share based upon such fraction. I direct that any invasions of corpus shall be distributed from the marital deduction share before any such invasions are distributed from the non-marital deduction share. I exonerate my Executor from any liability for such election and direct that no beneficiary or other person shall have any claim against my Executor or my estate by reason of the exercise of my Executor's judgment in this respect.

Revocable trusts that split the estate upon the grantor's death into credit shelter and marital trusts are sometimes referred to as "A-B" trusts. Although there's no compelling reason for this, the general convention is that the marital (QTIP) trust is designated as share A (or "Trust A") while the credit shelter trust share is designated as share B (or "Trust B").

Practice Tip: For a relatively young and healthy couple executing a will, there is generally no compelling reason to suggest a QTIP. On the contrary, clients may find it more convenient simply to allow the outright distribution of these funds to the surviving spouse. A QTIP should be recommended where there are potential disagreements about how the assets will be distributed upon the second death or where there's another good reason that the surviving spouse should not be able to access the trust funds outright upon the first death.

A QTIP can also be established and funded during the lifetime of the grantor. Gifts to a QTIP are exempt from adverse gift tax ramifications because of the unlimited gift tax marital deduction.[32] However, the assets in the QTIP are, of course, part of the taxable estate of the recipient spouse upon his or her death.

Qualified Disclaimers

Another important device in the repertoire of the estate planning attorney is the qualified disclaimer. A qualified disclaimer is a manner in which a recipient

---

32. 26 U.S.C. §2523(b).

of a gift (typically in a will or trust) refuses the gift. The procedure, if executed properly with all the formalities laid out under federal law,[33] causes the gift to pass as though the recipient were not alive and the gift passes to the next beneficiary in line.

Although disclaimers can be used for many reasons; they are most often used for estate tax purposes.

> *Example: Joan has an estate worth $5,000,000. When she is 84 years old, her brother Jim, passes away, leaving a bequest in a will that gives stocks and bonds worth $400,000 "to Joan, or, if she is not living, then to her children, in equal shares." Odds are that when Joan dies, a federal estate tax will take about half of this $400,000. Thus, Joan likely will want to disclaim the $400,000. If she does this, the stocks and bonds will be distributed directly to her children and will not be part of Joan's taxable estate.*

To be valid for purposes of federal taxation, a disclaimer must meet the following requirements:

- It must be in writing;
- It must be executed and delivered to the person who is otherwise receiving the property within nine months of the date that the person making the disclaimer was entitled to the asset (usually the death of the previous interest holder);
- The person making the disclaimer must not have received any interest in or benefit from the property disclaimed; and
- The property must pass entirely to someone other than the person making the disclaimer.[34]

An exception to this last requirement rule occurs when a surviving spouse disclaims. A surviving spouse can disclaim assets even if they will go to a trust of which she is a partial beneficiary.[35]

Disclaimers can be used to increase the flexibility of a gift to a spouse for estate tax purposes. For example, assets could be gifted to a spouse, but allow the spouse to "disclaim" assets so that they would go to the children or into a credit shelter trust instead. This can allow the decision of how much to hold in the

---

33. 26 U.S.C. §2518.
34. 26 U.S.C. §2518 (b).
35. 26 U.S.C. §2518(a).

surviving spouse's taxable estate to be delayed until after the first spouse dies. The concept is best illustrated by examples.

> **Simple Example:** *Susanna has a simple will that gives all of her assets to her husband, John, when she dies, or to their children if John is not alive. When she does die, the estate tax exemption amount is $1,000,000, but her estate is $2,000,000. If John accepts all $2,000,000, then when he dies, his estate may be subject to estate tax. So he accepts $1,000,000 and disclaims $1,000,000, which goes to the children. The remaining $1,000,000 goes to John. The $1,000,000 that went to the children was not subject to estate tax because it was covered by the exemption amount. The remaining $1,000,000 in John's estate will not subject his estate to estate tax because it is also covered by the exemption amount.*

> **More Complex Example:** *Jared lives in New York, where the state estate tax exemption amount is $1,000,000. Beyond that, the state assesses an estate tax that is generally under 10%. Jared has approximately $6,000,000 in assets. Jared's revocable trust allocates the maximum that can pass free of federal and state estate taxes to a credit shelter trust for his children, and the remainder to a QTIP for the benefit of his wife, Donna.*

> *When Jared dies, the federal estate tax exemption amount is $3,000,000. However, according to Jared's will, $1,000,000 passes to the credit shelter trust and $5,000,000 passes to Donna. When Donna dies, the $5,000,000 will be subject to a massive federal estate tax of almost $1,000,000, because her estate is $2,000,000 above the exemption amount.*

> *Therefore, Donna decides to "disclaim" $2,000,000 from Jared's estate. Assuming she does so, and meets the requirements of Section 2518, this $2,000,000 will go to their children as though she predeceased Jared. The remaining $3,000,000 will go to the QTIP and be part of Donna's estate. Now, upon Jared's death, $3,000,000 ($1,000,000 to credit shelter plus $2,000,000 disclaimed) passes outside of Donna's estate and is subject to estate tax. Although this $3,000,000 is fully covered on the federal level by the exemption amount, it will be subject to New York state estate tax of about $100,000. Upon Donna's death, her $3,000,000 that she did not disclaim is also covered by the federal exemption, although it will also be subject to a New York state estate tax of about $100,000.*

> *Thus, by disclaiming, Donna's entire family pays a total of $200,000 in estate tax.*

Now, let's see what would have happened had Donna not disclaimed.

Upon Jared's death, only $1,000,000 is subject to estate tax. Since that amount is covered by both the federal and state exemption amounts, there will be no estate tax upon Jared's death at all. However, when Donna dies, the remaining $5,000,000 is part of her taxable estate. That will subject her estate to a New York estate tax of almost $400,000 and a federal estate tax of about $700,000, for a total estate tax of about $1,100,000! By the relatively simple act of disclaiming, Donna saved her family $900,000 in estate taxes!

If provided for by a trust or will, a disclaimer by a surviving spouse can also serve to allocate the disclaimed funds to a credit shelter trust rather than directly to the children. Additionally, a spouse can disclaim not only assets that would be distributed to him or her outright, they can also disclaim an interest in a trust (such as a QTIP). A typical trust provision that anticipates a disclaimer in this manner reads as follows:

A. Upon the death of the Grantor, all of the trust assets shall be held for the benefit of the Grantor's husband, JAMES JONES, in a marital trust, under the following terms and conditions:

[QTIP qualifying trust provisions]

B. In the event that the Grantor's husband, JAMES JONES, or his legal representative, shall make a qualified disclaimer (as defined in Section 2518 of the Internal Revenue Code) on some or all of the assets allocated or designated for the marital trust, then the amount so disclaimed shall be transferred into a new trust which shall be known as the Credit Shelter Trust, which shall be held, administered and distributed under the following terms and conditions:

[credit shelter trust provisions]

Practice Tip: Putting disclaimer provisions in trusts and wills and relying on them for flexibility in estate tax planning is an excellent strategy for clients who are conscientious and who will consult a lawyer shortly after the first death. However, keep in mind that disclaimers must be done, if at all, within nine months of death. Therefore, it is important to tell the clients, in writing, that a lawyer (such as your firm) should be consulted as soon as possible after the first death. Not only is this sound tax planning advice, but it may help garner more business for your firm.

Generation Skipping Transfer Tax ("GSTT")

To ensure that wealthy families do not avoid a level of estate taxation by transferring assets directly from grandparent to grandchild, federal law applies a generation skipping transfer tax (GSTT) on transfers that skip a generation.[36] Such transfers are called "direct skips" and the recipient of the gift is called a "skip person." For unrelated parties, a transferee who is 37½ years younger than the transferor is considered a skip person.[37] The GSTT rates are generally the same as the estate tax rates.[38]

> *Example:* Ken is a 92-year-old widower with an estate of $10,000,000. He has one child, Monica, who is 69 years old. Monica has four adult children. He realizes that if he dies and leaves his estate to Monica, it will be subject to estate tax. Then, when Monica dies, it will be subject to estate tax again. So, he decides to alter his will to give all of his money directly to Monica's children, so as to avoid one level of estate tax. Unfortunately, the GSTT renders this strategy ineffective. When Ken dies and his assets go to his grandchildren, a regular estate tax will be assessed and a comparable generation skipping transfer tax will be assessed on the remainder. In effect, both estate taxes will be paid at the same time.

The GSTT applies to gifts made during lifetime and to gifts made at death (by will or trust or other mechanism that is considered part of the taxable estate of the grantor) and it is subject to the same exemption amount as the estate tax exemption amount. If the estate tax exemption amount is $3,500,000, there is likewise no GSTT on gift transfers made of up to $3,500,000 over the course of a lifetime and at death. Unlike estate tax, there is generally no GSTT on the state level. This is a federal tax only.

Practice Tip: Gifting some assets directly to grandchildren can be a good estate planning strategy. Just make sure that the total amount of taxable gifts to grandchildren is less than the applicable generation skipping transfer tax exemption amount.

---

36. 26 U.S.C. §601, *et seq.*
37. *See* IRS Form 709 Instructions, page 7, column 1 (http://www.irs.gov/pub/irs-pdf/i709.pdf).
38. 26 U.S.C. §2641.

Direct and Indirect Skips

Outright gifts to "skip persons" are considered direct skips and are subject to GSTT, if over the exemption amount. However, what about a transfer to a trust or similar device that has both skip persons and non-skip persons as beneficiaries?

> *Example: Don establishes a family trust. The trust provides, "Until termination of the trust, the trustee may distribute trust income and/or principal to any of the children and/or grandchildren of the grantor to the extent the trustee deems appropriate for their health, education, maintenance and support." This trust clearly has both skip persons (Don's grandchildren) and non-skip persons (Don's children) as beneficiaries.*

The general rule regarding such trusts is that GSTT exemption is not used when the assets are gifted to the trust initially. Instead, when and if assets are given from the trust to a skip person, that is considered a "taxable distribution" (if during the trust's existence) or a "taxable termination" (if upon termination of the trust). At that point, a generation skipping transfer has taken place.

The danger here is that GSTT exemption must be allocated for a person's estate on his or her estate tax return.[39] In other words, on the estate tax return of the person who passes away and who made generation skipping transfers during life or at death must decide how to divide and use the GSTT exemption amount. At the time of the person's death, it may not be clear whether it is necessary to use GSTT exemption on a trust with skip persons as beneficiaries. If the executor uses GSTT exemption on all of the trust assets, there may be insufficient exemption to cover other generation skipping transfers. If the executor uses no GSTT exemption on the trust, then if the trust makes a generation skipping distribution later on (a "taxable termination"), then the distribution will be subject to GSTT.

Although the complexities of GSTT allocation is beyond the scope of this text, suffice it to say that transfers to trusts that have skip persons and non-skip persons as beneficiaries can cause unnecessary risks and complexities. Therefore, it is usually advisable to ensure that trusts do not have both skip persons and non-skip persons as beneficiaries.

---

39. *See* pages 24–27 of the Instructions for Schedule R of U.S. Estate Tax Return (Form 706) (http://www.irs.gov/pub/irs-pdf/i706.pdf).

Example: In Don's case above, the trust should instead provide, "Until termination of the trust, the trustee may distribute trust income and/or principal to any of the children of the grantor to the extent the trustee deems appropriate for their health, education, maintenance and support." If Don wants to benefit his grandchildren he should do so in a separate trust.

Testamentary Generation Skipping Trusts

As you'll recall, the credit shelter trust device seeks to take advantage of both spouses' estate tax exemptions by splitting the estate into two shares upon the death of the first spouse. The maximum amount that can pass free of estate tax passes to the credit shelter trust and the remainder to the spouse or a QTIP. The same basic strategy can be employed to allow wealthy families to take advantage of both the estate tax exemption and the GSTT exemption in passing assets to the third generation. This is best illustrated by way of example.

Example: Samantha is 90 years old, has a $15,000,000 estate, has no spouse, and has three children: Alan, Beth and Carla. The estate tax exemption amount is $3,000,000. Samantha knows that her estate is going to be subject to a hefty estate tax and wants her children to avoid estate tax. As we have seen, transferring the assets directly to the grandchildren is a bad idea because of the GSTT. In addition, passing all $15,000,000 to the children would give them each taxable estates.

Samantha's will thus divides her estate as follows. The maximum amount that can pass free of GSTT passes to three trusts, each for the benefit of the children of one child. The remainder passes directly to the children. When Samantha dies, Alan will get $4,000,000 outright and $1,000,000 will be outside of his estate as it will pass to a generation skipping trust for the benefit of Alan's children. This distribution is repeated for Samantha's other two children and their children. Thus, there is estate tax on $12,000,000 on Samantha's estate ($4,000,000 in each of Alan, Beth and Carla's estates). This maneuver saves each of their estates from having to pay estate tax on $1,000,000 since each child's taxable estate will only be $4,000,000 instead of $5,000,000. In addition, there is no GSTT when Samantha dies since only $3,000,000 (an amount within the exemption amount) was transferred to skip persons.

Practice Tip: Generation skipping trusts can have other benefits, aside from estate tax issues. The money set aside in the generation skipping trusts can be protected from creditors of the "middle" generation and it can ensure that the grandchildren receive at least some benefit from the estate. Therefore, a generation skipping trust may be considered even for clients without such large estates.

Review Questions

1) Why do the gift and estate tax depend on each other?

2) What is the "estate" of a person and when is it created?

3) Aside from assets owned by a person outright, give two other examples of assets that would be counted as part of one's taxable estate.

4) Why is a revocable trust no more effective than a will regarding estate tax planning?

5) Is a gift to a trust that is a "completed gift" for gift tax purposes always outside of the estate of the grantor? Explain.

6) Is a gift to a trust that is outside of the estate of the grantor always a "completed gift" for gift tax purposes? Explain.

7) What is the distinction, from an estate tax perspective, between a general power of appointment and a limited power of appointment?

8) What is necessary for a GRAT to be considered a "zeroed out" GRAT?

9) Name one major advantage of the Intentionally Defective Grantor Trust strategy over the GRAT strategy.

10) Why is the IDGT established intentionally as a grantor trust?

11) Why is it sometimes important to ensure that trust assets are *in* the taxable estate of the grantor?

12) Why should the grantor's power over trust assets be severely limited in an estate tax planning irrevocable trust?

13) Explain how the "credit shelter trust" strategy serves to take advantage of both spouses' estate tax exemption.

14) How can a gift to a trust qualify for the estate tax marital deduction even though it is not given outright to the surviving spouse?

15) What are the requirements for a disclaimer to be "qualified" under Section 2518 of the Internal Revenue Code?

16) Give an example as to how the qualified disclaimer can be used to save estate tax in the long run.

17) Why is gifting assets to one's grandchildren potentially a dangerous idea?

18) What is the difference between a transfer that is a "direct" skip and an "indirect" skip?

CHAPTER 5

INCOME TAXATION OF TRUSTS

Taxation of income earned by trusts can be complex. Primarily, this is because it is often unclear exactly who will be taxed on what income earned by a trust. In addition, the rate at which income tax is paid often depends on to whom the income is attributable. Proper planning can allow attorneys and their clients to plan the manner in which trust income will be taxed at the time of the formation of the trust.

Regarding terminology, for the purpose of this chapter, trust "income" means money earned by trust assets within a given year. This can be in the form of interest, dividends, rents from real estate earned by the trust, etc. Trust "principal" means all trust assets over and above trust income. If trust income is held from year to year and not distributed, it becomes trust principal.

> *Example:* XYZ Trust *earns $50,000 in interest and dividends during the year 2010. None of that amount is distributed to the trust beneficiaries. For 2010, the $50,000 is considered trust income. However, as of 2011, the $50,000 will become part of the trust principal.*

Trust Rates of Taxation

Like individuals, trusts have their own progressive federal income tax rates.[1] The general trust income tax brackets are similar to those brackets for individuals. Trust income earned during the year 2010 starts at the 15% bracket (for income up to $2,300) and progresses to 35% for income over $11,200.[2]

The bad news is that the "bracket creep" is extremely fast when is comes to trust income. For example, for 2010, the federal income tax rate for individuals does not reach 35% until $373,650 of income. By contrast, trusts pay 35%

---

1. 26 U.S.C. §1(e).
2. Rev. Proc. 2011–12 (http://www.irs.gov/formspubs/article/0,,id=188575,00.html).

federal income tax on all income above $11,200. Trusts, in effect, pay much higher income tax rates than do individuals.

The good news, however, is that trust income is not combined with other income belonging to the grantor or beneficiary of the trust. This can save money for people with high incomes.

> *Example: Jennifer earned $400,000 in 2010. She also is the beneficiary of a trust that earned $10,000 in 2009. Because Jennifer's income is more than $373,650, she is in the 35% tax bracket. If the $10,000 were taxable as part of Jennifer's income, it would be taxed at the 35% rate. However, the trust will pay less than 20% in federal income tax, based on the applicable trust income tax rates.*

The other good news is that with a minimal amount of forethought, a trust can be drafted with the flexibility to allocate income in a manner that is most advantageous for the client's family as a whole. The manner in which this can be done is the subject of the next several sections.

Income Taxation of Simple Trusts

A "simple" trust is a trust that must, under its terms, distribute all of its income each year. A simple trust may not hold or accumulate income.

> *Example: ABC Trust is established for the benefit of Adam, Bertha and Carl. The trust instrument states, "The trustee shall distribute all trust income to Adam, Bertha and Carl, in equal shares, in quarterly or more frequent installments." This is a simple trust because it must distribute all of the trust income and may not accumulate trust income from year to year.*

A simple trust may allow the trustee discretion to determine exactly how the trust income may be distributed. As long as the trust income must be distributed every year, it is a simple trust.

> *Example: ABC Trust is established for the benefit of Adam, Bertha and Carl. The trust instrument states, "The trustee shall distribute all trust income to Adam, Bertha and/or Carl, at intervals and in amounts and proportions that the trustee shall determine in his or her sole discretion, provided that all trust income must be distributed annually." This is a simple trust. Even though the trustee has discretion to allo-*

cate and distribute trust income, the beneficiaries must receive all trust income each year. Therefore, this trust is a simple trust.

It is important to note that a trust may be drafted so that the trustee may distribute trust principal at his discretion and still be a simple trust. As long as the income must be distributed each year, it is a simple trust.

> *Example:* ABC Trust *is established for the benefit of Adam, Bertha and Carl. The trust instrument states, "The trustee shall distribute all trust income to Adam, Bertha and Carl, in equal shares, in quarterly or more frequent installments. In addition, the trustee may distribute trust principal for the benefit of the beneficiaries' health, education, maintenance and support to the extent that the trustee deems advisable." Even though the trustee has discretion to distribute additional trust principal (and how much to distribute and to whom), this trust is a simple trust since all income must be distributed.*

Income taxation of simple trusts is, in fact, quite simple. The trust itself pays no income tax since it may not retain any trust income. Instead, the trust income is taxable to the beneficiaries that actually receive the trust income.[3]

> *Example:* ABC Trust *is established for the benefit of Adam, Bertha and Carl. The trust instrument states, "The trustee shall distribute all trust income to Adam, Bertha and Carl, in equal shares, in quarterly or more frequent installments. In addition, the trustee may distribute trust principal for the benefit of the beneficiaries' health, education, maintenance and support to the extent that the trustee deems advisable."*
>
> *In 2010, the trust earns $60,000 of income. The trustee is required to distribute $20,000 to each Adam, Bertha and Carl. Therefore, $20,000 of income is taxable to each beneficiary. Note that if the trustee distributes an additional $10,000 of principal to Adam under his discretionary authority to do so, that amount is not taxable to anyone. Only income earned by a trust is subject to income tax. Distributions of trust principal are not subject to income tax.*

Although simple trusts do not pay income tax, they are required to file their own income tax returns. The trustee must file a Form 1041 (United States Income Tax Return for Estates and Trusts) each year and should check the box

---

3. 26 U.S.C. §651.

in the upper left hand corner of the front page of the return that indicates that the trust is a simple trust.[4] Similar tax returns must generally be filed in the state in which the trust is located.

This return gives notice to the IRS of how much income (and what types of income) was earned by the trust. The preparer must also fill out and file Schedule K indicating how much of the trust income was allocated to each beneficiary. Schedule K-1s must be sent to the IRS and to the beneficiary to assist the beneficiaries in preparing their own personal tax returns. The Form K-1 notifies the beneficiary of how much income to report on the beneficiary's personal income tax return.

Practice Tip: When drafting a trust, you can control whether a trust is a simple trust or not. A complex trust allows the most flexibility on a year-to-year basis. However, if the trust beneficiaries earn low incomes and are thus in low tax brackets and if your client does not want to have to deal with complex income allocation decisions each year, a simple trust may be the best strategy. In addition, some types of trusts must be simple trusts to be effective. For example, a marital deduction trust must distribute all income to the grantor's spouse. Therefore, it must be a simple trust.

Income Taxation of Complex Trusts

Complex trusts are trusts that allow (or require) the trustee to hold some or all of the trust's income.

Example: ABC Trust *is established for the benefit of Adam, Bertha and Carl. The trust instrument states, "The trustee shall distribute as much of the trust income to or on behalf of the beneficiaries, as the trustee deems necessary and appropriate for their health, education, maintenance and support." ABC Trust is a complex trust because the trustee need not distribute all of the income each year.*

Example: ABC Trust *is established for the benefit of Adam, Bertha and Carl. The trust instrument states, "The trustee shall hold all trust income until the youngest beneficiary reaches the age of 18 years old.*

---

4. See page 15 of the Instructions for Form 1041 (http://www.irs.gov/pub/irs-pdf/i1041.pdf).

*At such time, the trustee shall distribute all trust assets to the benefi-
ciaries, in equal shares." ABC Trust is a complex trust because the
trustee need not distribute all of the income each year. Even though the
trustee has no discretion (i.e., he cannot distribute trust income), it is
still a complex trust.*

In a complex trust, income that is distributed to beneficiaries is taxable to
the beneficiaries as their personal income. Assets not distributed during the
course of a given year are taxable at trust income tax rates. Trust income can
be also be distributed within the first 65 days of the calendar year and be
counted as though they were distributed during the previous year.[5]

*Example: ABC Trust is established for the benefit of Adam, Bertha
and Carl. The trust instrument states, "The trustee shall distribute as
much of the trust income to or on behalf of the beneficiaries, as the trustee
deems necessary and appropriate for their health, education, maintenance and support." In 2010, the trust earns $50,000 in bank in-
terest as its entire net income. The trustee distributes $10,000 to Adam,
$20,000 to Bertha and nothing to Carl. Adam must report his $10,000
as his personal income. Bertha must report her $20,000 as her per-
sonal income. The remaining $20,000 must be reported as trust income.
Because trust income is taxed at the trust tax rates, the trust will pay
almost $6,000 in federal income tax, plus additional state income
taxes, where applicable.*

*Example: ABC Trust is established for the benefit of Adam, Bertha
and Carl. The trust instrument states, "The trustee shall distribute as
much of the trust income to or on behalf of the beneficiaries, as the trustee
deems necessary and appropriate for their health, education, maintenance and support." In 2010, the trust earns $50,000 in bank in-
terest as its entire net income. On February 15, 2011, the trust distributes
$5,000 to Carl. The trustee has the option to treat this distribution as
having been made in 2010 or 2011.*

In determining how much income to distribute to beneficiaries during each
given calendar year, the trustee should consider the income tax consequences
of making (or declining to make) a distribution. A trust with little income that
distributes income to a beneficiary in a high tax bracket may cost the family money.

---

5. 26 U.S.C. §663(b).

Conversely, distributing money to a beneficiary in a low tax bracket may save the family money.

> *Example:* ABC Trust *is established for the benefit of Bertha and Carl. The trust instrument states, "The trustee shall distribute as much of the trust income to or on behalf of the beneficiaries as the trustee deems necessary and appropriate for their health, education, maintenance and support." In 2010, the trust earns $10,000 in bank interest as its entire net income. Assume that Bertha is single and earns $100,000 per year in income. Her tax bracket is 28% (every marginal dollar she makes will be taxed at 28%). Carl, on the other hand, is married and earns $50,000 in family income, thus putting him in the 15% tax bracket.*
>
> *Based on the trust income tax rates, if the trust were to hold its income and not distribute it, it would be taxed at roughly 25%. Distributing the $10,000 to Bertha would thus cause the money to be taxed at a higher rate (28%). On the other hand, distributing the assets to Carl would cause it to be taxed at a lower rate (15%). Obviously, other factors have to come into play when determining whether to make a distribution. However, from an income tax perspective, distributing assets to Carl would save money, while distributing assets to Bertha would cost money.*

One way to increase the flexibility of a trustee to deal with income tax is to give the trustee the discretion to distribute trust income OR principal, at the trustee's discretion. This allows the trustee to allocate distributions as distributions of principal or income, as the circumstance may warrant.

> *Example:* ABC Trust *is established for the benefit of Bertha and Carl. The trust instrument states, "The trustee shall distribute as much of the trust income and/or principal to or on behalf of the beneficiaries, as the trustee deems necessary and appropriate for their health, education, maintenance and support." In 2010, the trust earns $10,000 in bank interest as its entire net income. Assume that Bertha and Carl have the same incomes as indicated in the previous example.*
>
> *The trustee would like to distribute $5,000 to each beneficiary in 2010. The smartest way to do this would be to distribute $5,000 to Carl from the trust income and $5,000 to Bertha from the trust principal. The $5,000 given to Carl is taxed at Carl's income tax rate (to be paid by Carl). The other $5,000 of income is taxed to the trust at the trust rates. The $5,000 distributed to Bertha is not taxed at all, since it is a*

distribution of principal. Of course, this benefits Bertha to the exclu-
sion of Carl; but the trustee could always make an additional distri-
bution of principal to Carl to compensate for the income tax that he
will have to pay based on the $5,000 distribution.

Practice Tip: If your clients are sophisticated and/or have competent ac-
countants working for them, it generally makes sense to draft a complex
trust rather than a simple trust and to give the trustee as much discretion
as possible to distribute income and/or principal to beneficiaries. This increases the flexibility that the trustee has to work with and to make decisions on a year-to-year basis to best protect the interests of the family as a
whole.

Another provision that many clients may want to consider is a provision
that allows the trustee to distribute trust income to charitable organizations.
If this is allowed, the trustee can take advantage of the income tax charitable
deduction by donating trust income to charity, thus taking advantage of the income tax charitable deduction.

However, it is important that trust drafters limit this ability to contribute
assets to tax exempt charitable organizations only. Giving the trustee discretion
to distribute assets to any cause that he or she deems "charitable" is giving the
trustee too much power and the IRS (and creditors, for that matter) may consider the trust assets to be the trustee's money.

This should only be done if the client has complete confidence in the trustee's
judgment. The last thing any practitioner wants is for the grantor of the trust
to become angry with the trustee for giving too much trust money to charity
and to blame the practitioner for giving the trustee this authority.

A sample charitable trust provision may read as follows:

> The Trustee shall also have the authority to distribute trust income for
> charitable causes that the Trustee deems worthy; provided, however,
> that such charitable distribution may only be made to tax exempt char-
> itable organizations under Section 501(c) of the Internal Revenue Code.

Grantor Trusts

Between the 1930s and the 1980s, the top marginal tax bracket for high
earners was much higher than it is today. Compared with today's top marginal

federal income tax rate of 35%, during that era the top tax bracket was rarely below 60% and reached as high as 94% in the 1940s. Because of this, the incentive was great for high wage earners to shift income to other people or devices to avoid these high tax rates.

To prevent people in high tax brackets from putting assets into trusts that they control in order to shift the income away from themselves and their high tax brackets, Congress passed a series of rules that are now known as the "grantor trust" rules.[6] The upshot of these rules is that if the grantor (or the grantor's spouse, in many cases) retains certain powers or interests in a trust, then any income earned by the trust is taxed as income to the grantor. For income tax purposes, it is as though the trust does not exist. All trust income is directly attributable to the grantor.

> **Example:** ABC Trust *is established by Mom, as grantor, for the benefit of Adam, Bertha and Carl. Mom earns $100,000 in income in 2010. The trust earns $10,000 in bank interest as its sole income in 2010. Assume that the trust is considered a grantor trust. Mom must report the $10,000 as her own personal income, meaning that her total income is $110,000. Note that this is true even if trust income is distributed to Adam, Bertha and/or Carl during 2010. Neither the trust nor the beneficiaries will pay any income tax on this income, as it is all considered income of Mom.*

Powers that Create Grantor Trusts

The grantor trust rules are spelled out in Sections 671–679 of the Internal Revenue Code.

Although an exhaustive analysis of all the different circumstances that can create a grantor trust is beyond the scope of this work, a brief discussion of the most common of these circumstances is in order.

A trust is a grantor trust if the grantor retains any "reversionary" interest in the trust that is worth at least 5% of the trust's value. In other words, if trust assets will at some point in the future, go back to the grantor, it is likely a grantor trust.[7]

---

6. *See generally,* http://www.bwwlaw.com/downloads/mvb/2002%20aliaba/2002%20G Tv12.htm.

7. 26 U.S.C. §673.

Example: ABC Trust *is established by Mom, as grantor, for the benefit of Adam, Bertha and Carl. The trust states "During the period of the trust's operation, the trustee shall distribute as much of the trust income and/or principal to or on behalf of the beneficiaries, as the trustee deems necessary and appropriate for their health, education, maintenance and support. After a period of ten (10) years elapses from the date of the execution of this trust, the trust shall terminate and the trust assets shall be distributed to Mom." This is a grantor trust because Mom (the grantor) has a reversionary interest.*

A trust is a grantor trust if the grantor or any "nonadverse" party has the ability to control beneficial enjoyment of the trust assets.[8]

Example: ABC Trust *is established by Mom, as grantor, for the benefit of Adam, Bertha and Carl. The trust states "During the period of the trust's operation, Mom shall direct the distribution of trust assets to or on behalf of the beneficiaries in amounts and at intervals that she shall determine." This is a grantor trust because the grantor can control beneficial enjoyment of the trust.*

An "adverse party" is a party who would be adversely affected by the use of trust assets.[9] In most cases, beneficiaries of a trust are all "adverse" to each other since a distribution to one means that there are fewer trust assets available for the others.

Example: ABC Trust *is established by Mom, as grantor, for the benefit of Adam, Bertha and Carl. The trust states "During the period of the trust's operation, Mom shall direct the distribution of trust assets to or on behalf of the beneficiaries in amounts and at intervals that she shall determine; provided, however, that any distribution under this paragraph shall require the consent of at least one beneficiary other than the beneficiary who is receiving the distribution." This is not a grantor trust under Section 674(a) since Mom cannot give trust assets to Adam, Bertha or Carl without the consent of at least one other beneficiary. Each beneficiary is an adverse party with respect to the others. Therefore, a distribution cannot be made by Mom to one of them without the consent of an adverse party.*

---

8. 26 U.S.C. §674(a).
9. 26 U.S.C. §672(a).

Subsections (b), (c) and (d) of Section 674 create a long list of exceptions to the general rule of subsection (a). Therefore, if you do want to give the grantor some authority to determine how trust assets are spent without making the trust a grantor trust, this is possible in many cases. Just make sure that the authority given to the grantor or trustee of your trust fits into one of the litany of circumstances described in subsections (b), (c) and (d).

A trust is also a grantor trust if the grantor retains any one of various powers over the trust assets, including

- The power to exchange trust assets with private assets of the grantor for less than adequate consideration.
- The power to borrow trust assets without posting adequate security for the loan.
- Certain administrative powers to control the trust assets.[10]

Like the other grantor trust rules, this rule contains various caveats and exceptions. As we will see later on, Section 675 is not as important in that it limits powers that grantors would otherwise want, but in that it allows trusts to be intentionally created as grantor trusts so easily and conveniently.

A trust is also a grantor trust if the grantor retains the power to revoke the trust.[11] Therefore, revocable trusts are, by definition, grantor trusts.

A trust is likewise a grantor trust if the trust may be used for the benefit of the grantor or the grantor's spouse (or be used to pay premiums on the life insurance policies of the grantor or the grantor's spouse) without the consent of an adverse party.[12]

There are also circumstances under which trust income is automatically treated as income of a beneficiary rather than the income of the grantor.[13] Essentially, if a beneficiary can control the disposition of trust income and can give it to him or herself without another person's consent, then that person is taxable as the owner of such income. Under Section 679, if an American person transfers property to a foreign trust, then he or she is taxable for the income generated by that property.[14] There are a litany of exceptions and caveats in both sections, so make sure to review the sections if these scenarios come up.

---

10. 26 U.S.C. §675.
11. 26 U.S.C. §676.
12. 26 U.S.C. §677.
13. 26 U.S.C. §678.
14. 26 U.S.C. §679.

When Using a Grantor Trust Can Be Advantageous

Although Congress initially passed the grantor trust rules to serve as a limitation on people removing assets from their own income tax liability, the grantor trust rules can often be a boon to clients. There are several reasons that it may be in the client's best interest to intentionally ensure that a trust is a grantor trust.

The first reason is that it avoids the high trust income tax rates described earlier in this chapter. Causing trust income to be considered the income of the grantor may decrease the level of income taxation on that income.

> *Example:* ABC Trust *is established by Mom, as grantor. Mom earns $50,000 per year in net income (after deductions). The trust earns $30,000 per year in net income. If the trust paid its own income tax, based on the rates laid out in Rev. Proc. 2011–12, it would pay $9,464.50 in federal income tax. However, if the trust is a grantor trust, Mom's income would increase from $50,000 to $80,000. This would result in an increase of federal income tax of less than $5,600. The family would save $3,864.50 in federal income tax simply because this trust was drafted as a grantor trust.*

A variety of other reasons to ensure that a trust is a grantor trust exist, many of which are discussed elsewhere in this book. Briefly, these reasons include:

- Grantor trusts may hold S Corporation shares,[15] while most other types of trusts cannot.[16] Therefore, if your client wants to place S Corporation shares into the trust, the simplest way to allow that is to ensure that the trust is a grantor trust.
- If real property is placed into a grantor trust, having the grantor be treated as the owner of the trust may keep the grantor eligible for various income and property tax advantages that are given to owner occupied real estate. These will be discussed more fully in chapter 9.
- Grantor trusts allow trust income to be treated as part of the grantor's income. This may allow the grantor to offset trust income with losses or deductions that are generated by other property belonging to the grantor.

---

15. 26 U.S.C. §1361(c)(2)(A)(i).
16. 26 U.S.C. §1361(b)(1)(B).

Example: Adam wants to establish trusts for the benefit of his children, in which to place two investment properties that he owns, Blackacre and Whiteacre. For asset protection purposes, he wants to place them into separate trusts. So, he creates Trust A for Blackacre and Trust B for Whiteacre. In 2010, Blackacre generates net taxable income of $25,000. Whiteacre generates a net loss of $10,000. If Trust A and Trust B were non-grantor trusts, Trust A would pay income tax on its entire gain. Trust B's loss, save for the possibility of carrying over some of it to offset future gains (which would be subject to all the limitations of carry over losses), would be wasted. On the other hand, if both Trust A and Trust B were grantor trusts, Adam could use the $10,000 loss from Whiteacre to partially offset the $25,000 gain from Blackacre in preparing his personal income tax return.

Practice Tip: Even if it is unclear whether a grantor trust will be advantageous to your client, this is an issue that should be discussed with the client during the trust preparation process. The client should be presented with the benefits and drawbacks of the grantor trust and should make the final decision (with advice from the attorney, of course). Whatever the decision, the document itself should make crystal clear whether the trust is a grantor or non-grantor trust. Ambiguity on this question can create confusion and consternation later on when the trust has to file income tax returns.

How to Ensure That a Trust Is or Is Not a Grantor Trust

The convenient thing about the grantor trust rules is that the practitioner can almost always choose, at the time of the drafting of the trust, whether the trust is a grantor trust or not.

Ensuring that a trust is a non-grantor trust requires that the trust avoid giving the grantor or trustee any power or interest that would cause the trust to be considered a grantor trust under the rules described in the previous section. Even if clients often want authorities or interests in their trusts that would create grantor trust status, grantor trust status can often be avoided by requiring the consent of an adverse party.

Example: Sandy wants to create a trust to hold cash assets and life insurance policies on her life, for the eventual benefit of her children, Mark and Jane. She wants to appoint her friend, David, as trustee. After discussion, Sandy decides that she does not want the trust to be *a grantor trust. Section 677, however, states that a trust is a grantor trust if its "income without the approval or consent of any adverse party is, or, in the discretion of the grantor or a nonadverse party, or both, may be ... (3) applied to the payment of premiums on policies of insurance on the life of the grantor." So, to avoid Section 677, the practitioner puts the following language into the trust:*

> *"The trustee may use trust income and/or principal to pay the premiums of life insurance policies held by the trust; provided, however, that the trustee may not use trust income to pay the premiums of life insurance policies on the life of the grantor without the approval of Mark or Jane."*

Since Mark and Jane are "adverse parties" (since any expenditure of trust assets decreases the availability of those assets for eventual distribution to them), and approval of one of them is necessary before the trust income can be spent on life insurance premiums for policies on Sandy's life, Section 677 does not apply. The trust can (subject to its other provisions, of course) be a non-grantor trust.

Any trust that is a non-grantor trust may (and, if this status is important to the client, should) specifically state that it is intended to be a non-grantor trust. In addition to ensuring that the grantor has no interest that would cause the trust to be a grantor trust, the drafter might add language along the lines of the following:

> It is the intention of the grantor that this trust not be treated as a "grantor trust" under Sections 671–679 of the Internal Revenue Code. Any power, authority or interest vested in the grantor hereunder shall be null and void if it would cause this trust to be considered a "grantor trust" for federal income tax purposes. All provisions hereunder shall be construed in accordance with this intent.

Ensuring that a trust is a grantor trust requires only that the trust give the grantor one or more interests or powers referenced in Sections 673 through 677. This means that you can choose any of the powers or interests described in those sections and give those to the grantor. This will cause the trust to be considered a grantor trust.

As a practical matter, however, one must be extremely careful not to give the grantor interests or authority that might jeopardize other purposes of the trust. For example, if the trust is designed to be outside of the taxable estate of the grantor, it is important to avoid giving the grantor power over the trust that might cause the trust assets to be considered part of his taxable estate.[17] If a purpose of the trust is to render the grantor eligible to receive Medicaid assistance or other government benefits, the grantor trust provision must likewise not jeopardize this purpose.

One convenient administrative power that can be used to ensure that a trust is a grantor trust without risking other adverse consequences is the power, under Section 675, to reacquire the trust corpus by substituting other property of an equivalent value. This is such an insignificant authority that there is little risk that it would cause the trust assets to be considered the grantor's for estate tax or Medicaid eligibility purposes. The author typically uses this power to ensure that a trust is a grantor trust while minimizing the possibility of other negative consequences.

A typical trust provision taking advantage of this rule might read something like this:

> The grantor shall have the authority, without the consent of any other party and in a non-fiduciary capacity, to remove trust assets from the trust by substituting other assets of reasonably equivalent value.

> It is the intent of the grantor that this trust shall be treated as a grantor trust for federal income tax purposes under Section 675 of the Internal Revenue Code. All provisions hereunder shall be construed in accordance with this intent.

Kiddie Tax

Trust income from a non-grantor trust is taxed to the trust itself if not distributed, or to the recipient if income is distributed. Because trust beneficiaries are often in lower tax brackets than the grantor or the trust itself, distributing assets can be an excellent way to save on income tax.

However, practitioners should be aware that this method of "shifting income" to people with lower tax liabilities has an important limitation when the recipient is a child. That limitation is what is known as the "kiddie tax."[18] The kiddie tax applies to all children under the age of 18 and can apply to children as old as 24, depending on their status.

---

17. *See* 28 U.S.C. § 2038.
18. *See* 26 U.S.C. § 1(g).

The rule states that unearned income (such as distributions of trust income) above twice the standard deduction for dependents[19] (a total of $1,900, as of 2010) is taxed at the child's parents' marginal rate.

> **Example:** ABC Trust *is established by Mom, as grantor, for the benefit of Adam, Bertha and Carl. Mom's income is such that her marginal dollar of income is taxed at 28% on the federal level. Adam is 15 years old. In 2009, Adam received $3,000 in distributions of income from the trust. The first $1,900 is taxed as Adam's income (which means that, unless Adam has other income from other sources), it will be taxed at a very low rate). However, the last $1,100 of income will be taxed at 28% on the federal level.*

Capital Gains Tax on Trust Assets

Capital gains earned by trusts are treated similarly to those earned by individuals. Under the 2010 rules, this means that short term capital gains (gains earned by assets sold within one year of having been purchased) are treated as ordinary income. Long term capital gains (gains from assets held for one year or longer) are taxed at a maximum rate of 15% (and can be taxed at less than that, depending on the total taxable income of the trust).

Another critical rule for the practitioner to be aware of involves the "step up" in cost basis that occurs upon death. Generally, the capital gain realized upon the sale of an asset equals the sales price minus the purchase price. The purchase price (which also includes any money spent on capital improvements) is known as the "cost basis" of the asset, and is used as a reference point in computing capital gain (or loss).

If assets are given as a gift, the recipient of the gift takes over the cost basis of the donor.[20] If the property is later sold, capital gain (or loss) must be computed by subtracting the cost basis from the sales price.

> **Example:** *Doug purchased a painting in 1985 for $1,500. In 2010, he sells the painting for $3,500. Doug has realized a capital gain of $2,000.*
>
> **Example:** *Doug purchased a painting in 1985 for $1,500. In 1997, when the painting is worth $2,500, he gave the painting to his daugh-*

---

19. *See* 26 U.S.C. §911(d)(2).
20. 26 U.S.C. §1015(a).

ter, Darla, as a gift. In 2010, Darla sells the painting for $3,500. Darla has realized a capital gain of $2,000. The value of the painting when it was transferred in 1997 is irrelevant.

An important exception occurs, however, with the assets of a decedent. When a person dies and his or her assets pass to his or her heirs, the cost basis of the recipients becomes the value of the asset on the date of death.[21] This is sometimes referred to as a "step up" in cost basis or a "stepped up" basis.

Example: Doug purchased a painting in 1985 for $1,500. In 1997, when the painting is worth $2,500, Doug died and the painting passed to his daughter, Darla, under his will. In 2010, Darla sells the painting for $3,500. Darla has realized a capital gain of $1,000. Her cost basis was $2,500 — its fair market value on the day that Doug died.

Applying this rule to assets held in trust becomes somewhat complex. If an elderly client owns an appreciated asset, it becomes of paramount importance that the asset receive the benefit of a "step up" in cost basis upon the client's death.

Example: Mary purchased an investment property in 1980 for $15,000. In 2011, the property is worth $500,000. Mary comes to you and, after consultation, decides to remove the property from her name for purposes of allowing her to become eligible for Medicaid assistance. If she were to give the property to her children, then their cost basis would only be $15,000. When the property is later sold, the family is looking at an enormous capital gains tax. If Mary died while still the owner of the property, the new cost basis would be $500,000; eliminating or minimizing capital gains tax upon its later sale.

So, the question becomes: Is it possible to place the appreciated asset into trust and to nevertheless secure the benefit of a step up in cost basis after the death of the client?

The answer, perhaps surprisingly, is yes. More surprisingly, even, is how relatively easy it is to do. The general rule has been that as long as an asset is considered part of the taxable estate of the grantor of a trust when the grantor dies, the assets also gains the benefit of the step up in cost basis.

[Note: Under the rules temporarily in effect until 2013, to ensure a step up in cost basis, the trust should also be drafted as a grantor trust (in addition to

---

21. 26 U.S.C. § 1014.

being part of the taxable estate of the grantor).[22] In fact, under the temporary rules that were scheduled to expire on January 1, 2011 (but were extended until January 1, 2013 by legislation passed and signed by President Obama in December of 2010), it is not entirely clear what is necessary for trust assets to be eligible for the step up in cost basis. Further research should be done when this situation arises.]

As discussed in chapter 4, keeping trust assets in the taxable estate of the grantor is a relatively simply maneuver. For example, the grantor can be given a limited power of appointment over the trust assets upon the grantor's death. This power keeps the trust assets in the taxable estate of the grantor, thus allowing for the step up in cost basis. At the same time, allowing a limited power of appointment to the grantor upon his or her death is not an authority that would interfere with the trust's Medicaid planning purposes; thus allowing the client the best of both worlds.

The downside to keeping the trust asset in your client's taxable estate is that the trust asset will be part of your client's taxable estate. However, if your client's total estate is at or below the estate tax exemption amount, this may not be much of a concern.

> *Example:* Mary purchased an investment property in 1980 for $15,000. In 2011, the property is worth $500,000. Mary comes to you and, after consultation, decides to remove the property from her name for purposes of allowing her to become eligible for Medicaid assistance. You determine that, even with this property, Mary's total taxable estate should be no more than about $900,000. Thus, estate tax is not a concern.

> To allow Mary her Medicaid planning objectives while allowing her to keep her step up in cost basis, you prepare a standard Medicaid trust with the following provision:

> Upon the death of the grantor, the trust assets that were contributed by the grantor shall be distributed to whomever among the children of the grantor that the grantor shall appoint said assets by a will that specifically references this limited power of appointment. In default of appointment, the trust assets shall be distributed to the children of the grantor, in equal shares, per stirpes.

Under the post-January 1, 2013 rules, the assets in this trust will receive a step up in cost basis upon Mary's death. Until then, the trust should be also

---

22. *See* 26 U.S.C. §2511(c).

drafted as a grantor trust and additional research should be done to determine what other steps may be necessary under the circumstances to ensure that the trust assets are eligible for a step up in cost basis.

Review Questions

1) How do the income tax brackets for trusts compare with those for individuals?

2) What is the fundamental difference between a simple trust and a complex trust?

3) How can a trust be used to shift income and thus lower the overall income tax burden on a family?

4) What yearly income tax form must a trust file with the Internal Revenue Service?

5) What is the purpose of requiring a simple trust to file income tax returns?

6) How does a trustee let the beneficiaries of a trust know how much income they received from the trust in a given year and thus must report on their personal tax returns?

7) What advantage do trusts have over individuals in terms of the income tax charitable deduction?

8) Why is it important to give a trustee discretion to determine what type of income to distribute to which beneficiaries and which to hold in the trust?

9) In what way is a grantor trust taxed differently than a non-grantor trust?

10) Name a possible advantage of creating a non-grantor trust over a grantor trust.

11) Name a possible advantage of creating a grantor trust over a non-grantor trust.

12) Name three powers retained by the grantor that would cause a trust to be considered a grantor trust.

13) What types of trusts would typically have to worry about the "kiddie tax"? Explain.

14) What is the "step up" in cost basis and why is it important?

15) Under the 2013 rules, what condition must be satisfied for a trust asset to receive a step up in cost basis upon the death of the grantor?

CHAPTER 6

ASSET PROTECTION
FEATURES OF TRUSTS

Protecting trust assets from creditors for the eventual distribution to family members is often as important as securing tax advantages. While poor tax planning can generally result in a portion of trust assets being lost, poor creditor protections can result in the depletion of the entire trust via payments to creditors of the grantor or beneficiary. Fortunately, protecting trust assets from potential creditors is generally not as complex as securing favorable tax treatment.

Fraudulent Transfers

The first thing that must be addressed in a discussion of creditor protection trusts is the fraudulent transfer rule. In short, the fraudulent transfer rule prevents clients from gifting away assets to avoid existing creditors. The general rule of thumb is that if the client has creditor problems before he or she comes to you, there is probably little you can and should do to help your client shield his or her assets from these existing creditors. Spousal obligations, such as equitable distribution and alimony, are similarly difficult to evade through creditor protection steps.

There are two types of fraudulent transfers (also called "fraudulent conveyances") to avoid when transferring assets to a trust or any other recipient. The first is an *actual fraudulent conveyance.* The rules regarding what is considered an actual fraudulent conveyance are set forth both in the Uniform Fraudulent Transfer Act[1] (which has been adopted by most states) and in the United States Bankruptcy Code, where the debtor declares bankruptcy after the transfer.[2]

---

1. http://www.law.upenn.edu/bll/archives/ulc/fnact99/1980s/ufta84.htm.
2. 11 U.S.C. §548.

The most common types of actual fraudulent transfers occur when the debtor transfers assets after the debt arises with the purpose of ensuring that the creditors do not have access to these funds.[3]

> **Example:** *Tina owes $28,000 in credit card debts. She has only $10,000 in cash in her bank account. Since she does not want the credit card companies to be able to seize this, she gifts the $10,000 to her sister, Angie. This is a fraudulent transfer. A court will most likely invalidate this transfer and force Angie to return the money if Tina cannot otherwise pay her creditors in full.*

> **Example:** *Donald comes to your office and says "I was in a car accident last month when I had no car insurance and Doug, who got hurt, is threatening to sue me for $250,000. I only have $100,000 in the bank, but I really want my children, not Doug, to get that money. Can you help me put that money into a trust so that my children will benefit from it and Doug won't have access to it?" Even though no lawsuit has yet been filed, a potential debt exists and any transfer of the $100,000 to a trust will likely be considered a fraudulent transfer.*

> **Example:** *Donna comes into your office and says "I'm married to this creep, Troy, and I have $100,000 in my personal account. I figure that Troy and I will be divorcing some time in the near future and I really don't want him to get any of my money. Can we do a trust to keep the money away from Troy?" The answer to Donna's question is most likely a resounding "no." A transfer of marital assets to a trust (including assets held by one individual spouse during the marriage) would most likely be undone in the event of a divorce and the assets would be included in the equitable distribution of the marital property.*

The other type of fraudulent conveyance is the *constructive fraudulent conveyance*. Under federal bankruptcy law, a constructive fraudulent conveyance occurs when the debtor makes any transfer or assumes any liability for less than fair market value and, at the time of the transfer was "insolvent," was about to engage in or already engaged in a business or transaction "for which any property remaining with the debtor was an unreasonably small capital,"[4]

---

3. 11 U.S.C. §548(a)(1) defined an actual fraudulent transfer as being any gift when the donor "made such transfer … with actual intent to hinder, delay, or defraud any entity to which the debtor was" indebted to.

4. 11 U.S.C. §548(a)(1)(B)(ii)(II).

or intended to incur debts that could not be repaid.[5] For this purpose, a debtor is "insolvent" when "the sum of the debtor's debts is greater than all of the debtor's assets, at a fair valuation."[6]

The Uniform Fraudulent Transfers Act also specifies that a transfer can be considered fraudulent, even if the debtor has other assets, if the transfer is a gift and the donor:

i) Was engaged or was about to engage in a business or a transaction for which the remaining assets of the debtor were unreasonably small in relation to the business or transaction; or

ii) Intended to incur, or believed or reasonably should have believed that he would incur, debts beyond his ability to pay as they became due.[7]

> *Example:* Levan owes $75,000 in credit card debt to First Bank. He has $200,000 in cash in his savings account. He gives $100,000 to a family trust for the benefit of his children and uses the other $100,000 to fund a speculative real estate venture. After the venture fails, First Bank sues to set aside the gift to the trust. Under the standards of the Uniform Fraudulent Transfer Act, it's possible that the transfer to the trust could be set aside as a fraudulent conveyance. Since Levan knew (or should have known) that the investment of the $100,000 in the speculative real estate venture might be lost, transferring the other $100,000 to the trust could be viewed as an attempt to insulate that money from his creditor, First Bank. Even if Levan can show that he had no intent to evade his creditors, the transfer may be considered a constructive fraudulent transfer.

Practice Tip: As a trusts and estates professional, it is not your responsibility to ensure that your client never makes what is later deemed to be a fraudulent transfer. If a gift is questionable as to whether it will later be deemed fraudulent, there may be little to lose by making the transfer. However, a practitioner should not advise a client to intentionally make a transfer to evade a creditor or spouse. A good rule of thumb is that if the client lists the desire to avoid a current or looming creditor as the major purpose of a transfer to a trust, the transfer is likely ill-advised.

---

5. 11 U.S.C. §548(a)(1)(B)(ii)(III).
6. Uniform Fraudulent Transfer Act Section 2.
7. Uniform Fraudulent Transfer Act, Section 4(a)(2).

Practice Tip: Above all, it is critical that the practitioner never advise a client to conceal assets or lie as to their whereabouts, whether in response to a lawsuit, during a divorce proceeding, or on a bankruptcy petition. The financial consequences of a fraudulent transfer are likely to be limited to an undoing of the transfer and possibly the assessment of administrative costs and/or attorney's fees. However, the consequences of lying on a bankruptcy application or the like could include severe sanctions up to and including disbarment for attorneys and felony charges for both attorney and client.

Conversely, there is nothing wrong with transferring assets to avoid creditors whose debts may arise in the future. On the contrary, this is sound estate planning. Fraudulent transfer rules protect pre-existing creditors, not creditors that may arise at some point after the transfer.

> *Example: Doctor Phil, a neurosurgeon, comes into your office for estate planning. He mentions that doctors in his profession routinely get sued. He has malpractice insurance but is worried that his coverage may not be sufficient in the event of a large judgment against him. You can certainly suggest that he place significant assets into a family trust that will be protected against potential future plaintiffs.*

Spendthrift Trusts and Spendthrift Provisions

Assuming that a gift to a trust is not a fraudulent conveyance, the transfer of an asset should remove that asset from the grantor for purposes of creditor protection. However, in most states, it is critical that the grantor not retain any possible beneficial interest in the trust. In most states, if the grantor retains even a possibility of receiving benefit from the trust, the entire trust corpus will be vulnerable to the grantor's creditors, at least up to the maximum possible interest afforded to the grantor.[8] This is known as a "self-settled" spendthrift trust, which, in most states, is ineffective to shield the trust corpus from creditors of the grantor.[9]

> *Example: Brian Jones creates* The Jones Family Trust. *Under the trust terms, the trustee "may, at his or her discretion, distribute trust assets*

---

8. See, e.g., Texas Property Code—Section 112.035.

9. The states that do allow self-settled spendthrift trusts to be effective against creditors are discussed later in this chapter.

to the grantor, his wife, and/or any of his children, to the extent that the trustee deems necessary and appropriate for their health, education, maintenance and support." First Bank and Trust Company is named as trustee of the trust. Although the decision as to whether to give Brian anything from the trust resides in the hands of an independent trustee, the entire trust assets will be vulnerable to Brian's creditors if he later incurs debts or is sued.

The grantor's spouse or children can be beneficiaries of a trust without endangering the trust assets to the creditors of the grantor. However, the trust should ensure that the grantor cannot benefit from the trust by having the trust pay for expenses he or she would otherwise be responsible for.

Example: Brian Jones creates The Jones Family Trust. *Under the trust terms, the trustee "may, at his or her discretion, distribute trust assets to the grantor's children, to the extent that the trustee deems necessary and appropriate for their health, education, maintenance and support." If Brian has minor children, the trust assets may be used to pay for things that Brian would otherwise be legally obligated to pay, such as their shelter and food. Therefore, this trust may be considered a self-settled spendthrift trust and be vulnerable to Brian's creditors.*

To avoid this problem, the trust should specify that the trust assets cannot be used for the benefit of the grantor. In the above examples, Brian's trust might instead say:

During the trust term, the trustee may, at his or her discretion, distribute trust assets to or on behalf of the grantor's children, to the extent that the trustee deems necessary and appropriate for their health, education, maintenance and support; provided, however, that no trust asset shall be used in a manner that provides any pecuniary benefit for the grantor or in any manner that displaces any legal obligation of the grantor.

The Beneficiaries' Creditors

The rules regarding creditor access to the trust are easier to deal with when it comes to the beneficiaries' creditors. As long as the trust clearly states such, trusts assets will generally not be vulnerable to the creditors of any of the beneficiaries.[10] To ensure this, trusts should generally state something to this effect:

> To the extent permitted by law, the beneficiaries' interests will not be subject to their liabilities or creditor claims or to assignment or anticipation.

Indeed, the author has never drafted an irrevocable trust without this simple yet powerful provision. The provision also ensures that the beneficiary cannot sell or give away his or her beneficial interest, in the trust, which is almost always consistent with the grantor's intention.

One pitfall to watch out for is to avoid giving any beneficiary a "general power of appointment" over the trust assets. If any beneficiary can distribute trust assets to himself or his creditors, he or she may be deemed to have a general power of appointment over the trust assets. This will not only cause these assets to be counted as part of his taxable estate,[11] but it will also likely subject the trust assets to the claims of his creditors.[12]

This problem may arise when a trust beneficiary is also the trustee. If the trustee has the power to distribute trust assets to a class of people that includes herself (or even to distribute assets to her children in a manner that would displace expenses that she would otherwise be responsible for), it is possible that the trustee will be considered to have a general power of appointment over the trust assets.

> **Example:** *Darren establishes the* Darren Family Trust. *The trustee is his daughter, Francine. The trust states, "The trustee may distribute trust income and/or principal to whomever among the children of the grantor that the trustee deems appropriate from time to time." Since Francine has unlimited discretion to give herself assets from the trust, she will be considered to have a general power of appointment over the trust assets. If creditors sue Francine, they can likely attach and collect from the trust assets. Furthermore, if Francine makes a distribution to another sibling from the trust, it may be considered a fraudulent transfer if Francine has creditors. In short, the whole situation is one big mess.*

There are multiple ways that this problem can be avoided. The first and probably simplest manner is to require the consent of another person (for ex-

---

10. *See, e.g.,* Nichols v. Eaton, 91 U.S. 716 (U.S. 1875); Broadway Nat'l Bank v. Adams, 133 Mass. 170 (Mass. 1882).

11. 26 USCS § 2514(c).

12. *See, e.g.,* Mich. Comp. Laws Section 556.123.

ample, another trust beneficiary) before the trustee may make a distribution. In the above case, the trust might be changed to say:

> The trustee may distribute trust income and/or principal to whomever among the children of the grantor that the trustee deems appropriate from time to time; provided, however, that no trustee may distribute assets to him or herself or to displace any of his or her legal obligations without the consent of at least one other child of the grantor.

Appointing two or more co-trustees to serve as trustees of the trust (and thus requiring the consent of both trustees to make a distribution) would have the same effect. However, this may not be the best option for some clients, and they may want to preserve the efficiency and ease of administration that is associated with having a single trustee.

Another option is to limit the ability of the trustee-beneficiary to make distributions by subjecting the distribution authority of the trustee to an ascertainable standard. The most common of these is the "health, education, maintenance and support" formula that is so common in the other contexts discussed earlier in this book. A power to make distributions limited by an ascertainable standard is not a general power of appointment.[13] In the case of Darren's trust above, the trust provision could simply be changed to:

> The trustee may distribute trust income and/or principal to whomever among the children of the grantor that the trustee deems appropriate from time to time for their health, education, maintenance and support after taking into account, to the extent that the trustee deems advisable, the other resources available to the beneficiary.

To be doubly certain that no trustee holds a general power of appointment over the trust assets, a provision is often included in trusts that states the following:

> Notwithstanding any other provision hereunder, no power of authority granted to any trustee or beneficiary hereunder shall be valid if holding such power or authority would be deemed to be a "general power of appointment" under the Internal Revenue Code.

A provision such as this one should not be relied upon exclusively, however. One also must be careful to avoid having the trust allocate powers that could be construed as granting a general power of appointment.

---

13. See 26 U.S.C. §2041.

Another important point to be aware of is that some states have rules which allow courts to order that a discretionary trust power be used to support a beneficiary.[14] Such laws may potentially be used by courts to require trusts to pay the debts necessary for a beneficiary's support or to displace expenses that may otherwise be paid for by government assistance.

> **Example:** *Jason establishes a trust for the benefit of his children, Abe, Brenda and Cary. A trust provision allows the trustee to "spend or apply trust funds for the benefit of the beneficiaries' health, education, maintenance and support." Brenda is later sued by a hospital for medical bills that she incurred after a skiing accident. In some states, a trust may force the trustee to pay the medical bills (which are included in her health) if Brenda cannot pay them on her own.*

Because some of these rules, such as the one cited above, may be expressly disclaimed by the trust instrument, a trust may contain a clause doing so. This clause may read as follows:

> To the extent allowed by law, no law of any relevant jurisdiction shall be available to allow any court to force the trustees to make any discretionary distribution hereunder.

Protecting Beneficiaries' Eligibility for Government Assistance Programs

Most beneficiaries are, of course, happy to receive a cash inheritance. However, if not planned properly, a sudden cash infusion may have adverse impacts on the beneficiaries. In other places, we discuss the impacts of cash infusions on the taxable estate and creditor vulnerability of the beneficiaries. Here we focus on the impact on eligibility for government assistance that an inheritance can have.

There are many forms of government assistance that beneficiaries may be receiving. Some benefits, such as Medicare, social security and social security

---

14. See, e.g., New York Estate Powers Trust Law Section 7-1.6.

Notwithstanding any contrary provision of law, the court having jurisdiction of an express trust, heretofore created or declared, to receive the income from property and apply it to the use of or pay it to any person, unless otherwise provided in the disposing instrument, may in its discretion make an allowance from principal to any income beneficiary whose support or education is not sufficiently provided for, *etc.*

disability are asset irrelevant. That is, income and/or assets will not affect the recipient's eligibility. Other programs (e.g., food stamps and Section 8 housing assistance) apply only an "income" test but not an asset test. That is, a low income person can be eligible even if he or she has significant savings or other assets. Still other programs apply both an income and an asset test (e.g., Medicaid).

The exact qualification tests applicable to each program, even federally funded ones, are usually determined by the individual states. Many northeastern states, for example, do not apply asset tests for some government funded healthcare programs for people under 65, while states in many other areas of the country do. In addition, the income limitations for programs vary from state to state. A comprehensive look at eligibility requirements for government programs around the country is beyond the scope of this text. However, it is important that the practitioner know (or at least know where to look for) the eligibility requirements in the jurisdiction for government programs such as Medicaid, food stamps, Section 8 housing assistance, etc.

Practice Tip: Don't make the mistake of ignoring government program eligibility concerns just because a trust beneficiary is not, at the time of the planning, receiving assistance. Based on the beneficiaries' financial situations and prospects for future income, it may be foreseeable that one or more beneficiaries will eventually require government assistance. Planning for this possibility is often relatively easy and should be done where even the possibility of its benefit exists.

The basic planning device to preserve the eligibility of the beneficiaries is to take assets that would otherwise be distributed to them outright and instead place them into trust for the benefit. This also must be done in a manner that does not cause the trust assets to be considered an available resource for purposes of government assistance programs. More specifics regarding Medicaid eligibility are discussed in chapter 7.

Crummey Powers and Asset Protection

Many trusts serve multiple purposes, such as asset protection and estate tax planning. It is very important to recognize where these interests may conflict with each other so you modify your drafting accordingly.

In chapter 3 we discussed "Crummey" rights of withdrawal. Allowing the beneficiaries to withdraw a proportionate share of the contributions to the trust allows gifts to the trust to be considered gifts of "present interest" and thus eligible for the gift tax annual exclusion. This right of withdrawal, however, may cause those assets to be vulnerable to creditors of the beneficiaries.

> *Example: George and Martha create the* Washington Family Trust *for the benefit of their five children. The trust provides that each year, each child can withdraw up to the amount that is available under the federal gift tax exemption amounts allowable to both George and Martha. In 2011, George and Martha contribute $100,000 to the trust. Each child now has the right to withdraw his share of the $100,000 ($20,000) of this contribution (since, as of 2011, a married couple can transfer up to $26,000 to each beneficiary under the gift tax annual exclusion).*

> *Fred, who is George and Martha's son, is currently being sued by a creditor for $20,000. Since he has little money available, he is negotiating a settlement with the plaintiff. However, once the creditor becomes aware of Fred's withdrawal, the creditor seeks an injunction to force Fred to exercise his withdrawal power so as to have the necessary funds to pay his debts. Since the withdrawal power belongs to Fred, it is possible that a court* will *force Fred to withdraw the money to pay his creditors.*

This is especially problematic if the trust holds liquid assets. In theory, a creditor of a beneficiary holding a Crummey withdrawal power may have the right to demand that the beneficiary exercise the withdrawal power and give the proceeds of the withdrawal to the creditor. If the trust holds only illiquid assets, such as shares of an LLC, family partnership, or share of a real estate holding, this may be less of an issue. However, the best strategy to avoid these problems is to ensure at the outset that no trust beneficiary who is vulnerable to creditors' claims holds a withdrawal power in the trust. There is nothing wrong, for example, with specifically excluding a certain child of the client from holding a withdrawal power in anticipation that that child may become subject to creditors' claims.

Self-Settled Spendthrift Trusts

As stated previously in this chapter, trusts for which the grantor is a beneficiary are not protected against the creditors of the grantor. The interest that is subject to the grantor's beneficial enjoyment will be vulnerable to the creditors. This is true in most states. For example, Texas Law provides:

If the settlor is also a beneficiary of the trust, a provision restraining the voluntary or involuntary transfer of his beneficial interest does not prevent his creditors from satisfying claims from his interest in the trust estate.[15]

California law, even more explicitly, provides:

Where settlor is a beneficiary
(a) If the settlor is a beneficiary of a trust created by the settlor and the settlor's interest is subject to a provision restraining the voluntary or involuntary transfer of the settlor's interest, the restraint is invalid against transferees or creditors of the settlor. The invalidity of the restraint on transfer does not affect the validity of the trust.
(b) If the settlor is the beneficiary of a trust created by the settlor and the trust instrument provides that the trustee shall pay income or principal or both for the education or support of the beneficiary or gives the trustee discretion to determine the amount of income or principal or both to be paid to or for the benefit of the settlor, a transferee or creditor of the settlor may reach the maximum amount that the trustee could pay to or for the benefit of the settlor under the trust instrument, not exceeding the amount of the settlor's proportionate contribution to the trust.[16]

Thus, when forming a creditor protection trust (or any trust which is supposed to have the advantage of protecting its assets from the grantor's creditors), the best strategy in general is to avoid having the grantor as a beneficiary. Unfortunately, this is not satisfactory for many clients who, for whatever reason, want to be beneficiaries of their own trusts.

> *Example: Jim, a heart surgeon, has recently been divorced and has five adult children. He has savings of $200,000 and earns a steady income. After paying alimony, he still earns surplus income that he would like to put away for his children's eventual benefit. However, Jim wants some benefit from his own savings as well. Also, Jim has concerns about issues he may face in the near future (e.g., he is nearing retirement age, he believes he could lose his job at some point involuntarily, he fears the possibility of a medical malpractice lawsuit that could bankrupt him, etc.).*
>
> *After Jim comes to you and explains his dilemma, you suggest establishing an irrevocable trust for the benefit of his children (who would*

---

15. Texas Property Code—Section 112.035(d).
16. Cal Prob Code § 15304.

hold rights of withdrawal for gift tax purposes, etc.). Jim says he has a good friend and neighbor whom he would be happy to designate as trustee. You tell Jim that to protect against possible future creditors, he should not be a potential beneficiary of the trust. Jim says that is unacceptable. He has a rocky relationship with some of his children and he has little confidence that they would support him if necessary. He further has no interest in putting himself in a position where he would essentially need to beg for money from his own children. Jim is fine with establishing an asset protection trust, but he needs his trustee to be allowed to distribute money to him if he needs it. Is there anything that could be done for Jim?

The answer is that there are two possible trust strategies Jim could employ that would allow him to be a trust beneficiary and may allow him to keep the creditor protection advantages of an irrevocable trust.

Foreign Trusts

The first possibility is to set up a trust in a foreign jurisdiction, such as the Bahamas, Bermuda or the Cayman Islands. These and other jurisdictions may have laws that are more favorable than American law for purposes of creditor protection. Many such jurisdictions have rules that allow self-settled spendthrift trusts that are not vulnerable to the grantor's creditors. Some may even allow the trust to be *revocable* and still afford some asset protection.[17]

Other advantages of establishing an "offshore" trust include the lack of jurisdiction over the trust by American courts. Thus, even if a creditor convinces an American court to order that trust assets be used to satisfy a judgment or other debt, there may be no mechanism by which the creditor can enforce this judgment. There may even be certain tax advantages to establishing trusts in other countries, though a discussion of these potential advantages is beyond the scope of this text.

There are, however, some important negatives associated with establishing foreign trusts. The first issue is the cost. An attorney who is an expert in the laws of the jurisdiction in which the trust is being established may have to be retained to oversee the process of opening and managing the trust. A foreign bank or trust company may charge significant fees to hold and manage the trust's accounts. Income or excise taxes and/or various administrative fees and

---

17. http://www.rpifs.com/protection/ap9401.htm (current as of May, 2011).

taxes may apply depending on the trust's activities and the rules of the jurisdiction.

A second issue area of potential concern is stability. American banks are usually insured by the Federal Deposit Insurance Corporation (FDIC) and investors may additionally be protected under various securities rules. The same may not be true in a foreign jurisdiction. It is important to assess the likelihood of bank failure and research whether such a foreign account will be protected in that event.

Finally, the Internal Revenue Code imposes strict and burdensome reporting requirements on foreign trusts. A foreign trust and its beneficiaries may be required to file various annual reports and returns with the IRS.[18] These requirements, which were established as part of the effort to prevent the offshore hiding of assets to avoid income tax,[19] can be complex and compliance can cost a significant amount in accountant and/or attorney's fees. Therefore, a foreign trust may not be suitable for clients seeking to fund a trust with only a small amount of assets.

Practice Tip: Unless you are knowledgeable in the foreign trust reporting rules and understand the rules of the foreign jurisdiction at issue, it would be unwise and perhaps even unethical to establish a client's foreign trust. That doesn't mean that you cannot recommend a foreign trust to your client; only that you should refer the client to another professional with more expertise to handle the establishment and operation of the trust.

Domestic Asset Protection Trusts

There are several states that have amended their creditor-debtor rules to allow assets held in a trust to be protected from the creditors of the grantor even if the grantor is a trust beneficiary. Alaska, Delaware and Nevada, in an attempt to lure assets from other states, were among the first states to make this rule modification. As of this writing, other states that allow asset protection trusts to be effective where the trustee is a beneficiary are Oklahoma, Colorado, Missouri, Wyoming, Tennessee, South Dakota, Rhode Island, Utah and New Hampshire. It should be emphasized, of course, that not all of these states' statutes are alike and some of these states may be more protective of trusts than others. For brevity, we will refer to these states as "DAPT states" ("Do-

---

18. See http://www.irs.gov/businesses/international/article/0,,id=185295,00.html.
19. See http://www.irs.gov/businesses/small/article/0,,id=106493,00.html.

mestic Asset Protection Trust" states). We will refer to other states as "non-DAPT states."

If a person resides in a DAPT state, establishing a DAPT is likely a sound strategy. This is especially true if the client's assets are held in her home state and the trustee resides and works in the DAPT state. A creditor from a different state suing the client who lives in a DAPT state would almost certainly be bound by the rules of the grantor's state.

> *Example: Darren lives in Dover, Delaware. He holds his assets in Delaware banks and Delaware branches of national banks and brokerage firms. He establishes* The Darren Irrevocable Trust *for the benefit of his children. The trust gives the trustee the authority to distribute assets to Darren "to the extent that the trustee deems necessary and appropriate to provide for Darren's health, education, maintenance and support, after taking into account, to the extent that the trustee deems advisable, other resources that are available to Darren." Since Delaware is a DAPT state, as long as Darren complies with other Delaware rules for domestic asset protection trusts, the principal of this trust should be protected from his creditors.*

Of higher complexity is when a resident of a non-DAPT state wishes to take advantage of the friendly rules of a DAPT state and thus establishes a trust in a DAPT state with the grantor as a potential beneficiary. Can the grantor still achieve the creditor protection benefits of the trust rules of a DAPT state without actually living there?

> *Example: Assume that Darren, from our previous example, lives in Pennsylvania and not Delaware. He wants to establish a trust that will be protected from his creditors—but with himself as grantor and a potential beneficiary. So, he has a DAPT drafted for him by a Delaware attorney and holds all of the trust assets in a Delaware bank. The trust agreement states that the trust is to be governed by Delaware law. Can this effectively protect the trust from Darren's creditors and if so, what other steps should Darren take to ensure this favorable treatment?*

At the outset, it should be made clear that there is certainly not unanimous consent among legal practitioners that creating a DAPT in a state in which you don't reside is a viable strategy.[20] There are several problems that may be en-

---

20. *See, e.g.,* http://www.assetprotectionbook.com/domestic_APT_analysis.htm.

countered by the user of this device. We will discuss these problems and some potential solutions below.

1) Jurisdiction of the Courts of the Grantor's Home State

> *Example: In the scenario above, Darren established a Delaware DAPT and funds it with $250,000. Seven years later, Darren is sued in Pennsylvania by a creditor for $100,000. Because the debt arose after the trust was funded, there is no suggestion of fraudulent transfer. The creditor is granted a judgment for the full $100,000. Since there is nothing else to collect from, the creditor seeks to collect the debt from the trust.*

The first rule of thumb in this situation is that if the Pennsylvania court manages to get jurisdiction over the Delaware trust, it will likely exercise that jurisdiction and force the trust to pay the judgment. Needless to say, an important order of business should be to establish the trust so that the Pennsylvania court has the minimum possible basis upon which to establish jurisdiction over the trust.

To do so, some basic steps should be taken. First, the trustee of the trust should not reside in the same state as the grantor. Otherwise, the state in which the grantor resides may assert personal jurisdiction over the trustee and force him or her to use trust assets to satisfy a judgment against the debtor. Keep in mind that the trustee has legal title to the trust assets. Therefore, any court that has jurisdiction over the trustee may have indirect jurisdiction over the trust.[21]

Often, a professional trustee in the DAPT state will be named as trustee. This prevents other states from having jurisdiction over the trust assets.[22] If the grantor insists that a friend or relative that lives in his or her own state be able to direct distributions (as is most often the case), that person may be named as a trust advisor or trust protector, with the power to advise the trustee regarding trust distributions.

> *Example: Ruth lives in Virginia. She wishes to establish a DAPT in Delaware that will not be vulnerable to her creditors, even though she is a potential beneficiary. She wants her brother, Dominic, to be able to direct distributions to beneficiaries. However, Dominic also lives in*

---

21. *See, e.g.,* Emberton v. Rutt, 2008 U.S. Dist. LEXIS 69074 (D.N.M. Mar. 31, 2008).
22. *See, e.g.,* Rose v. Firstar Bank, 819 A.2d 1247 (R.I. 2003).

Virginia. If Dominic were the trustee, a Virginia court may subject him to jurisdiction of the Virginia courts and force him to use trust assets to pay Ruth's creditors (as mandated by Virginia law). So, instead, Ruth hires the First National Bank of Dover, a Delaware professional trustee, to be the trustee of the trust. The trust document names Dominic as a trust advisor and states that he has the authority to recommend when and to whom distributions be made from the trust. Giving Dominic the authority to direct *(not just recommend) that distributions be made is also theoretically possible but is a little more risky; as it's possible that a court with personal jurisdiction over Dominic could assert jurisdiction over the trust as well.*

The assets themselves should also be held in the DAPT state, or at least outside of the state of the grantor. For example, the accounts held by the trust can be with branches of banks or brokerage firms in the DAPT state. This will help prevent the courts of the DAPT state from indirectly obtaining jurisdiction through "in-rem" or "quasi in rem" jurisdiction.[23]

A further protective device used by some is to create a business entity, such as a limited liability company (LLC) established in the DAPT state and to hold the trust assets in that company. The shares of the company are owned by the trust. Because assets held in LLCs are afforded additional creditor protections,[24] and because the fact that the assets are held by a company organized in the DAPT state establishing a clear nexus between the DAPT state and the trust assets, this is often safer than having the DAPT hold direct title to the trust assets.

2) Full Faith and Credit

The United States Constitution requires all states to give "full faith and credit" to the judgments of all other states.[25] Based on this, a creditor might sue

---

23. In rem jurisdiction (literally, jurisdiction over the thing) is a basis that allows a court to assert jurisdiction over a case because the case affects or involves something in the jurisdiction. Quasi in rem jurisdiction allows a court jurisdiction over a case by attaching property within its jurisdiction to indirectly force the defendant to defend the action even though the court may not have personal jurisdiction over the defendant. An assertion of quasi in rem jurisdiction must be exercised in a manner that is "fair" to the defendant and generally requires that the defendant have some nexus to the state other than the property's existence. *See* Shaffer v. Heitner, 433 U.S. 186 (1977).

24. *See, e.g.,* http://www.wyomingcompany.com/LLCS.htm.

25. U.S. Const. Art. IV Section 1.

the grantor in his or her home state, obtain a judgment against the grantor and then ask the DAPT state's court to enforce the judgment based on the full faith and credit clause.

However, if the DAPT is established properly this should not be an overwhelming concern. While courts of DAPT states must enforce judgments rendered by other states' courts, if the trust is properly set up, the courts should not both have authority over the same party. The home state of the grantor has personal jurisdiction over the grantor, but no jurisdiction over the trust (assuming the trust has no nexus to the grantor's state, as discussed above). The DAPT state will have jurisdiction over the trust but will not have jurisdiction over the grantor. A judgment against the grantor will not be enforced by the DAPT state since, under the rules of the DAPT state, the trust assets are *not* considered the assets of the grantor for creditor access purposes.[26]

3) Choice of Law

A domestic asset protection trust established in a DAPT state is worthless unless the courts of the DAPT state will apply the laws of the DAPT state rather than the laws of the grantor's state. It is therefore imperative to ensure that the courts of the DAPT state will apply its own state's laws.

As with many types of contractual agreements, the agreement may (and should) contain a choice of law provision. That is, the trust agreement should specifically state that the laws of the DAPT state should govern all aspects of the trust. However, that is not the end of the inquiry. A choice of law provision can be challenged on the grounds that it would be against public policy to apply the laws of a state with a very weak connection to the trust administration.

Under the Restatement Second of Conflict of Laws, a trust may choose the laws under which it is governed as long as the state whose laws are chosen "has a substantial relation to the trust and that the application of its law does not violate a strong public policy of the state with which, as to the matter at issue, the trust has its most significant relationship."[27] In other words, a trust may choose any state's rules as long as 1) The trust has a substantial relation to the chosen state; and 2) the public policy of another state that the trust relates to is not violated.

If the above discussed steps are taken, i.e., the trust is governed by a trustee in the DAPT state and the assets held by the trust are held in the DAPT state,

---

26. *See* Boxx, *Gray's Ghost—A Conversation About the Onshore Trust*, 85 Iowa L. Rev. 1195 (2000).

27. Restatement 2d of Conflict of Laws, §270.

there seems little danger of the trust being considered to have too slight a relationship to the DAPT state under this standard. This is likely true even if the grantor and the trust beneficiaries live in a different state.

As a final note, it is important to reiterate that while the establishment of an asset protection trust may secure creditor protection advantages allowed under the rules of another state or county, transfers to these trusts are still subject to the fraudulent transfer rules discussed at the beginning of this chapter. Therefore, an asset protection trust should be used to protect against future debts, but the strategy is unlikely to be effective against current debts, whether or not there is pending litigation.

Review Questions

1) What is the basic purpose behind the fraudulent transfer rules?

2) What are the two types of fraudulent transfers and what are the differences between them?

3) For which type of fraudulent conveyance must a debtor be "insolvent"? Why?

4) For purposes of determining whether a transfer was fraudulent, how is "insolvency" defined?

5) What is the purpose of a "spendthrift" provision in a trust?

6) What does a spendthrift provision prevent the beneficiary of a trust from doing?

7) Why is it important to avoid giving the beneficiary a general power of appointment over trust assets in a trust that is designed for creditor protection?

8) Explain the differences between a government assistance program that is asset tested, income tested, both and neither.

9) Of the types of government assistance programs referenced in question 9, beneficiary interest provisions in trusts are relevant to which one(s)? Explain.

10) What is the danger of a "Crummey" right of withdrawal in an asset protection trust?

11) Why should a grantor generally not be a beneficiary of a trust that is to be used for creditor protection?

12) What type(s) of asset protection trusts allow the grantor to be a potential beneficiary and nevertheless retain creditor protection advantages?

13) What are advantages of the foreign asset protection trust over the domestic asset protection trust?

14) What are advantages of the domestic asset protection trust over the foreign asset protection trust?

15) Name three potential pitfalls to the domestic asset protection trust strategy that can undo the benefits of the trust if the trust is not properly established.

16) Why is it important that the trustee of a DAPT and/or the financial institution at which the trust assets are held NOT be the same state as that in which the grantor resides?

17) When is a DAPT most likely to be effective? Explain.

18) Does a DAPT allow the grantor to circumvent the fraudulent conveyance rules? Explain.

CHAPTER 7

MEDICAID PLANNING TRUSTS

Medicaid Eligibility Rules: A Primer

Medicaid is a hybrid federal and state program that provides healthcare services for those who cannot afford to pay for their own. The program is administered by the states through local departments of social services. The program is typically funded roughly equally by the state and federal governments.

Although *state* law determines how Medicaid is administered in each individual state, federal funding is conditioned on adherence to a series of complex federal regulations. Therefore, the rules that govern Medicaid have a degree of uniformity throughout the country.

Practice Tip: The devices discussed in this chapter are based on complying with the applicable federal regulations. Where we divert into issues that are governed by state law, we will specifically say so. However, as there is quite a variation between Medicaid programs in different states, it is critical for the elder law practitioner to become familiar with the nuances involved in Medicaid law and administration in his or her state.

Most Medicaid programs apply both asset based and income based tests for determining Medicaid eligibility. That is, to be eligible for Medicaid a person must not have access to significant resources OR have too large an income.[1]

The exact income and asset limitations vary from state to state. However, asset limitations are typically only a few thousand dollars[2] and income limitations are typically under $1,000 per month for an individual (this amount goes up for additional family members).[3] Therefore, many of your estate planning

---

1. *See* http://www.cms.gov/MedicaidEligibility.
2. *See*, e.g., http://www.hhsc.state.tx.us/mbi.html#Q3.
3. *See*, e.g., http://www.hrsa.gov/reimbursement/states/California-Eligibility.htm.

clients are not likely to be immediately eligible for Medicaid assistance. Clients who have excess *income* may have to apply that excess toward their care before Medicaid will pay for such care. Similarly, clients who have access to excess *resources* will have to "spend down" these resources to a point below the resource limit if they are to become eligible.

The Need for Medicaid Planning for Your Clients

Unfortunately, many expensive healthcare costs incurred by seniors are not covered by Medicare or typical supplemental health insurance. For example, nursing home care (which costs in excess of $5,000 per month in most areas and more than $10,000 per month in some areas) is not covered by typical health insurance. Medicare (which almost all people over age 65 are eligible for) can cover a temporary rehabilitative nursing home stay, but will not cover a long term stay.

Long term care insurance will often cover nursing home stays and thus may be a viable means of planning for nursing home care. However, long term care insurance premiums can be very expensive, especially for clients who purchase the policy when they are older.[4]

Thus, in order to pay for expensive elder care costs, many clients are forced to seek Medicaid assistance. As previously mentioned, if they have significant assets they will have to spend them down before being eligible for Medicaid.

> *Example: Georgina is a 73-year-old widow with four children. She has saved $300,000 over the course of her life, all of which is held in a brokerage account. In addition, she receives $1,500 per month in social security payments. She pays her expenses primarily with these social security payments, but she also occasionally draws money from her brokerage account to cover her living expenses. Since her brokerage account assets generate about $15,000 in income and her living expenses are light, she is generally able to live without drawing down the $300,000 brokerage account principal. Georgina wants her children to inherit her money after she passes away. However, if she ever needs long term care services, such as a nursing home for a couple of years or more, this could lead to a diminution or even elimination of her assets while she is alive. Every dollar that is spent on her nursing home care is one less dollar that is available for her children's inheritance. As her elder care legal professional, it is your responsibility to help*

---

4. *See, e.g.,* https://www.ltcfeds.com/ltcWeb/do/assessing_your_needs/ratecalcOut.

Georgina take advantage of legal remedies that will allow her to receive government assistance for these services.

The Five Year "Look Back" Period

It is well settled in the congressional record and in case law that Medicaid was and has always been designed to be a "payer of last resort."[5] As such, federal law has takes steps to try to ensure that people don't use shortcuts to get the government to pay for healthcare services that the recipient really has the means to pay for.

For elderly clients, the key impediment to Medicaid eligibility is usually excess assets ("available resources"). It would seem that one particularly easy method to circumvent the asset test is to gift away one's assets at the time of a need for Medicaid assistance.

Federal law, however, imposes a five year "period of ineligibility" that is triggered by a gift. If a person gives a gift (including a gift to charity) and applies for Medicaid at any point during the five year period subsequent to the gift, a period of ineligibility for Medicaid will be assessed.[6] Note that this period of ineligibility applies to both spouses for a gift made by either spouse.[7]

> *Example: John is 82 years old and his children are thinking of sending him to a nursing home as he can no longer live alone safely. He has $200,000 in stocks and cash in a brokerage account. John's children ask him to give this account to them so that he can be eligible for Medicaid. This strategy will not work. If John gifts the $200,000 to his children and then applies for Medicaid within five years, a period of ineligibility will be assessed against him and the government will not pay for his nursing home care.*

The length of this period of ineligibility depends on the size of the gift and the cost of the average nursing home in the area. The length of ineligibility is calculated by the value of the gift divided by the average monthly nursing home cost in the area. The period of ineligibility starts when the client applied for Medicaid assistance and would otherwise be eligible to receive Medicaid assistance.[8]

---

5. Costello v. Geiser, 85 N.Y.2d 103, 106 (N.Y. 1995).

6. 42 USCS § 1396p(c)(1)(B)(i).

7. 42 USCS § 1396p(c)(1)(A).

8. 42 USCS § 1396p(c)(1)(B)(ii).

Example: John gifted $200,000 to his children on July 1, 2011. The average nursing home in his area (as published by the local Department of Social Services) costs $10,000 per month. On November 1, 2011, John requires nursing home care and applies for Medicaid. He has no other assets. Because the $200,000 gift divided by the $10,000 per month is 20, he will be ineligible for nursing home care for 20 months, or until July 1, 2013. Until then, his family will have to make their own arrangements to pay for his care.

Community Medicaid vs. Long Term Care Medicaid

Medicaid services can vary greatly from recipient to recipient. Younger people who have low income and asset levels often need Medicaid assistance because they cannot afford to pay for their own health insurance. For these recipients, the Medicaid program simply provides them with health insurance with no or drastically reduced premiums. As with any other health insurance program, these services may require small co-pays and participating providers may be limited.

Older or severely disabled recipients, on the other hand, may require much more significant and expensive care. While the cost of family health insurance often exceeds $2,000 per month, healthcare costs often exceed $10,000 for an individual elder care patient. Thus, while Medicaid resource and asset allowances are fairly constant, some states do distinguish between Medicaid programs based on services provided.

Some states account for this difference by bifurcating their Medicaid administration into two systems. "Community Medicaid" administration systems may be used to provide less costly healthcare services such as health insurance and even home health aide coverage for older recipients.[9] "Nursing home Medicaid" or "long term care Medicaid" is used to administer nursing home and similar services.

The key difference between these programs is that some states do not apply a five year period of ineligibility for gift transfers for community Medicaid applications. This means that in those states, clients who meet the income requirements can gift all of their assets and become eligible for some Medicaid services.[10]

---

9. *See, e.g.,* http://jfs.ohio.gov/OHP/consumers/HCBS.stm.
10. *See* 18 NYCRR § 360-4.4.

Example: Stuart is 78 years old and lives alone in New York City. He owns $400,000 in assets in a brokerage account. He does not want to enter a nursing home as long as he can avoid it, but he does need a home health aid to care for him. His only income is a $1,500 monthly social security check that covers his rent and utilities. Since a home health aid costs about $18 per hour, this would be a substantial expense for him. So, he transfers his brokerage account to his children. Although he will not be eligible for nursing home Medicaid for five years, he will be eligible to receive benefits under New York's "community" Medicaid program.

Medicaid Trusts

With that as background, we segue now to the main focus of this chapter: the Medicaid planning trust. The Medicaid planning trust is a device that can serve as a vehicle to hold a person's (gifted) assets for the benefit of a person's children or heirs (or whomever) while allowing the grantor(s) to become eligible for Medicaid. Medicaid trusts are valuable when, for any number of reasons that may apply, it is unwise to gift assets directly to a person's beneficiaries.

Forms of Medicaid trusts vary greatly. There are, however, two defining characteristics that apply to all Medicaid trusts. The first is that they are irrevocable. This means that the grantor has no power to revoke, modify, or alter the trust. The second is that the trust principal may not be used for the general support or healthcare expenses of the grantor. For a married client, the trust should not allow trust principal to be used for the general support or healthcare expenses of either spouse. If the trust is revocable or if the trust principal could be used to pay for the healthcare of the grantor, the entire trust principal would almost certainly be considered an "available resource" for the grantor, thus rendering him or her ineligible for Medicaid assistance.

Whether the grantor can be a possible beneficiary of a Medicaid trust is not clear in every state. The best way to be safe in this regard is to ensure that the grantor is not a potential principal beneficiary at all.

Example: Mike and Theresa, who are each 70 years old, establish a Medicaid planning trust for the benefit of their children. The trust agreement gives the trustee the authority to spend trust assets "for the benefit of the grantors, at the discretion of the trustee." Even if the trustee refuses to spend money for Mike and Theresa's healthcare, the local de-

partment of social services will likely consider the entire corpus of the trust as an "available resource" for Medicaid eligibility purposes. Since Mike and Theresa funded the trust and they are potential beneficiaries, this is a poor Medicaid planning tool.

Example: *Mike and Theresa, who are each 70 years old, establish a Medicaid planning trust for the benefit of their children. The trust agreement gives the trustee the authority to spend trust assets "for the benefit of the children of the grantors, at the discretion of the trustee." Although the trustee has the authority to distribute assets from the trust, they are not authorized to make distributions for the benefit of the grantors. This can be an effective Medicaid planning trust.*

Example: *Mike and Theresa, who are each 70 years old, establish a Medicaid planning trust for the benefit of their children. The trust agreement gives the trustee the authority to spend trust assets "for the benefit of the grantors, for their housing expenses and for their education, but NOT for their healthcare or general maintenance." It is unclear whether the principal of this trust will be considered an available resource for Medicaid purposes. The best practice is avoid this risky provision and not to give the grantor(s) any rights to the trust principal.*

To ensure that assets in a Medicaid trust are not available resources, many drafters of these trusts go out of their way to specify that the grantors are not potential beneficiaries of the trust. Language allowing distributions to other beneficiaries but not to the grantor may be phrased as follows:

> During the lifetime of the grantor, the trustee may pay to or apply trust assets for the benefit of the children of the grantor, for their health, education, maintenance and support, after taking into account, to the extent that the trustee deems advisable, the other resources available to them. However, no distribution may be made to this trust that would result in any benefit to the grantor or the grantor's spouse; nor shall any distribution be made from the trust that would displace any legal support obligation of the grantor.

The last sentence is particularly important if the clients have minor (or disabled) children living with them. In such case, if the trust had the authority to spend assets for the children, this could be considered to the benefit of the grantor since it would require the grantor to spend less on such care. For both Medicaid and creditor protection purposes, this possible benefit could have adverse consequences.

Practice Tip: The client should be made to clearly understand that the client will not have any rights to the trust funds in a Medicaid planning trust. Clients, especially older ones, are often reluctant to cede control over their assets. If a client is not going to want to cede control over the assets, perhaps a Medicaid planning trust is not ideal for that client. The last thing you want is a client blaming you for loss of control of their assets.

In other respects, Medicaid planning trusts share features with other irrevocable trusts, discussed elsewhere in this text.

Considerations Involving the Family Home

Chapter 9 is devoted to dealing with issues that are specifically relevant to trusts that hold real estate. However, it is also important to discuss certain Medicaid eligibility ramifications of owning one's own home when discussing the Medicaid eligibility rules.

The first important rule is that as long as a person is residing in a home, the home itself is not generally considered an available resource for Medicaid purposes.[11] That is, the government does not expect a person to sell his or her home to pay for healthcare before Medicaid will step in with assistance.

Therefore, for younger people who are interested in Medicaid primarily for health insurance and related expenses, owning a family home should not be a problem. It is important to note, however, that this applies only if the applicant's home equity is not more than $500,000 ($750,000 in some states). Equity in excess of that is considered an available resource.[12]

Example: Peggy and Alan are 45 years old and have four children living with them. They own a nice house that has a fair market value of $600,000. The house is subject to a $200,000 mortgage. Because of a recent layoff, Peggy and Alan are having trouble financially and they wish to seek Medicaid help for their family's health insurance. Assuming they are otherwise eligible for Medicaid, the fact that they own this house will not impact their Medicaid eligibility, since they have only $400,000 in equity in the house.

Example: Peggy and Alan are 45 years old and have four children living with them. They own a nice house that has a fair market value of

---

11. *See* 42 USCS § 1382b (a)(1).
12. 42 USCS § 1396p(f)(1).

$800,000. The house is subject to a $200,000 mortgage. Because of a recent layoff, Peggy and Alan are having trouble financially and they wish to seek Medicaid help for their family's health insurance. If they live in a state that limits the exemption to $500,000, they are $100,000 over this amount. Therefore, $100,000 is considered an available resource for Medicaid eligibility purposes.

Money that can be accessed from a home equity line of credit is not considered an available resource if the total home equity is less than the $500,000/$750,000 limit.

Example: Manon, age 67, owns a two bedroom condominium that has a market value of $250,000. She has a home equity line of credit that has a maximum line of credit of $100,000. As of now, Manon only owes $20,000 on the line. The additional $80,000 that Manon can access is not considered an available resource for Medicaid eligibility purposes.

Please note that in some cases, it is a viable Medicaid planning strategy to use excess cash resources (that are over the Medicaid asset limit) to pay down a mortgage. As long as this payment does not drive the client's equity beyond the $500,000/$750,000 limit, this could work to make a client eligible for Medicaid without reducing his or her overall wealth.

Example: Manon, age 67, owns a two bedroom condominium that has a market value of $250,000. She owes $150,000 on a mortgage on the condominium. Manon has $80,000 in cash assets that puts her well in excess of the asset limit for Medicaid eligibility. She can use $75,000 of her cash assets to pay half of the principal she owes on her mortgage. She is now eligible for Medicaid since she is not over the resource limit and the value of her home equity is still far less than the $500,000 threshold. In addition, spending the $75,000 to pay down her mortgage is not a gift (and so does not start a five year period of ineligibility), since it was not given to another person.

A home is also not considered an available resource if the applicant's spouse lives in the house. Therefore, if a client's wife or husband lives in the house, the client can successfully apply for Medicaid (assuming the other resource and asset limitations are met).

The danger occurs when a client requires nursing home care and no spouse lives in the home. In this case, the home will be unprotected. While government authorities may not require that the house be sold (especially if a reasonable claim can be made that the client eventually intends to return), they almost certainly will put a lien on the house up to the value of the Medicaid services provided.[13]

> *Example: Donald is 86 years old and lives alone. Because of his deteriorating health, he is forced to enter a nursing home. His sole valuable asset is his home, which is worth $350,000. In the three years between his entry into the nursing home and his death, Medicaid pays $200,000 towards his medical care. The local department of social services will likely (and, in many states, is required by law to) attach a lien to the house up to the value of the services that Medicaid provided. When the house is sold after Donald's death, the first $200,000 will be applied to reimburse Medicaid for the expenses paid on behalf of Donald.*

To avoid this, transferring the family residence to an irrevocable Medicaid planning trust is a strategy that is appropriate for many clients. As long as the clients wait out the five year period of ineligibility following the transfer, this strategy should protect the residence from being subjected to a lien by the Medicaid authorities.

Practice Tip: Although a person of any age can conceivably need chronic nursing home care because of catastrophic injury or illness, clients often are unwilling to cede control of their assets until the prospect of needing nursing home care is realistic. Suggesting that a healthy 55-year-old client start worrying about nursing home Medicaid requirements is likely to annoy the client and is most likely unnecessary. On the other hand, you want your clients to complete their Medicaid planning transfers at least five years before they are likely to need Medicaid assistance. In the experience of the author, clients in the mid to late 60s and early 70s are in the ideal time frame to engage in comprehensive Medicaid planning. As people reach retirement age, they are more willing to engage in discussions about elder care issues. Waiting beyond that age increases the risk of the clients not being able to remain out of a nursing home for five years after the transfers.

With regard to a family home, it is often wise to allow the client certain controls over the residence, including the right to live in the property and to

---

13. 42 USCS § 1396p (a)(1)(B).

disallow its sale. Apart from the property and income tax benefits that can be preserved through such provisions (discussed later, in chapter 9), it can help increase a client's comfort with a plan if the client knows that he or she retains the right to live in the property. The next chapter discusses the best manner in which to do this.

Individual Retirement Accounts and Other Deferred Assets

Many clients, especially elderly clients, have significant assets in tax deferred accounts, such as Individual Retirement Accounts (IRAs) and 401(k) plans, etc. These accounts are usually funded with pre-tax dollars (i.e., the initial contribution was tax deductible). Except in the case of the Roth IRA, the assets are taxed as income when they are withdrawn from the account.

Account holders who are under age 59½ are, with limited exceptions, subject to a 10% penalty if they withdraw deferred account assets. Clients who are older than 59½ years old can withdraw as much of their deferred account as they like without penalty, although such withdrawals are taxable as income (again, except for Roth IRAs).[14]

To keep their tax deferred status, an IRA must be held by an individual. If an IRA is transferred to a trust or the assets are withdrawn and transferred to the trust, the entire amount of the IRA will be taxable as income that year.[15] That could have disastrous consequences for your client.

> *Example: Derek owns a traditional IRA that is worth $400,000. He is 64 years old and currently earns $100,000 per year. While doing some Medicaid planning, he transfers the money in the IRA to his children in 2011. All $400,000 will be counted as part of his 2011 taxable income. Depending on the applicable state and federal income tax rates, close to 40% of the $400,000 can be lost to income taxes.*

Because of these income tax ramifications, it rarely pays to transfer tax deferred accounts to another person or a trust for Medicaid planning purposes. Even with a Roth IRA, which is not tax deferred, but grows tax free, it is often unwise to withdraw the assets as this ends their ability to grow tax free.

The good news is that IRAs and other tax deferred retirement accounts receive favorable treatment for Medicaid eligibility purposes. Rather than con-

---

14. *See* I.R.S. Publication 590 (http://www.irs.gov/publications/p590/).
15. *See id.*

sidering the entire value of the retirement account as an available resource, Medicaid authorities in many states will only consider the fraction of the trust that is equal to one divided by the number of years remaining on the client's life expectancy.[16]

> *Example:* Christine is 67 years old and needs Medicaid assistance in 2011. She owns a 401(k) account that is worth $200,000. Assume that under applicable government promulgated tables, her life expectancy is 20 years. In many states, the Medicaid authorities will only consider 1/20 of the account's value ($10,000) as an available resource. Therefore, while this money may need to be "spent down" for the client's healthcare before Medicaid will start paying for Christine's healthcare (depending on her other resources), the existence of the account and the $190,000 remaining in the account should not make her ineligible for Medicaid.

Practice Tip: The point of this section is that, because of the confluence of the favorable treatment that IRAs get from Medicaid and the adverse tax consequences of transfer, IRAs should generally not be transferred to Medicaid planning trusts. However, the circumstances of your case may determine differently. Also, make sure to learn how your state and local Department of Social Services treat assets in retirement accounts as this is not a subject where there is necessarily nationwide uniformity.

Irrevocable Burial Trusts

An irrevocable burial trust is, as the name implies, a trust that is established to fund the eventual burial expenses for the client. Assets in an irrevocable burial trust are not considered available resources to the client. In addition, federal law provides that transfers to an irrevocable burial trust are not considered gifts for purposes of the five year period of ineligibility.[17]

> *Example:* Gerry and Donna have $50,000 in cash assets. They both realize that Gerry needs to be transferred imminently to a nursing

---

16. This is similar to the "minimum required distribution" rules that apply to most tax deferred accounts. These rules require that, beginning at age 70½, the account holder must withdraw, each year, a fraction of the trust that is one divided by the person's remaining life expectancy. *See* 1–6 Bender's New York Elder Law §6.06 [1][f].

17. 42 USCS §1382b(d).

*home because of his failing health. They cannot transfer their assets
to their children or an ordinary Medicaid planning trust because Gerry
cannot wait out the five year period of ineligibility. Instead, they can
each transfer a reasonable amount (say, $10,000) to an irrevocable
burial trust that will pay for their funeral expenses after death. This
is not considered a gift for Medicaid purposes. Thus, they will only
have $30,000 left that needs to be spent down when applying for Med-
icaid.*

Income Only Trusts

Clients often rely on the income generated by their financial assets (such as
stocks or bonds) to help defray their day to day living expenses. Therefore, it
might be unwise to transfer all of a client's assets to a trust from which they receive no benefit. In addition, an estate plan that leaves the clients no means of
support is inherently suspect and may cause Medicaid authorities to carefully
investigate whether the trust (or other sources) are, in fact, being used to support the grantors. If it is determined, for example, that the clients' children
are, in fact, using trust assets to help their parents, the authorities could reasonably consider the entire trust an available resource.

An alternative to establishing a Medicaid trust that gives the client no beneficial interest is the "income only" Medicaid trust. An income only trust gives
the grantor(s) the right to all of the income generated by the trust (such as interest and dividends earned from cash assets held by the trust or rentals earned
by property owned by the trust, etc.). The principal can still be used for other
purposes, but should not potentially benefit the grantor(s). A typical income
only trust clause would be as follows:

> During the lifetime of the grantor, the trustee shall pay to or apply for
> the benefit of the grantor all of the net income of the trust, in quarterly
> or more frequent installments. However, in no event shall any of the trust
> principal be applied in any manner that would provide the grantor any
> pecuniary benefit or in a manner that would displace any legal obligation
> of the grantor.

The advantage of an income only trust is that it gives the grantor a source
of income to live off of. In addition, an older grantor is more likely to be comfortable with a trust that allows her the income.

The disadvantage, of course, is that the income generated by the trust will
be vulnerable in the event that the client needs Medicaid assistance. Depend-

ing on the client's other income sources, the client may have to "spend down" this income on his or her healthcare before Medicaid assistance kicks in. In addition, if the client does not spend all of the income on an ongoing basis, it will accumulate and become an available resource to the client.

> *Example:* Sam and Diane, each age 66, establish an income only Medicaid planning trust. The trust allocates the income to Sam and Diane. They fund the trust with $500,000 in cash and securities. Each year, the trust funds earn about $30,000 in income. Sam and Diane, however, do not use this money, as their social security and pension checks are enough to live on. This money accumulates, and thus becomes an available resource. If either Sam or Diane requires nursing home care, these savings will be lost.

> In this case, it would have been better for the trust not to allocate income to Sam and Diane. As it is, however, the best strategy for Sam and Diane would be to spend these funds on themselves or on expenses that will eventually increase the benefit to their children without increasing their resource pool. For example, they might spend these assets on improvements to their home.

> It may be tempting for Sam and Diane to give the $30,000 income each year to their children. However, such gifts would renew their five year period of ineligibility each year, thus negating the benefits of their trust. If gifts are given to family members, it should be done in small increments and should be done by purchasing small items for their family members. In other words, it should not be done in a manner that will be easily noticed on their bank statements, as such statements will be reviewed by Medicaid officials in the event of a later application.

If the client does choose an income only trust, he or she should be carefully counseled that the income may be vulnerable in the event of a Medicaid need. If the client needs some income to live on, but not as much as his or her assets will generate, consideration may be given to establishing two Medicaid trusts: one "income only" trust (to give the client the necessary income) and one trust where the client has no right to the income.

> *Example:* Jason and Eve are 70 and 68 years old respectively and are considering some Medicaid planning. In addition to their social security checks, they figure they need an additional $2,000 per month to live comfortably. They own $800,000 in cash assets and their port-

folio generates about 5% income per year. If they put all of their assets into an income only trust, the trust will generate $40,000 per year in income, which is more than necessary. The additional income will be vulnerable in the event of a Medicaid need. Therefore, Jason and Eve should consider creating two trusts. An income only trust would hold about $480,000, which would generate the needed $2,000 per month in income. The remaining amount can be held in a Medicaid trust that does not afford the grantors an income interest.

Another issue to consider when forming and funding an income only Medicaid trust is the treatment of capital gains. Capital gains, which are the profits that one makes on a sale of an appreciated asset, can often be treated as income *or* as principal. Since Medicaid planning trusts often contain homes and/or other appreciated assets, it should generally specify that capital gains are NOT to be treated as income. Otherwise, the capital gain might be considered an available resource to the grantor. For example, the trust might stipulate:

During the lifetime of the grantor, the trustee shall pay to or apply for the benefit of the grantor, all of the net income of the trust, in quarterly or more frequent installments. For this purpose, the term "income" shall not include capital gains that are realized based on the sale of any appreciated trust asset.

Example: *Rikki is 74 years old and owns a home that she purchased in 1974 for $32,000. In 2011, she transferred the home (and other assets) into an income only Medicaid trust. In 2014, the trust sells the house for $300,000. If capital gains were considered income, Rikki would be entitled to $268,000, which would be a disaster for her Medicaid planning strategy. If the trust specified that the grantor is not entitled to capital gains (i.e., that capital gains are not income for purposes of the trust), there would be no such problem.*

Long Term Care Insurance

Although not part of trust preparation per se, the competent elder law professional should have a working awareness of all of the Medicaid planning alternatives that are available to clients. The purchase of long term care insurance is one such alternative to divesting oneself of one's assets so as to qualify for Medicaid. This insurance is designed to pay for the client's nursing home, home health aide and similar elder care needs. A client may come to you with one or more quotes for long term care policies and/or you may know or work with insurance professionals who may be selling long term care policies.

At first glance, long term care insurance policies seem attractive. They allow clients to pay for their elder care needs without having to undergo the time consuming and often worrying process of impoverishing themselves. For some clients this strategy *will* be the best choice, especially if the client has large pensions or other retirement incomes or assets that cannot easily be held in trust, as these might render income reduction difficult to the point of Medicaid eligibility.

However, there are a couple of pitfalls to watch out for regarding long term care insurance.

First, it is critical that the client purchase insurance with a benefit package that is likely to meet his or her long term care needs. In evaluating the benefits offered by a long term car insurance policy, there are three factors that must be evaluated:

> **The maximum benefit amount:** This is defined as the maximum benefits per day of care. If the client is purchasing insurance to protect against the possibility of needing nursing home care and the average nursing home in the area charges $300 per day, the policy should cover at least $300 per day in benefits.
>
> **The duration of the coverage:** Long term care insurance plans will not pay benefits indefinitely. They are limited in duration in terms of how long they will continue to pay benefits once the care is needed. Typical maximum lengths of coverage are 2, 3, 4 and 5 years. A healthy client with a relatively long life expectancy may need coverage for several years and should plan accordingly.
>
> **Protection against inflation:** Some policies allow (for an additional premium) a policy's benefits to increase to correct for inflation between the time that the policy is purchased and when the benefits are needed.

Of course one can never predict with certainty how much care one will eventually need. However, a client should not purchase a long term care insurance policy unless he or she is confident that it will most likely meet his or her needs.

The other factor to be aware of is that the premiums can be quite high, especially if clients first purchase the plan when they are older. As of the time of the writing of this text, a 65-year-old client purchasing a long term care policy with a maximum daily benefit of $300 and a maximum benefits term of three years and protected against inflation to a maximum of 4% per year would pay almost $400 per month for the premiums.[18] Many clients would prefer to avoid paying this type of premium, even if it means giving up control over their assets.

Beneficiaries of a Medicaid Planning Trust

Until this point we have been discussing Medicaid trusts and how they relate to the Medicaid eligibility of the grantor. Consideration should also be given to the potential impact a trust may have on the beneficiaries' eligibility for government assistance. As the beneficiaries of a Medicaid planning trust are typically the clients' children, questions about the financial status of the clients' children must be asked during the course of the representation.

If children of the clients are themselves receiving asset or income based government assistance, such as Medicaid, Section 8 housing assistance, food stamps, or other state welfare programs, it is as important that the assets in the Medicaid trust not be considered available resources to the children as it is to do the same for the parents.

> *Example: Teri is 73 years old and has engaged your firm for Medicaid planning services. She has $300,000 in cash assets that will be transferred to a Medicaid trust pursuant to your suggestion. Teri trusts her son, Mike, who is receiving Medicaid assistance for his health insurance, to be the trustee of the Medicaid planning trust. The Medicaid trust contains the following provision that is common to Medicaid planning trusts:*
>
> *During the lifetime of the grantor, the trustee may pay to or apply for the children of the grantor, as much of the trust income and/or principal as the trustee deems necessary to pay for their health, education, maintenance and support, after taking into account, to the extent that the trustee deems appropriate, the other resources available to the said trust beneficiaries.*
>
> *In this case, Mike has the discretion to use the trust assets for his own healthcare. Therefore, all of the income and assets of the trust will now most likely be considered an available resource to Mike. Mike will now have to give up his Medicaid assistance. Certainly, this is not a result that the client intended.*

---

18. *See* https://www.ltcfeds.com/ltcWeb/do/assessing_your_needs/ratecalcOut.

Even if there is another co-trustee whose permission is required to disburse trust assets, there is no guarantee that this is sufficient to protect the assets.

> *Example: Assume, in the above example, that Mike and his sister Lisa were named as co-trustees. Assume further that the trust stipulates that no distributions to any child of the grantor could be made without the consent of both trustees. Even with these restrictions, Mike has some control over distributing assets for his own healthcare and Medicaid authorities may take the position that the trust assets are available to him.*

Even, where the beneficiary receiving government assistance is not the trustee at all, but merely a beneficiary, there may still be an adverse impact on the beneficiary's eligibility. As long as the trustee *may* distribute assets to a beneficiary, a local department of social services may assert that the trust assets are available to the beneficiary.[19]

> *Example: In the above example, Mike and Lisa have another sibling, Ron, who receives Medicaid assistance. Ron is not a trustee, but he is a trust beneficiary. Because the trust has the authority to pay for Ron's healthcare, some Medicaid offices in some jurisdictions may either require the trust to pay for Ron's healthcare or count the trust assets as an available resource to Ron. New York law, for instance, would allow a court to order that the trustee pay for Ron's healthcare, unless the trust specifically demands otherwise.[20]*

To avoid these potential problems, the safest thing to do is to specifically disallow the trust assets from being used to pay for services that government assistance would otherwise provide for the beneficiaries. For example, the trust may specify that assets can be used for education expenses, housing expenses and other expenses, but NOT reference healthcare or general support needs. A sample provision that does this might look something like this:

> During the lifetime of the grantor, the trustee may pay to or apply for the children of the grantor, as much of the trust income and/or principal as the trustee deems advisable for their education expenses, housing expenses and expenses related to desirable luxuries such as travel and other

---

19. *See, e.g.,* 18 NYCRR 360-4.5 which provides as follows:
Any portion of the trust principal, and of the income generated from the trust, which can be paid to or for the benefit of the applicant/recipient, under any circumstances, must be considered to be an available resource.
20. *See* N.Y. E.P.T.L. §7-1.6.

entertainment. However, the trust assets may not be used to pay for the beneficiaries' healthcare or general support expenses.

Attention should also be paid to the distribution of assets after the death of the grantor. Many Medicaid trusts simply provide that after the death of the grantor (or of the second grantor for a trust set up by a married couple), the trust assets are to be distributed to the children in equal shares (or in whatever proportions the grantor chooses). If a child is receiving asset or income based government assistance, such an infusion of capital may not be welcome or advisable, as it may impact the child's continued eligibility for these valuable assistance programs.

In such a case, the trust may be established so that the share of any beneficiary receiving assistance after the death of the grantor has his or her share remain in trust in a manner that will allow the child to benefit without the cost of losing eligibility for government assistance. An example of a trust provision that could accomplish this is as follows:

> C. Upon the death of the Grantor, the remaining trust assets shall be distributed to the children of the Grantor, in equal shares, per stirpes; provided, however, that if any beneficiary under this Paragraph certifies to the trustee that, at the time of the death of the grantor, such beneficiary was receiving government assistance, including but not limited to, Medicaid, food stamps, Section 8 housing assistance, etc., then such beneficiary's share shall be held by the Trustee of a EDUCATION, MARRIAGE and LUXURIES trust, hereinafter named, for the primary benefit of the issue of such beneficiary, in accordance with the provisions outlined below in ARTICLE VI.

> ARTICLE VI

> Education, Marriage and Luxuries Trusts

> All EDUCATION, MARRIAGE and LUXURIES TRUSTS established under Paragraph C of ARTICLE V, shall be maintained and distributed in accordance with the following provisions:

> A. The primary Trustee of each such Trust shall be that beneficiary whose issue the trust is intended to benefit. In the event that such beneficiary is unable or unwilling to serve as trustee, then the spouse of such beneficiary shall serve as trustee. In the event that the primary Trustee is deceased, then the surviving spouse of such beneficiary (who was married to such beneficiary at the time of his/her death) shall serve as successor trustee. The beneficiaries of each trust shall consist of the class of individuals who are the issue of the primary Trustee of each

Trust. Whenever the term "Beneficiary" or "Beneficiaries" is referred to in this ARTICLE, it shall be deemed to refer to the issue of such primary Trustee.

B. The trust assets, including trust income and trust principal *may only be expended for certain limited uses*, including:

- The marriage expenses of any of the Trust beneficiaries may be paid for (in whole or in part) from trust assets. Such expenses may include the cost of the wedding ceremony, reception, and dinner, the purchasing or renting and furnishing of a suitable apartment for the newly married couple, the purchase of any new apparel needed because of said marriage, and the purchase of any dishes, kitchens utensils, linens, or other items that is reasonably necessary for a newly married couple.

- The furtherance of the education of the trust beneficiaries may also be paid for (in whole or in part) from trust assets. This includes, but is not limited to, tuition costs at the primary, secondary and higher education levels, costs of room and board where appropriate, the purchase of computers, books, tutoring, etc., as is reasonably necessary for the education of the trust beneficiaries.

- Luxury expenses for the trust beneficiaries to the extent that the trustee deems advisable from time to time. This may include the purchase of vacations, jewelry, entertainment systems, etc., and any other item that is beyond the day to day support needs of the trust beneficiaries. The day to day support needs of the trust beneficiaries may not be paid from this trust, nor shall assets from the trust be used to pay the beneficiaries' debts, such as credit card debts, etc.[21]

C. The Trust shall be terminated upon the *earlier* of:

- The depletion of Trust assets;

AND

- Twenty-one (21) years after the death of the last descendant of the Grantor who is alive at the time of the execution of this Trust. If the Trust is terminated in this manner, the remaining proceeds of the trust shall be distributed to the issue of the primary trustee, in equal shares, per stirpes.

---

21. This sentence is to ensure, to the extent possible, that the trust assets are not available to the creditors of the beneficiaries.

The assets in this trust will not be considered "available" to the trust beneficiaries for purposes of eligibility for government assistance. Although this does decrease the control that the beneficiary has over the trust assets, the trade-off is often worth it. Of course, this trade-off should be discussed with the client prior to drafting the trust.

Review Questions

1) Are Medicaid rules based on federal law or state law? Explain.

2) Why are elder clients often in need of Medicaid in addition to Medicare and other health insurance?

3) To become eligible for Medicaid, why can't a client simply wait until he needs the services and then gift away all of his assets?

4) Why is it important that a Medicaid trust not allow the grantor to benefit from its assets?

5) When is a home that the client lives in considered an "available resource" for Medicaid eligibility purposes?

6) Why is it a good idea to transfer a home to a Medicaid trust even if the home is not considered an available resource?

7) Why is it often a bad idea to liquidate an IRA to transfer the assets to a Medicaid planning trust?

8) In what way are IRA assets given favorable treatment for Medicaid eligibility purposes?

9) How can an irrevocable burial trust be used as part of a Medicaid planning strategy?

10) What is one advantage of using an "income only" Medicaid trust rather than giving the grantor no beneficial interest in the trust?

11) What is one disadvantage of using an "income only" Medicaid trust rather than giving the grantor no beneficial interest in the trust?

12) How can long term care insurance accomplish the same basic goals as a Medicaid planning trust strategy?

13) Name three aspects of any long term care policy that should be investigated before purchasing one.

14) In what way can a beneficiary's eligibility for government assistance be hurt by a Medicaid planning trust?

15) Identify one solution to ensure that the danger expressed in your answer to question 14 does not come to fruition.

CHAPTER 8

SUPPLEMENTAL NEEDS TRUSTS

Supplemental Needs Trusts: An Introduction

A supplemental needs trust (which is also sometimes called a "special needs trust"[1]) is a legislation-created device that allows chronically disabled people to benefit from income and asset-based government assistance programs even when they might have other sources of revenue.

There are various types of special needs trusts that will be discussed in this chapter, but they all share a common purpose and many common features. All such trusts must be for the benefit of a person who is defined as being under a chronic disability under the applicable statute.[2] All such trusts must specifically be drafted so that they pay assets only to "supplement and not supplant" government assistance.[3] In other words, the trust assets may be used only to pay for expenses that government assistance would not otherwise pay for.

> **Example:** *Cindy suffers from severe schizophrenia and is confined to a psychiatric hospital. Various federal and state programs pay for most of her care. Brad, her uncle, wants to give Cindy a $10,000 gift. But, he does not want to hurt Cindy's continued eligibility for government assistance. He thus establishes a supplemental needs trust that will pay only for Cindy's "supplemental" expenses (i.e., expenses other than those that government assistance will pay for).*

Assets held by a supplemental needs trust are typically used to pay for things like the education, clothing and luxuries of the beneficiary (such as travel, entertainment, etc.). The trustee may certainly be given discretion within this

---

1. Although it can be, and often is, referred to by either name, for the sake of simplicity, we will refer to it as a "supplemental needs trust" throughout this chapter.

2. *See, e.g.,* N.Y. E.P.T.L. §7-1.12.

3. *See id.*

range of possible uses of the trust funds, as long as the trustee may not pay for expenses that government assistance would pay for.

The theory behind the allowance of this device is that if a disabled person's assets were required to pay for his or her healthcare, there would be nothing left to pay for quality of life expenses. In addition, the inability to create this type of trust would greatly discourage gifts to people with disabilities.

Practice Tip: It is true that just being the beneficiary of other types of trusts may not cause a disabled person to lose benefits. This is especially true if the trustee's discretion to give assets to the beneficiary is limited. However, where the share or gift of a single disabled beneficiary can be isolated in a special needs trust, it is often best to do so. The main reason is that, while local social services officials may question whether other trust assets are considered "available" resources, assets in supplemental needs trust are often protected by state or federal statute.

A supplemental needs trust can be established as inter-vivos trust or as a testamentary trust. That is, a supplemental needs trust can be set up either while the trustee is living or by a will, to take effect only upon the death of the client. The latter is a common approach for people who have disabled children. Rather than giving them an inheritance outright, thereby potentially threatening their eligibility to receive government assistance, the disabled child's share can be held for his or her benefit in a testamentary supplemental needs trust.

> *Example: Tom suffers from chronic paralysis of his legs. Because of this, he is confined to a wheelchair and cannot work. Therefore, he applies for and receives Medicaid and Supplemental Security Income[4] ("SSI"). Tom's mother, Gail, wants to give him a gift in her will. However a cash gift (or gift of any cash equivalent) may compromise Tom's ability to continue receiving government assistance. So, she provides in her will that Tom's share of her estate will not be distributed to Tom outright, but will instead be held for him in a supplemental needs trust.*

The provision establishing that one child's share is held in trust need not even specifically reference the disabled child. It can be worded something to this effect:

---

4. This provides additional social security benefits to poor disabled people.

Upon my death, my assets shall be distributed among my children, in equal shares, per stirpes, provided, however, that if any beneficiary under this Paragraph suffers from a severe and chronic disability, then his or her share shall not be distributed to the beneficiary outright, but shall instead be held for the benefit of the beneficiary in a "supplemental needs trust" under the terms and conditions set forth hereinafter in ITEM FIVE.

The actual language of the testamentary supplemental needs trust can then be similar to the inter-vivos provisions discussed below.

Supplemental Needs Trusts: The Provisions

The exact language by which a supplemental needs trust should be established may vary from state to state. However, a common thread among supplemental needs trusts, as established by applicable federal law, is that the trust must evince a clear intent that the trust assets are intended to supplement, and not supplant, government assistance to the disabled beneficiary. In addition, the trust may be used only to pay expenses that would not otherwise be paid for by government assistance programs.[5]

Although this type of trust was respected by courts even before gaining statutory recognition,[6] many states have given formal statutory recognition to supplemental needs trust.[7] In addition, since the passage of the Omnibus Budget Reconciliation Act of 1993, there is federal statutory recognition of supplemental needs trusts.[8]

Below, we will reproduce sample language that can be used by a trust to clearly indicate this intent. This is an example of a standard supplemental needs trust established by a will or other trust upon the death of the grantor, when one or more of the beneficiaries may be disabled at the time of the grantor's death.

Any provision hereof to the contrary notwithstanding, if any person (other than the Grantor) with a severe and chronic or persistent disability as defined under applicable state law is entitled to a trust share hereunder,

---

5. *See generally*, Rosenberg, *Supplemental Needs Trusts for People with Disabilities: The Development of a Private Trust in the Public Interest*, 10 B.U. Pub. Int. L.J. 91 (2000).

6. *See, e.g.*, Matter of Escher, 75 A.D.2d 531 (1980); aff'd. 52 N.Y.2d 1006 (1981).

7. *See, e.g.*, Ohio's O.R.C. § 5815.28.

8. 42 U.S.C. § 1396p(d)(4)(A).

then said beneficiary's interest in the trust share shall be held and managed by the Trustee in a supplemental needs trust for the benefit of said beneficiary, as provided for herein.

A. The Trustee shall collect the income therefrom and, after deducting all charges and expenses properly attributable thereto, shall, at any time and from time to time, apply for the benefit of the beneficiary, so much (even to the extent of the whole) of the net income and/or principal of this Trust as the Trustee shall deem advisable, in his or her sole and absolute discretion, subject to the limitations set forth below. The Trustee shall add to the principal of such Trust the balance of net income not so paid or applied.

B. It is the Grantor's intent to create a supplemental needs trust which conforms to the provisions of applicable state and/or federal law regarding supplemental needs trusts.

C. The Grantor intends that the Trust assets be used to supplement, not supplant, impair or diminish, any benefits or assistance of any federal, state, county, city, or other governmental entity for which the beneficiary may otherwise be eligible or which the beneficiary may be receiving. Consistent with that intent, it is the Grantor's desire that, before expending any amounts from the net income and/or principal of this Trust, the Trustee consider the availability of all benefits from government or private assistance programs for which the beneficiary may be eligible and that, where appropriate and to the extent possible, the Trustee endeavor to maximize the collection of such benefits and to facilitate the distribution of such benefits for the benefit of the beneficiary.

D. None of the income or principal of this Trust shall be applied in such a manner as to supplant, impair or diminish benefits or assistance of any federal, state, county, city, or other governmental entity for which the beneficiary may otherwise be eligible or which the beneficiary may be receiving.

E. The beneficiary does not have the power to assign, encumber, direct, distribute or authorize distributions from this Trust.[9]

F. Notwithstanding the above provisions, the Trustee may make distributions to meet the beneficiary's need for food, clothing, shelter or health care even if such distributions may result in an impairment or diminution of the beneficiary's receipt or eligibility for government ben-

---

9. This is a standard spendthrift provision which should appear in most trusts; not just supplemental needs trusts.

efits or assistance but only if the Trustee determines that (i) the beneficiary's needs will be better met if such distribution is made, and (ii) it is in the beneficiary's best interests to suffer the consequent effect, if any, on the beneficiary's eligibility for or receipt of government benefits or assistance; provided, however, that if the mere existence of the Trustee's authority to make distributions pursuant to this paragraph shall result in the beneficiary's loss of government benefits or assistance, regardless of whether such authority is actually exercised, this paragraph shall be null and void and the Trustee's authority to make such distributions shall cease and shall be limited as provided above, without exception.

G. Upon the demise of said beneficiary, any balance remaining of the Trust share shall be distributed to said beneficiary's issue, per stirpes; and if none living, to Grantor's issue, per stirpes.

Third Party Supplemental Needs Trusts

A third party supplemental needs trust is the most straightforward of the supplemental needs trusts. A supplemental needs trust is a "third party" trust when assets *other than* those assets belonging to the disabled person are used to fund the trust. To keep its status as a third party trust, no funds belonging to the disabled person nor funds to which the disabled person is entitled, should be used to fund the trust.

> **Example:** Linda suffers a severe and chronic disability and receives government assistance to help pay for her medical care. Her father, Jerry, wants to ensure that she has assets that will help pay for her additional expenses, such as education and leisure. Therefore, he establishes a supplemental needs trust for Linda's benefit. He transfers $100,000 of his own assets to the trust. This is a third party supplemental needs trust.

A testamentary supplemental needs trust is almost by definition a third party trust since a testator has the right to dispose of his or her assets as he or she sees fit. The only exception would be where the testator's provision is giving assets to the disabled person that the disabled person is legally entitled to (e.g., if the testator owed money to the disabled beneficiary).

A testamentary supplemental needs trust can be quite broad in the discretion it gives to the trustee, while protecting the eligibility of the disabled beneficiary. As long as the disabled beneficiary does not have control over the distributions from the trust (i.e., the decision is made by an independent trustee), the assets in the trust should not be considered an available resource to the disabled beneficiary.[10]

It is important to avoid directing the trustee to pay for the healthcare (or similar) expenses of the beneficiary. Where the trustee is directed to pay for the healthcare or general support needs of the disabled beneficiary, or perhaps even where the trustee has the authority to do so, it is possible that a local department of social services will consider the trust assets to be an available resource to the beneficiary.

It is important to note, however, that even when the provisions of a third party trust (or will) do not conform to the supplemental needs trust requirements, courts do have the authority to reform a provision to turn a trust into a qualifying supplemental needs trust.

> **Example:** *Michael established a will that provides that upon his death his assets shall be divided among his children, Adam, Ben and Cindy. The trust also provides that if any of them are younger than age 35, that child's share will be held in trust for his or her benefit until age 35. The provisions of the age 35 trusts require the trustee to pay trust assets to the beneficiaries for their "health, education, maintenance and support" to the "extent the trustee believes reasonably necessary" for the benefit of the beneficiary.*
>
> *Michael died when Ben was 26 years old. At age 29, Ben was involved in major car accident that causes him to sustain a chronic disability. As it stands, when he turns 35 years old he is going to receive all of the money. Even before he turns 35, since the trustee is directed to pay his healthcare expenses, the trust assets may be considered an available resource to Ben.*
>
> *Because of this unforeseen changed circumstance, the trustee can (and should) apply to a court with jurisdiction (like the surrogate's court or probate court) for judicial permission to reform the trust. The court can reform the trust to change its provisions so that it qualifies as a supplemental needs trust. Furthermore, the court may have the trust last perpetually rather than having it terminate when Ben reaches 35 years of age. This is because it is likely that, had Michael known of the circumstances that would occur after his death, he would have rather*

---

10. *See* Goldfarb, *Supplemental Needs Trusts for Disabled Persons,* http://www.senior-law.com/snt.htm.

*had the assets held for Ben's benefit in a supplemental needs trust than
to be dissipated paying for healthcare expenses that government assistance
would otherwise pay for.*[11]

Self-Settled Supplemental Needs Trusts

Things become a bit more complex when supplemental needs trusts are established using the assets of the disabled person. In spite of the general rule that assets held in self-settled trusts are vulnerable to the creditors of the grantor, federal law (and corresponding state laws) specifically exempt the assets in certain qualifying supplemental needs trusts from inclusion as "available resources" to the disabled person who funded it. In other words, if a disabled person has resources that would make him or her ineligible for government assistance, he or she can create a supplemental needs trust, use those assets to fund it and then continue receiving government assistance.[12]

> **Example:** *Kramer suffers from a severe disability and he receives Medicaid and SSI benefits. After a car accident, Kramer receives an insurance settlement of $50,000. Were he to simply keep that money, he would be ineligible to receive Medicaid and SSI and the money would have to be spent down towards his care before he could receive more government assistance. Instead, Kramer can establish (or a close relative can establish for him) a supplemental needs trust and transfer the $50,000 to the trust. In this way, the assets can still be used for Kramer's benefit (e.g., for his education or leisure) and will not affect his eligibility for Medicaid and SSI.*

Unlike the third party trust, however, there are strict conditions that must be followed for a self-settled trust to gain the benefits of the supplemental needs trust.[13] First, the trust must be established by the disabled person himself, by the disabled person's parent, grandparent or legal guardian or by a court on behalf of the disabled person. Second, the trust must be established for a disabled person under the age of 65.

Third and most significantly, the trust must contain a "payback provision." This provision must dictate that, upon the death of the disabled beneficiary,

---

11. *See* Matter of Ridell, 157 P.3d 888 (WA Ct. of App. 2007).

12. *See* 42 U.S.C. § 1396p(d)(4)(A).

13. *See id.*

any money that is remaining in the trust will be used to reimburse the state(s) that paid healthcare costs for the beneficiary up to the amount that they paid on behalf of the beneficiary. Any amount left over after this reimbursement can be distributed in accordance with whatever the trust dictates (e.g., to the beneficiary's heirs).

Essentially, the government is saying, "we'll let you (the disabled person) keep your money for supplemental expenses for yourself, but if there's anything left over when you don't need it anymore (because you're dead), we get first crack at whatever is left." The logic behind this is simple. The purpose of the supplemental needs trust statute was to allow the disabled person quality of life that would be lacking if he or she had to use all of his or her resources to pay for healthcare expenses. The purpose was not to allow the disabled person's family a windfall while the government pays for the healthcare of the disabled person.

A typical "payback" provision may read as follows

> Disposition of Trust on Death of Beneficiary: The Trust shall terminate upon the death of [the disabled beneficiary] and the Trustee shall distribute any principal and accumulated interest that then remains in the Trust as follows:
>
> The various public agencies that provided benefits and assistance to the beneficiary shall be reimbursed for the total expenditure and support provided to [the disabled beneficiary] during his lifetime, as consistent with federal and state law. If [the disabled beneficiary] received assistance in more than one state, then the amount distributed to the agencies of the various states shall be based on the proportionate share of the total amount of benefits paid by all the agencies of the various states on the behalf of the beneficiary, as required by statute.
>
> All remaining principal and accumulated income shall be paid to the issue of [the disabled beneficiary], or if he leaves no issue, then to the heirs of [the disabled beneficiary] under the local rules of intestacy.

Without this provision, a trust will not qualify as a supplemental needs trust. In that case, the entire trust corpus will be considered an available resource to the disabled beneficiary, likely disqualifying him from receiving many types of government assistance.

Practice Tip: If the disabled client has assets that he or she owns and assets coming from a third person, two separate supplemental needs trusts should be established. A self-settled trust should be established for the disabled person's assets and a third party trust should be established for the other assets. The main reason for this is, of course, that the self-settled trust must have a payback provision which is unnecessary for the third party trust. Using a single trust and allocating to the payback provision only the assets that the beneficiary owned is too complex and of questionable validity.

The family should also be advised that if any family member wants to give substantial gifts to the disabled person he or she should do so by giving gifts to the third party trust. This applies both to lifetime gifts and to testamentary gifts. In the case of the latter, the family member (including a parent) should be counseled to put a provision in his or her will that leaves the share of the disabled beneficiary to the beneficiary's lifetime third party supplemental needs trust. Alternatively, as discussed above, a will can create a separate third party supplemental needs trust for the benefit of the disabled beneficiary.

Supplemental Needs Trusts with Other Beneficiaries as Well as the Disabled Beneficiary

The next question is whether a supplemental needs trust may benefit additional parties in addition to the disabled person.

A standard trust, whether a qualifying supplemental needs trust or not, can benefit a disabled person as well as other third parties. As long as the trustee is not required (and certainly, if s/he is not allowed) to pay expenses for the disabled beneficiary that would be covered by government assistance, the trust should not adversely affect the disabled person's benefits eligibility.

The same applies to supplemental needs trusts. Although supplemental needs trusts typically benefit only the disabled person, there is probably no problem with having other people potentially benefit from a third party supplemental needs trust.

> *Example: Doris has a disabled son, Mike, and two healthy children, Cindy and Bobby. Doris wants to leave 1/3 of her estate to a supplemental needs trust for the benefit of Mike. However, to the extent that Mike doesn't use the money on an ongoing basis, she would like her other children to benefit from those trust assets. Therefore, she establishes a will with a supplemental needs trust to hold Mike's share. The trust provides that each year, the income from that trust shall be used for the supplemental needs of Mike. The trust provides that, at the end of each calendar year, any remaining trust income from that year will be distributed to Cindy and Bobby, in equal shares. As long as it's*

otherwise drafted properly, this trust should not adversely affect Mike's eligibility for government assistance and can be effective as a supplemental needs trust.

In addition, in a third party supplemental needs trust, third parties may (and should) be named as remainder beneficiaries in the event that trust assets remain after the death of the disabled beneficiary.

> **Example:** *In the above case, the trust can provide that, after Mike's death, the proceeds of the trust will be distributed to Cindy and Bobby, in equal shares.*

A self-settled supplemental needs trust, on the other hand, is another matter. Since the state must, by definition, have a remainder interest in the trust assets, it naturally has an interest in preserving the trust assets. As such, in a self-settled supplemental needs trust no person other than the disabled beneficiary may be a beneficiary of the trust, whether during the lifetime of the disabled beneficiary or after his death.[14]

Hobbs, referenced in note 14, was an interesting case that involved a comprehensive discussion of this requirement. In that case, assets from a self-settled supplemental needs trust were used to help make extensive improvements on the home in which the disabled beneficiary and his relatives lived, to furnish the home and to pay the disabled person's mother a salary of $2,200 per month for taking care of the beneficiary.

The federal district court ruled that the state has an interest in preserving its remainder interest in the trust. Therefore, the state had the right to reasonably determine whether all expenditures from the trust were necessary for the disabled beneficiary. Since the state reasonably concluded that the trust in question benefitted parties other than the disabled person, the state was justified in considering the entire trust corpus as an "available resource" to the beneficiary and to therefore deny him benefits!

Practice Tip: Of course it is reasonable for the supplemental needs trust to reimburse third parties for expenses advanced for the benefit of the disabled person. However, great care needs to be taken to ensure that the trust is drafted to allow all expenses to be paid from the trust. In addition, all expenses that are actually paid by the trust should be strictly applied for the

---

14. *See* Hobbs v. Zenderman, 542 F. Supp. 2d 1220 (D.N.M. 2008), *aff'd* 579 F.3d 1171 (10th Cir. 2009).

> benefit of the disabled person. The risk of being aggressive in this manner (i.e., the risk that benefits will be denied to the disabled person) needs to be taken seriously and justifies great caution.

An important caveat to note is that the requirement that a self-settled supplemental needs trust be for the sole benefit of the beneficiary is based on state law (unlike, for example, the payback provision requirement, which is based on federal law). Thus, there may be states that would allow a self-settled supplemental needs trust to benefit other parties as well as the disabled beneficiary. Research into your own state's rules in this respect is worthwhile for practitioners working on self-settled supplemental needs trusts.

Miller Trusts

The "Miller Trust,"[15] is also referred to as a "qualified income" trust.[16] This trust serves as a vehicle to hold income of a disabled person from pensions or social security that exceeds the state limit for Medicaid eligibility. This excess income can be placed into the Miller trust rather than being held by the beneficiary and thus allow such person to become eligible for Medicaid. Named after a 1990 case of the same name, the Miller trust was codified as part of the 1993 Act that also established the rules for the self-settled supplemental needs trust discussed above.[17]

> *Example: Minnie is 72 years old and suffers from various disabilities, for which she requires the assistance of a home health aide. The income limitation for her to be eligible for Medicaid in her state is $700 per month. She receives $1,500 every month in social security payments. The extra $800 will make her ineligible for Medicaid (or, at least, will require that it be spent down before care is provided by Medicaid). To avoid this, she can establish a Miller trust that will be funded with $800 per month from her social security check.*

Unlike a self-settled supplemental needs trust, this device can be used by people over the age of 65. As with a self-settled supplemental needs trust, the trust assets may be used for the benefit of the disabled person, but only in a

---

15. Named for the case, Miller v. Ibarra, 746 F. Supp. 19 (D. Colo 1990) that initially allowed this type of trust before it was codified.

16. Also sometimes referred to as a "Utah gap" trust.

17. 42 U.S.C. § 1396p(d)(4)(B).

manner that will supplement, and not replace, payments that would otherwise be made by government assistance.

Also as with a self-settled supplemental needs trust, Miller trusts require a payback provision. So, any amount of the trust assets that are unused at the time of the beneficiary's death must be used to reimburse the state for expenses paid on behalf of the disabled person. Assets remaining after this reimbursement to the state may be distributed to the disabled person's heirs, in accordance with the wishes of the disabled person.

Pooled Trusts

An alternative to the Miller trust, also codified by the 1993 Act, is the "pooled trust" that is held by a non-profit organization.[18] The non-profit organization establishes a trust where many disabled people "pool" their resources to be managed and invested by the organization.[19] Separate accounts must be held for each disabled beneficiary and the separate account must be set up by the disabled beneficiary or the parent, grandparent, or legal guardian of the beneficiary (or by a court).

The disabled person can fund his or her account in the pooled trust with assets (so as to lower his or her asset holdings below the Medicaid asset threshold) and may consistently fund the pooled trust with income that exceeds the income threshold. The trust may use the disabled beneficiary's account to pay for the beneficiary's supplemental needs.

Unlike the self-settled trust and the Miller trust, after the death of the disabled beneficiary, there is some flexibility in the pooled trust. Essentially, the trust has two choices. The first choice is to have the beneficiary's account simply remain with the non-profit organization and be used as part of its general (non-profit) purpose. In that case, the state need not be reimbursed for the care provided to the beneficiaries. Alternatively, the trust may pay back the state for the care it provided to the beneficiary and the remainder may then be distributed to the heirs of the beneficiary.

In most states, there is no age restriction on who can fund a pooled trust. This is an important advantage over the self-settled supplemental needs trust. Of course, the downside to the pooled trust strategy is that the organization maintains control over the trust assets and must approve expenditures on be-

---

18. 42 U.S.C. § 1396p(d)(4)(C).

19. See, e.g., http://www.nysarc.org/family/nysarc-family-trust-services.asp.

half of the beneficiary. With a supplemental needs trust it will be recalled, a family member or friend can be the trustee and thus control distributions to the disabled beneficiary.

Transfers to Supplemental Needs Trusts

In addition to the important benefit of maintaining/preserving a disabled person's eligibility for government assistance programs, supplemental needs trusts provide another important statutory advantage. Recall from chapter 7 that gift transfers typically cause a five year period of ineligibility to receive Medicaid assistance. A transfer to a qualified supplemental needs trust, on the other hand, does not result in a period of ineligibility for the donor.[20] If the disabled beneficiary of the trust is a spouse or child of the grantor, the disabled beneficiary may be of any age.[21] If the disabled beneficiary is someone else, the beneficiary must be younger than age 65.[22]

> *Example: Brenda is 78 years old and has $150,000 in assets. She has a disabled son, Jim. If she were to transfer all of her assets directly to Jim, that would trigger a five year period of ineligibility for Medicaid assistance. On the other hand, if she creates a (or funds an existing) supplemental needs trust for Jim's benefit, she will be eligible for Medicaid assistance immediately.*

In addition to the other statutory requirements of a supplemental needs trust, to be eligible for this transfer exemption the trust must be for the "sole benefit" of the disabled beneficiary. This is true even though such transfer is made to a third party supplemental needs trust. In addition, unlike the sole benefit requirement discussed above in the context of the self-settled trust discussed earlier in this chapter, this requirement is mandated by federal statute and thus not subject to variation between states.[23]

> *Example: In the above case, the supplemental needs trust that Brenda transfers her assets to must be for the sole benefit of Jim. If another child can benefit from the trust, the transfer will cause the full period of ineligibility discussed in chapter 7.*

---

20. 42 U.S.C. § 1396p(c)(2)(B).
21. 42 U.S.C. § 1396p(c)(2)(B)(iii).
22. 42 U.S.C. § 1396p(c)(2)(B)(iv).
23. *See id.*

Practice Tip: If the client has other children aside from the disabled child, this strategy may be impractical. If the client transfers assets to the supplemental needs trust and other people at the same time, the transfers to the other people may cause a period of ineligibility in any case, minimizing the benefit of the transfer to the supplemental needs trust. This strategy works best when the disabled child is the only beneficiary or when a client wants to make an isolated large gift for the benefit of the disabled child.

Since a supplemental needs trust to which such a transfer is made is generally a third party supplemental needs trust, a "payback" provision (that requires that the state be reimbursed from the trust from assets remaining at the death of the beneficiary) is *not* required. However, the gift to the supplemental needs trust must be such that, based on sound actuarial data, it is reasonable to expect that the amount transferred will be spent over the course of the life of the disabled beneficiary.[24] Any gift over and above this amount will cause a period of ineligibility for Medicaid purposes. The reason for this is simple. If the gift is large enough that it will not likely be spent during the lifetime of the beneficiary, the entire gift cannot reasonably be considered to be for the benefit of the disabled beneficiary.

If the gift is made to a trust with a payback provision (e.g., a supplemental needs trust that was self-settled by the disabled beneficiary), then there is no such requirement (since the state has a remainder interest in the trust in any case).

Unfortunately, this only works to avoid the transfer ineligibility period. If a person has consistent income in excess of the Medicaid income limitations, transferring the excess income to a supplemental needs trust for the benefit of a disabled child will not prevent it from being considered available to the initial recipient of the income.

> *Example: Ken is 74 years old and requires long term care medical assistance. He receives $2,000 in social security income, which is far more than the $700 he is allowed under Medicaid eligibility limits. Therefore, he sets up a mechanism by which $1,300 of his income will be paid to a supplemental needs trust for the benefit of his disabled daughter, Karen, each month. Unfortunately, the $1,300 so transferred each month is still considered an "available" resource for Ken and will adversely affect Ken's Medicaid eligibility. Although the period of ineli-*

---

24. *See* CMS State Medicaid Manual § 3257(B)(6).

gibility caused by transfers can be avoided because the assets are trans-
ferred to a supplemental needs trust, the income as it comes in is still
considered available to Ken.[25]

One last possible benefit of transferring assets to a supplemental needs trust is that some states will not "recover" assets paid by Medicaid after the recipient's death if the assets are left to a supplemental needs trust for the benefit of a disabled beneficiary. Typically, if Medicaid pays for the care of a person who dies with assets, the state is required by law to seek recovery of the expenses that were laid out. However, at least one state, California, will not seek to recover such assets if they are left to a supplemental needs trust.[26]

Review Questions

1) What is the main criterion that allows a person to be the beneficiary of a supplemental needs trust?

2) What is the purpose of holding assets in a supplemental needs trust rather than having the beneficiary own them outright?

3) What key element is common to all supplemental needs trusts in terms of how and for what reason the trust may distribute its assets?

4) What is a third party supplemental needs trust?

5) What is a self-settled supplemental needs trust?

6) Is a testamentary supplemental needs trust usually a third party trust or a self-settled trust? Explain why.

7) What is the key difference between a third party supplemental needs trust and self-settled supplemental needs trust in terms of required provisions?

8) If a person wants to make a gift to a disabled beneficiary who already has a self-settled supplemental needs trust, should the person give the gift to the self-settled supplemental needs trust or establish a new supplemental needs trust to hold the gift? Explain.

9) Why should a self-settled supplemental needs trust have no beneficiary other than the disabled beneficiary?

10) What is a "Miller" trust and what purpose does it serve?

11) What is a "pooled" trust and how does it work?

---

25. Jennigs v. Commissioner, 71 A.D. 3d 98 (2d Dept. 2007).
26. *See* Shewry v. Arnold, 125 Cal. App. 4th 186 (Cal. Ct. of App. 2004).

12) Describe one advantage of the pooled trust over the Miller trust.

13) When does a gift transfer to a third party supplemental needs trust NOT cause a period of ineligibility for the person making the transfer?

CHAPTER 9

Trusts That Hold Real Estate

Jurisdictional Issues

As with most contracts, a trust can generally establish which state's rules control its administration. In addition, even absent a provision, the trust's operation will usually be governed by the state in which the grantor is domiciled.[1] It is therefore not necessary to worry about the rules of other states, such as the states of the beneficiaries

To ensure, however, that jurisdiction of other states does not come into play, choice of forum provisions are standard in trusts. Choice of forum provisions are simple to draft and to insert in trust agreements. In general, they are effective.[2] An example of such a provision is as follows:

> This trust and all trusts created hereunder shall be governed by and construed in accordance with the laws of the State of Texas, which shall also govern the conduct of fiduciaries appointed hereunder.

Things become more complex, however, when one deals with real estate. Regardless of where the grantor or trust is domiciled, public policy of each state requires that its law governs real estate within its borders.[3] This may complicate trusts that will hold real estate as trusts may be subject to the law of the jurisdiction in which the real estate sits.

> **Example:** *George lives in Brookline, MA. He has a winter home in Sarasota, FL. For Medicaid planning purposes, he decides to transfer all of his assets to a trust. He hires a Boston law firm to draft the trust for him. The firm's standard trust agreement contains a choice of law provision that stipulates that the trust agreement is governed under Mas-*

---

1. *See* Commonwealth v. Morris, 196 Va. 868 (Va. 1955).
2. *See* Carr v. Kupfer, 250 Ga. 106 (Ga. 1982).
3. *See* Pennoyer v. Neff, 95 U.S. 714, 734 (U.S. 1877).

sachusetts law. This provision will probably be valid. However, if the Sarasota home is transferred to the trust and a legal issue later arises with respect to the Sarasota property, Florida law will likely govern its disposition.

It is important to note, however, that this does not mean that a firm *cannot* draft a trust that will hold real estate located in another state. Quite the contrary, it is very common for firms to draft trusts that will hold assets such as vacation homes in other states. The key concern in such a case is that an attorney drafting a trust that will hold out of state real estate must be very careful not to dispense legal advice as to what might happen under the laws of the other state.

> *Example: In the case above, George asks his Boston attorney, what authorities his trustee will have with respect to dealing with potential tenants who rent out the Sarasota property. Assuming that the Boston attorney is not also licensed in Florida, he should be very careful when answering this type of question to avoid giving legal advice about Florida law.*

Practice Tip: If a client asks a question about the result of a hypothetical or real scenario under the law of a state in which he or she is not licensed, an attorney puts himself in a dangerous position by researching and/or answering the client's question. An attorney is better off explaining to a client that the attorney may not draw conclusions on the laws of other states even at the risk of seeming unhelpful or ignorant. Giving correct advice about the law of a state in which one is not licensed is unauthorized practice of law. Giving incorrect advice about the law of a state in which one is not licensed is unauthorized practice of law and legal malpractice.

Capital Gains Tax Implications— Step-up In Cost Basis

A major tax issue to be considered with regard to any trust that will hold real estate relates to capital gains tax. Capital gains tax (as discussed in chapter 5) is assessed on the profit a person makes when selling an appreciated asset. In this chapter we will focus specifically on the capital tax implications relevant to real estate held in trusts.

While securities and other appreciating assets are often bought and sold relatively quickly, people tend to hold real estate for long periods of time (especially when the real estate serves as the client's residence or vacation home). Real estate sales therefore tend to generate large capital gains, especially with older clients. Therefore, capital gains tax implications are exceptionally important to real estate trusts.

> *Example:* Doris bought a house in 1966 for $42,000. In 2011, that house is worth $450,000. If the house is sold, it will generate an enormous taxable capital gain. This is a fairly common scenario. By contrast, it is less usual for individual securities or other assets to be held for more four decades and appreciate this significantly.

Long term capital gains (gains on assets held for one year or more[4]) are taxed at a lower rate than ordinary income.[5] Nevertheless, the sale of a property held long term can cost a client an enormous amount in capital gains tax. The good news is that there are two favorable capital gains tax rules that can be used to greatly benefit clients with appreciated real estate:

1) The "step-up" in cost basis rule that takes effect upon the death of the client (discussed previously in chapter 5).[6]
2) A capital gains tax exemption of up to $250,000 per person ($500,000 for a married couple) under Section 121 of the Internal Revenue Code.[7]

The step-up in cost basis is applicable only if the property is sold after the client dies. It is generally wise to ensure that appreciated property is included in your client's taxable estate so that if the client dies before the property is sold, the heirs receive the benefit of the step-up in cost basis. The methods by which to accomplish this are discussed in chapter 5.

Capital Gains Tax Implications— Section 121 Exemption

Perhaps an even more critical aspect of dealing with clients who would like to place their homes in trust is the capital gains tax exemption under Section 121 of the Internal Revenue Code. This rule exempts the first $250,000 of capital gains ($500,000 for a married couple) from being taxed. The key requirements of this rule are:

---

4. 26 U.S.C. § 1222(a).
5. 26 U.S.C. § 1(h).
6. 26 U.S.C. § 1014.
7. 26 U.S.C. § 121.

1) The seller must have resided in the property as his or her "principal residence" for at least two of the previous five years.[8]
2) The seller must be the owner at the time of the sale.

This exemption can save clients over one hundred thousand dollars in federal and state capitals gains tax. It is therefore critical that this be taken into account when thinking through the estate planning options of a client. Because this issue does not directly involve estate taxation or Medicaid eligibility, it can be overlooked if one is not careful.

> *Example: Don and Rhonda purchased a house in 1974 for $35,000. In 2011, that same house is worth $500,000. To become eligible for Medicaid, Don and Rhonda gifted their house to their children in 2005. In 2011, they want to move out of the house. So, the children go out and sell the house for $500,000. Because Don and Rhonda did not own the house at the time of the sale, they are not eligible for the Section 121 exemption. The children will be forced to recognize $465,000 in capital gains. Depending on the applicable federal and state rates, this may cost them more than $100,000 on income tax! In essence, they sacrificed over $100,000 for some Medicaid eligibility benefits that could have been accomplished in a much less destructive manner.*

> *Example: In 2011, Don and Rhonda make an appointment to see R. Quick, Attorney, about their estate plan. Because Mr. Quick has listened to all sorts of seminars and taken classes in estate planning that focus on Medicaid eligibility and estate tax avoidance, he overlooks the Section121 exemption. He directs Don and Rhonda to place the home in an irrevocable "Crummey" trust for the eventual benefit of their children. If the trust later sells the property, the trust may not be eligible for the Section 121 exemption. Mr. Quick's failure to look at the whole picture may have cost his clients $100,000 and subjected him to a hefty malpractice lawsuit.*

This does not mean that houses should not be transferred to Medicaid planning trusts. This can certainly be done safely if done properly. In addition, the same trust can protect the client's house from vulnerability to creditors. The

---

8. 26 U.S.C. §121(a).

An in depth discussion of the residency requirements that make a "principal residence" are beyond the scope of this text. However, these are issues worth studying as they will invariably some up in discussions with clients who have vacation homes or who split their residency through the year.

key is to allow the client to maintain the Section 121 exemption while still removing the house from the client's ownership for Medicaid and credit protection purposes.

The simplest method by which to do this is to ensure that the trust one establishes for the client is a "grantor" trust, for income tax purposes. Under
Section 121, the property must be "owned" by the seller. Since capital gains
tax is a form of income tax, "owned" for purposes of income tax is the same
as "owned" for purposes of capital gains tax.[9] As your client will be the grantor
of the trust that you establish for his or her benefit, a trust is considered "owned"
by your client if it is a grantor trust.

As discussed in chapter 5, there are many methods under Sections 671–679
of the Internal Revenue Code to create a grantor trust. These include allowing
the grantor or his or her spouse the income, giving the grantor or any nonadverse
party power to distribute trust assets, etc.

For purposes of confirming the 121 exemption, it is very important to ensure that the *entire* trust is considered a grantor trust and not just the income.
Otherwise, Section 121 might not apply to the real estate, since it is part of
the trust principal.

> **Example:** *Brenda transfers her residence to a trust. The trust states
> that "During Brenda's lifetime, she shall be entitled to determine who
> among her family members shall receive the trust income." Under Sec
> tion 674, this makes the income taxable to the grantor. However, it is
> not clear that this makes the trust a grantor trust with respect to the
> income only or with respect to the principal as well. As such, it is un
> clear if Brenda will be eligible for the Section 121 exemption if the
> residence is sold during Brenda's lifetime.*

Therefore, the practitioner should draft into the trust a provision that renders the entire trust a grantor trust, not just the income. The easiest way to
ensure this is to use a provision that does not reference the income. For example, the administrative powers under Section 675 provide that the "grantor
shall be treated as the owner of any portion of a trust in respect of which ..."
thus clearly referring to both income and principal.[10]

> **Example:** *Brenda transfers her residence to a trust as in the above
> case. To ensure that the principal trust is a grantor trust for Section*

---

9. Treas. Reg. 1.121-1(c)(3)(i).
10. 28 U.S.C. §675.

121 purposes the trust contains a provision that "the grantor shall have a power, in a nonfiduciary capacity and without the approval or consent of any person in a fiduciary capacity, to reacquire any and all trust corpus by substituting other property of an equivalent value." The entire trust is now treated as owned by the grantor under Section 675(4)(C). Therefore, if the property is sold during Brenda's lifetime, it should be eligible for the Section 121 exemption.

Practice Tip: The power "to reacquire trust corpus by substituting other property of an equivalent value" is a convenient way to make sure a trust is a grantor trust. It is minimally intrusive in that it rarely frustrates other estate planning objectives. If, for whatever reason, this power cannot be used, the practitioner must choose another power listed in Section 674 or 675 to ensure that the trust is a grantor trust. One must be careful, however, not to frustrate other estate planning objectives. For example, giving the grantor power over distribution of trust assets can lead to inclusion in the grantor's taxable estate and/or may have disadvantageous effects regarding creditor protection or Medicaid planning.

Medicaid Issues

The main discussion of the Medicaid eligibility rules relevant to trust drafting and planning are covered in chapter 8. In this chapter, we focus on the Medicaid eligibility rules that are specifically relevant to real property ownership.

Real estate holdings are generally considered "available resources" for purposes of Medicaid eligibility. Thus, if a client owns a parcel of real property, the resource may make him or her ineligible for Medicaid. This is true of any investment property, even that which may not be accessible at the moment.

Example: In 1997, Clara's son, Ryan, wished to purchase a home. As Ryan's credit score prevented him from obtaining a mortgage loan, Clara took out the mortgage for him. Each month, Ryan pays the mortgage as his "rent" while the home remains in Clara's name. Although one may argue that the home is "really" Ryan's and although Clara has no immediate way to access cash from the property, the home will be considered an "available resource" for Clara. Therefore, its existence will likely disqualify Clara from Medicaid eligibility.

The rules are a bit more lax when it comes to owning one's own residence. A person's residence is generally *not* considered an available resource for Medicaid purposes unless the person has more than $500,000 in equity in the home.[11] Some states have increased this threshold to $750,000 as allowed by the relevant federal statute.[12]

> *Example: Meredith and John own and live in a home that is worth $600,000. They owe $150,000 on a mortgage associated with the property. Because their equity in the home is less than $500,000, this home would not be considered an available resource and would not disqualify them from Medicaid eligibility.*

It should be noted, however, that for this exemption to apply, at least one of the following people must be residing in the residence:

- The Medicaid applicant (i.e., the client doing the Medicaid planning);
- The applicant's spouse;
- A minor or disabled child of the applicant; or
- A sibling with an equity interest in the home and who has been living in the home for at least one year prior to the admission of the applicant to a nursing home.[13]

Because of this exemption, if the client or his or her spouse (as is more common than children in the case of elder law clients) lives in a personal residence, one must be very careful before transferring the property to anyone, including an irrevocable trust. As discussed in chapter 8, a gift to a trust creates a five year period of ineligibility for Medicaid for the transferor and his or her spouse. This is true even if the transferred property is a personal residence. If a community spouse is living in the house anyway, it may be counterproductive to transfer it to a trust.

> *Example: Brian and Amanda are each 68 years old and own a home worth $400,000. They have little in terms of other assets. Amanda is in good health, but Brian is suffering from advanced Alzheimer's disease and is rapidly losing his mental faculties. As it stands, if Brian needs a nursing home, the couple will be eligible for Medicaid. Since Amanda (a community spouse) is living in the house, it is not an available resource for Brian. On the other hand, if they transfer the house to their children or to an irrevocable trust, both spouses will be ineligible for*

---

11. 42 USCS § 1396p (f)(1)(A).
12. 42 USCS § 1396p (f)(1)(B).
13. 42 USCS § 1396p (a)(2).

nursing home assistance for five years following the transfer. Transferring the house to a trust would most likely be counterproductive in this case.

Practice Tip: It is impossible to know with certainty whether a transfer, and its attendant five year period of ineligibility, will be in the best interest of the client. It is up to the practitioner to ask the appropriate questions and make an informed recommendation. Additionally, it should always be kept in mind that a transfer can usually be "undone" for Medicaid eligibility purposes. If Medicaid is needed within the five year period, the gift that caused the period of ineligibility can be undone by returning the gift to the client. This will negate the benefits of the transfer; but is an option in an emergency. The option should be kept in mind in the event that circumstances do not play themselves out as anticipated.

If no community spouse (or other eligible relative) lives in the house with the client (or if there is a fear that both spouses may need nursing home care), options to protect the residence are much weaker. In such a case, Medicaid will still almost certainly not deem a primary residence as an available resource (since it is unreasonable to expect a person to sell a primary residence that he or she may eventually want to return to). However, the local Medicaid administrators will put a lien on the residence and recover their paid costs after the death of the client.[14]

Example: Randall is 74 years old and lives alone. He is reasonably healthy and does not anticipate needing Medicaid assistance in the near future. He has four adult children who all live elsewhere. Randall owns his home, which is worth $325,000, and has few other assets. If Randall does not transfer his home and requires a nursing home in the future, the house may be jeopardized. This is because, while Medicaid will likely pay his nursing home bills, they will also put a lien on the house. After Randall's death or when the house is sold, Medicaid will recover from the proceeds the value of the care it provided to Randall. If Randall transfers the home now to a trust for his children, however, he will not be eligible for Medicaid for five years. After the five years, he will be eligible for Medicaid assistance and receipt of such assistance will not jeopardize the house. Therefore, in this case, it would be to Randall's family's advantage for him to gift the house

---

14. 42 USCS § 1396p(a)(1)(B).

to his children or an irrevocable trust for their benefit. If nursing home care is needed, say, two years later, the transfer to the trust can be undone, rendering him eligible to receive nursing home care immediately (subject, however, to Medicaid's lien on the house).

Caregiver Child Rule

An important exception to the transfer ineligibility period discussed in chapter 8 occurs where the transfer of a residence is to a "caregiver child." If the client lives with his or her child who cares for the client, then the transfer of their shared residence to the child at the time that the parent moves to a nursing home does NOT result in a period of ineligibility. Therefore, a parent with a caregiver child living with him or her who is expecting to need nursing home care may want to avoid transferring the property to a trust or to other children and thus avoid the five year period of ineligibility.[15]

> *Example: Mildred is 83 years old and lives with her son Drew. The home, which Mildred owns, is her principal asset. Mildred's health has been deteriorating and she is worried that she may need nursing home care shortly. Transferring the house and trying to wait out the five year period of ineligibility may be unrealistic. Therefore, the best strategy might be to simply hold the house until nursing home care is needed and then transfer the house to Drew.*

Of course, using the caregiver child exemption is not without risks. If the house is transferred to the child, benefits such as the step-up in cost basis, the Section 121 capital gains tax exemption and the property tax benefits of home ownership (discussed below) will be lost. As with so many Medicaid eligibility decisions, the best strategy will depend on a variety of factors that must be carefully weighed based on the individual circumstances.

Maintaining Property Tax Exemptions

Many states give property tax benefits to people who own their residences.[16] These reductions in property taxes can take a variety of forms, including extra tax benefits for seniors.[17] Transferring property directly to children or to a

---

15. 42 U.S.C. §1396p (c)(2)(A)(iv).

16. *See, e.g.,* http://dor.myflorida.com/dor/property/taxpayers/exemptions.html#1.

17. *See, e.g.,* http://www.orps.state.ny.us/star/faq.htm.

poorly drafted trust for Medicaid planning purposes can cause the client to lose these valuable property tax benefits.

> *Example:* Aaron is a 70-year-old widower in good health with four children. He owns a house in which he resides worth $450,000 and few other valuable assets. Aaron receives a 25% discount each year under local law because he is a senior that resides in a residence that he owns. For purposes of Medicaid planning, Aaron gives the house to his children. Among the many potential problems that use of this strategy may cause is the near certainty that the house will lose the property tax discount. Since the house is no longer owned by its occupant and since its owners are no longer seniors, the children will pay full property tax rates.

Property tax exemptions can often be kept, however, when the client keeps a beneficial interest in the property, even if the property is removed from the client's assets for Medicaid planning purposes. Many states will allow the property tax exemptions to be maintained as long as the client retains the right to live in the property.

Practice Tip: Do not assume this to be the case in any particular jurisdiction. Property tax rules are complex and can vary from state to state and enforcement of property tax rules and procedures can even vary from county to county. It is imperative that the practitioner have some familiarity with the local rules and procedures before advising clients on how to maintain a property tax exemption. This is one area where informal conversations with people working in the local tax assessor's office and conversations with people who have previously tried maintaining tax exemptions after transferring property can be as important as researching the applicable statutes (which may be vague on this point) or case law (of which there is often little in regard to this issue).

When a client transfers a residence that benefits from an owner-occupied property tax benefit, it is often a good strategy to reserve an interest for the client that will allow the client to retain the property tax exemption. Retaining all "beneficial interest" for the client in the residence transferred is certainly sufficient to retain the property tax benefits for the client. However, such a broad reservation of rights in a trust may have other adverse estate planning effects.

> *Example:* Dave wants to remove his house from his name for Medicaid planning or creditor protection purposes. However, he is currently

receiving a school tax relief benefit that is allowable only to occupants of their own homes. If he gave the house to his children, he would lose this benefit. The children would have to pay the full property tax since they are not residents of the house. Therefore, Dave should retain the beneficial interest in the residence that is necessary to preserve this benefit.

To do so, Dave can retain a "life estate" in the property, which would retain the property tax benefits of owner occupation. However, the life estate may itself be considered an available resource since it can be sold on the open market to a third party.

Alternatively, if he puts the house in trust, the trust can give Dave the right to all "beneficial interest" in the house. However, the beneficial enjoyment of the house may be considered an available resource for Medicaid eligibility purposes. For example, if the house or a portion is rented out to a third party tenant, Dave will be entitled to this income and the income will thus be vulnerable if Dave requires Medicaid assistance.

Instead of either broad strategy, Dave should retain only the rights necessary to allow the house to be considered owner occupied for property tax purposes. He should relinquish the rights that could cause the house to be considered an available resource and/or make it vulnerable to his creditors. This may be accomplished as discussed below.

One common approach is to stipulate in the trust that the grantor has the right to live in the property for life, but to expressly disavow other rights that are associated with property ownership. For example:

> As long as the Grantor is living, the Grantor shall have the right to reside in the property located at 123 Main Street in Hypoville. However, this shall not include the right to receive income or any other benefit from the trust or any assets belonging to the trust.

As added protection (the necessity of which is doubtful), the trust can specify that the grantor is responsible to pay the real property tax associated with the property. This provision may be worded as follows:

> As long as the Grantor resides in the residential real property at 123 Main Street in Hypoville, the Grantor shall be responsible for property taxes that are assessed on the basis of such property.

Another important consideration in transferring client's residences to trusts is that clients are often insecure when it comes to their housing. Even though

clients may trust their children, it's a little disconcerting to many elderly clients
to give up the control over their housing that they've always enjoyed. Although
there is no way to completely avoid giving up control over a house when making it invulnerable in the event of a Medicaid need, there are ways to reassure
clients. For example, a trust can specify that it will pay for client's housing.
For example, the trust might state:

> As long as the Grantor is living, the Grantor shall have the right to re-
> side in the property located at 123 Main Street in Hypoville. The Grantor
> may also disallow any pending sale of the residence. If the residence
> is sold, then the Trust may use Trust income to provide alternative hous-
> ing for the Grantor. This may be accomplished by paying the Grantor's
> rent at a suitable alternative location or by purchasing other residential
> real property and allowing the Grantor to reside in such property rent-
> free. However, the Trust may not use Trust assets to pay for the Grantor's
> care at a nursing home or other facility that provides enhanced care for
> its residents.[18]

Practice Tip: It is important to reassure clients at every step that the client
will not be adversely impacted by your estate plan. However, it is equally
important not to mislead clients or imply that they will retain more power
or right over the trust assets than they, in fact, will. Promising a client that
he or she will retain full control over a trust over which another person is
trustee is malpractice and borderline fraud.

Qualified Personal Residence Trusts

Recall from chapter 4 that any property over which the grantor retains enjoyment of during his or her lifetime is included in his or her taxable estate.
Therefore, removing a personal residence from one's taxable estate is exceptionally
difficult if the client wishes to continue residing there. If the client gives away
his residence entirely but then continues living there, the IRS will no doubt
take the position that the grantor, in fact if not in name, retained beneficial enjoyment over the residence. In this case the IRS would assert that the property
is includable in the client's estate.

---

18. This last provision is to ensure that Department of Social Services officials do not
view the trust as having the ability to pay for nursing home care and thus being considered
an available resource in the event that the client needs nursing home care.

In many cases, this inclusion of the residence in the client's estate is not a problem. Often, estate taxes are not a factor for the client or can be avoided through other devices. In many cases, in fact, it is advantageous to keep the residence in the grantor's estate for capital gains tax purposes, also as previously discussed.

However, there is one tried and true way to remove residential real property from the taxable estate of the grantor while allowing the grantor to reside in the house. That is the Qualified Personal Residence Trust ("QPRT"). This is a somewhat complex device that involves considerations in income, gift and estate taxes. We will briefly discuss the basic strategy, requirements and features of a standard QPRT.

The basic structure of a QPRT requires that the grantor gift his or her residence to the trust while maintaining the right to live in (and enjoy, in all respects) the rights to the property for a fixed number of years. At the end of that fixed number of years, the trust expires and the residence is distributed outright to the remainder beneficiaries. Through use of a QPRT, the house can be removed from the client's taxable estate at a much reduced cost in lost gift tax exemption while remaining eligible (during the term of the QPRT) for some of the other benefits of property ownership.

> **Example:** *Joann is a single widow who is 70 years old and is in good health. Between her life insurance, stocks, cash, etc., her estate is worth $4,000,000. Her residence, which she owns outright without a mortgage, is worth approximately $600,000. If she were to gift her residence to a QPRT this could remove the house from her taxable estate, thus reducing the estate tax burden upon her death.*

The first issue to be aware of when drafting a QPRT is that certain qualifications are required for the device to be effective. The following are the key requirements:

1) The trust must be established for a limited duration (though this may be contingent on an event occurring, in some cases).

2) All income generated by the trust must be distributed to the grantor during the term of the trust.

3) No person other than the grantor (and his or her spouse and dependents may reside there rent-free) and no person other than the grantor may receive distributions of benefits from the trust.

4) The grantor may not be allowed to re-acquire the residence by purchasing it from the trust. By the same token, the grantor's interest may not be "bought out" earlier than the expiration of the term.[19]

At the time that the house is transferred to the QPRT, the grantor must report the value of the remainder interest as a gift by filing a federal gift tax return for that year. The value of the remainder interest is determined by IRS tables and is based upon the length of the interest of the grantor.[20]

> *Example: Joann gifts her house to a QPRT that allows her to live in and enjoy the house for five years. After that, the house is to be distributed to her children, in equal shares. According to applicable tables (which change from year to year), the value of the remainder interest will be approximately 2/3 the value of the entire house. So, if the house is worth $600,000, the taxable gift will be approximately $400,000. Assuming Joann has not previously used her gift tax lifetime exemption, this amount will be applied against her gift/estate tax lifetime exemption amount. In this way, Joann has effectively gifted a $600,000 asset while incurring only $400,000 in lost gift/estate tax exemption.*
>
> *If the term were to have been set at ten years, the value of the remainder interest would have been closer to 40% of the value of the house. The value of the remainder interest in that case would be closer to $240,000. A $600,000 asset will be gifted with only $240,000 used in gift/estate tax exemption!*

During the term of the trust, the QPRT is inherently a "grantor trust." Therefore, the grantor is taxed on any income generated by the trust. If the house is sold during the trust term, the grantor will still be eligible for the $250,000 capital gains tax exclusion under Section 121. In addition, since the grantor has beneficial interest in the property during the term, the grantor remains eligible for owner occupied property tax benefits during the trust term.

Unfortunately, an important drawback to the QPRT strategy is that if the grantor dies within the trust term, the entire value of the house is included in the grantor's taxable estate.[21] This essentially negates the advantage of the QPRT unless the grantor survives the term.

---

19. *See* 26 U.S.C. § 2702.
20. *See* 26 U.S.C. § 7520.
21. *See* 26 U.S.C. § 2036(a)(1).

Example: Joann gifts her house to a QPRT with a ten year term in 2012 when the house is worth $600,000. She dies in 2021 when the house is worth $900,000. The entire $900,000 is included in her taxable estate.

Therefore, it is important to choose a trust term that the client is likely to survive. The temptation is great to stretch the term as long as possible so as to give the grantor the tax benefits of home ownership and to reduce the value of the remainder interest. However, if the grantor does not survive the term, the estate tax benefits of the QPRT (i.e., the principal reason for its existence) are nullified.

After the Term

Once the QPRT term has expired, the residence (along with any other trust assets) must pass to the beneficiaries (typically the grantor's children). If the grantor wishes to remain in the residence, the client(s) must pay rent at fair market value (which can be another way to reduce the client's estate without using gift tax exemption). However, the grantor will not retain any of the tax benefits of home ownership as the grantor no longer has any beneficial interest in the residence.

Practice Tip: Although a QPRT may have some marginal benefits in terms of Medicaid planning and creditor protection, those goals have more efficient devices. The QPRT should be used strictly for clients for whom estate reduction is a priority. Also, if the house has appreciated significantly, a QPRT may not be a great idea, as there will be no step-up in cost basis if the client dies after the term. So, while a QPRT is a wonderful device to reduce a client's estate, be very careful about the other relevant considerations before recommending one.

Review Questions

1) Which state generally has jurisdiction over a trust and its assets?
2) What is the key jurisdictional difference between a trust that holds real estate and a trust that does not hold real estate?
3) Explain the benefit of a stepped-up cost basis.
4) Give an example of a Medicaid planning device regarding a family home that can lose the benefit of the step-up in cost basis.

5) Explain the capital gains tax benefit applied by Section 121 of the Internal Revenue Code.

6) What is required so that a house held in trust is nevertheless eligible for the Section 121 exemption?

7) Describe one practical way to ensure that a trust is a grantor trust to the extent necessary to ensure the Section 121 exemption.

8) Under what circumstance is a personal residence not considered an available resource to its owner?

9) What is the danger in allowing a client to receive Medicaid assistance while living in his or her owner occupied residence?

10) When and how can the "caregiver child" rule be used to protect a house from Medicaid recovery?

11) Describe one drawback to using the "caregiver child" rule to protect a personal residence.

12) Why can transferring a house to a client's children or to a trust have adverse property tax consequences?

13) Describe one way a trust can maintain a property tax exemption for a house held in the trust while not hurting the client from a Medicaid or creditor protection standpoint.

14) What conditions must be satisfied for a trust to qualify as a qualified personal residence trust?

15) How does a QPRT reduce the amount of gift/estate tax exemption that must be used at the time the house is transferred to a QPRT?

16) What key event must occur well after the QPRT is established in order for the QPRT to maintain its estate tax advantage?

17) If the client resides in the home after the end of the term of the QPRT, why is it important that the client pay fair market value in rent while continuing to reside in the home?

CHAPTER 10

Life Insurance Trusts

Forms of Life Insurance

It is very important that the estate planning legal professional understand the terminology involved in dealing with life insurance policies. Most life insurance policies can be divided into two basic categories: Term policies and whole life policies. Other types of insurance policies, such as variable life and universal life are similar to whole life policies, with slight modifications.[1]

A term policy is generally only good for a defined period of time (e.g., 10 or 20 years). During the term, the owner pays the same monthly premiums (which are generally low, especially for younger and healthier people) and a payout occurs only if the insured dies during the time that the policy is in effect and in good standing. Premiums are based on the age and health of the insured, along with other factors that may be decided upon by the insurance company (such as occupation, mental health history, etc.).

The advantage of this form of insurance is that the premiums are low, thereby allowing the client to purchase insurance with a large death benefit relatively cheaply. This form of life insurance is meant to be "insurance" in the true sense of the word—it is to protect against a catastrophic death, and little more. This is often the popular choice of younger working people who have families to protect and provide for.

The disadvantage of this form of insurance is that after the period of time that the insurance is in effect, it is worthless. In other words, unless the insured dies within the term, 100% of all premiums paid are lost. Term policies are not a form of investment, but rather a form of risk avoidance for the insured's family.

A whole life policy, on the other hand, while requiring the payment of much higher premiums, does not expire (unless the premiums are not paid) and does accumulate "cash value." Whole life policies often have relatively low death benefits and high premiums. When a premium is paid, some of it goes to pay

---

1. *See, e.g.,* http://www.insurancefinder.com/lifeinsurance/typeslifeinsurance2.html.

for the "insurance" component (i.e., to allow the insurance company to pay the death benefit if the insured dies). Some of it (especially early in the policy's term) may be used to pay the broker or other administrative fees. The remainder is saved (with interest) and accumulates as cash value of the policy. Whole life policies usually pay interest at a rate that is in excess of what is available from savings accounts or money market funds.

> *Example:* Jack is 34 years old and in good health. He works as an attorney and earns $85,000 per year. He has a wife, Maria, age 32, who works as a school teacher and earns $25,000 per year. The couple have three children, ages 5, 3 and 1. To protect themselves in the event of a catastrophic death, they decide to look into the possibility of purchasing life insurance. They want to ensure the lives of both spouses, but because of his higher income, they want to insure Jack's life to a greater extent than Maria's life.

> They meet with Bobby Broker to discuss strategy. After crunching the numbers, Bobby figures that the couple should have $1,000,000— $1,500,000 million in coverage on Jack's life and $500,000 to $1,000,000 on Maria's. He presents the following three alternative proposals:

> 1) **The term insurance route.** Because Jack and Maria are non-smokers in good health, hold low risk jobs and are without a history of major physical or mental illness, term insurance will be relatively cheap. Bobby proposes that they purchase $1,500,000 on Jack's life and $1,000,000 on Maria's life. Bobby has found a highly rated insurance company that will issue a 20 year level term (i.e., that guarantees that the premiums will be steady for 20 years). For $960 per year ($80 per month) it carries a $1,500,000 death benefit on Jack's life and for $600 per year ($50 per month) it carries a $1,000,000 death benefit on Maria's life.

> If they choose this route, Jack and Maria will protect their family's financial security against the potential death of either one of them at a cost of $130 per month for the next 20 years.

> If they do choose this route, however, they will need to start from square one in 20 years when Jack is 54 and Maria 52. Although their children will be adults and so there will be less need for protection against the loss of an income, presumably Jack and Maria will still be working and in need of protection against an untimely death.

> 2) **The whole life insurance route.** If Jack and Maria wish to purchase whole life insurance, the premiums will be much higher. If, for

example, they want $1,000,000 on Jack's life and $500,000 on Maria's life, the premiums will be well in excess of $1,000 per month. Because most middle class families are unwilling to pay that kind of money for life insurance, this option is often impractical.

3) The combination route. Finally, Bobby presents an option for a combination. Jack and Maria can purchase $1,000,000 and $500,000 term policies respectively. The total premiums for these two policies will likely be under $100 per month. In addition, they can each purchase a whole life policy with a death benefit of $250,000. The death benefits, however, are not the important thing for this policy. Instead, the insurance is purchased primarily as a savings vehicle. Jack and Maria hope to be protected in the event of death primarily by the term policies. The whole life policies are used as a safe method of saving money at a high interest rate while providing a little additional protection against a sudden death. The premiums on the whole life policies may be in the $500 per month range.

Cash value of whole life policies can be withdrawn by the policy owner as a means of "borrowing" from the policy. If premiums are not paid on a whole life policy, the cash value will be used to pay the premiums. In the case of both types of policies, unpaid premiums will cause the policy to lapse.

Practice Tip: Although a full discussion of life insurance and how the policies operate is beyond the scope of this text, an estate planning practitioner must have a working knowledge of life insurance and life insurance procedures since life insurance if often such a large part of estate planning. Much useful information can be obtained by speaking to life insurance agents. Not only can life insurance agents be an invaluable source of information, but they can also refer their insurance clients to you for estate planning services. Dealing with friendly insurance brokers can be a major source of business for an estate planning law firm.

Parties

There are three parties that are relevant to every insurance policy:

1) **Owner.** The owner of an insurance policy holds legal title to the policy and has complete control over the policy. The owner can change bene-

ficiaries and pay premiums. The owner can also borrow against the policy and/or withdraw cash value where applicable.

2) **Insured.** The insured is the person on whose life the policy is held. The insured's death triggers the payout of the death benefit.

3) **Beneficiary.** The beneficiary (or beneficiaries) is the recipient of the death benefit. The death benefit it paid to the beneficiary after the death of the insured.

The parties need not necessarily be three separate people. In fact, the owner and the insured are typically the same person at the outset of the policy. If the insured is also the beneficiary, then the insured's estate will receive the death benefit. This is also the default rule if there is no named beneficiary. Many life insurance companies, however, require that a beneficiary be named at the outset of the policy.

Insurable Interest

Life insurance policies are not meant to be speculative investments, but protection for the family (or business partner) of the insured. Therefore, state laws require that the purchaser of a life insurance policy have some "insurable interest" in the insured.[2] This means that the initial owner of the policy must have reasonable grounds to expect some benefit or advantage from the continuation of the life of the insured. Otherwise, the insurance policy would merely be a wager that the insured will die, which is against public policy.[3]

The precise definition of "insurable interest" varies from state to state. Obviously, one person has an insurable interest in oneself. Therefore, a person can purchase an insurance policy on his or her own life. The other people who have an insurable interest in an insured fall into one of three categories:

1) Blood Relatives. The definition of this category may vary from state to state. However, this includes, at a minimum, parents, siblings, children, grandchildren, etc. More distant relatives may also be included, depending on the state.

2) Spouses. Spouses clearly have an insurable interest in each other. Domestic partners, in states that recognize these, also have insurable interests in each other. Some courts have ruled that engaged couples have

---

2. *See, e.g.,* Fla. Stat. §627.404.
3. *See* United Sec. Life Ins. & Trust Co. v. Brown, 270 Pa. 270 (Pa. 1921).

insurable interests in each other as well. Unmarried couples living together are less clear.

3) Business Relations. Since the death of a business partner may hurt a business' ability to function, business partners are considered to have insurable interests in each others' lives. Even if not a partner, a company
stakeholder is also considered to have an insurable interest in the lives of
key personnel, such as the managing officers and directors of the company.[4]

Please note that the owner of a policy can generally sell the policy to someone without an insurable interest. The owner does not necessarily have to have
an insurable interest at the time of the death of the insured.

No insurable interest requirement exists with respect to the policy beneficiaries. Once a person with an insurable interest owns the policy, he or she
can designate anyone as a trust beneficiary.

Income Taxation

Life insurance death benefits are not subject to income taxation, as long as
the recipient of the proceeds has an insurable interest in the insured.[5] This
tremendous tax advantage of the life insurance policy is based on the idea that
the death benefits merely compensate the beneficiaries for services or income
that would otherwise have been provided by the decedent. If, however, the beneficiary is merely an investor with no relationship to the insured, then any profit
made on the policy (over and above the initial investment) is taxable income.[6]

> **Example:** Paul purchases a $1,000,000 term life insurance policy on
> the life of his mother, Sandy. Paul names himself and his children as
> the beneficiaries. When Sandy dies, Paul and his children will receive
> the death benefit free of income tax since they have an insurable in-
> terest in Sandy, as her children and grandchildren.

> **Example:** Paul purchases a $1,000,000 term life insurance policy on
> the life of his mother, Sandy. After Sandy is diagnosed with kidney
> problems, Kelli, a stranger, offers Paul $400,000 for the policy. Paul
> agrees. After Kelli pays an additional $100,000 in premiums over the

---

4. *See* Stillwagoner v. Travelers Ins. Co., 979 S.W.2d 354 (Tex. App. 1998).

5. 26 U.S.C. § 101(a)(1).

6. 26 U.S.C. § 101(a)(2).

course of a few years, Sandy dies. Kelli must pay income tax on her $500,000 profit. Since she has no insurable interest in Sandy, she does not get the benefit of the life insurance death benefits exemption. Since she invested $500,000 in the policy and earned a $1,000,000 death benefit, the $500,000 difference is treated as ordinary income.

The Life Insurance Trust — Structure

A life insurance trust is an irrevocable trust (in fact, it is often referred to as an "irrevocable life insurance trust" or "ILIT") that is designed to hold one or more life insurance policies. An insurance policy can be purchased in the name of the trust or it can be transferred to the trust after it is purchased — even after it has existed for many years. In most cases, the trust is named as both the owner and the beneficiary of the trust.

In many respects, the ILIT is structured in the same manner as is any other irrevocable trust. The grantor does not retain any authority to direct the disposition of the trust assets. Yet the grantor's spouse and the grantor's children may be potential beneficiaries of the trust. The extent to which they can be beneficiaries of the trust and the extent of the trustee's discretion in distributing trust assets is governed by other concerns discussed in this text.

After the trust is established, the grantor typically uses forms provided by the life insurance company to transfer the policy ownership to the trust. Just as importantly, the beneficiary of the policy should be changed as well to reflect that the trust is the beneficiary of the policy. The insured remains the same, typically the grantor. Alternatively, if the trust is being established at the time that the policy is purchased, the initial policy paperwork can list the trust as the owner and the beneficiary.

Practice Tip: A life insurance trust is generally useless unless the relevant policies are transferred to the policy AND the trust is named as the policy's beneficiary. As a legal professional, it is your responsibility to help the client ensure that this occurs. Clients often assume that once they've signed the trust documents (and paid your fee), they're done and that you will take care of everything else. That doesn't mean that the client is generally incapable of handling the paperwork necessary to make the trust the owner and beneficiary of the policy. It does, however, mean that the firm should inform the client of this necessary step and follow up to make sure it is done. A firm is justified in charging extra for its time if the firm is asked to take care of this.

The ILIT as a Device in Estate Tax Planning

Irrevocable life insurance trusts have historically been used primarily as an estate tax planning device. The trust serves in this capacity by being a vehicle to hold the policy in a manner that it outside the taxable estate of the grantor. In fact, when properly done, the policy should be outside of everyone's taxable estate. ILITs often state this intent from the outset. The following is a sample opening article of an ILIT.

A. The Grantor creates this trust as a means by which assets, which may include one (1) or more policies of insurance on his life, may be held for the benefit of his family, on the terms and conditions set forth in this instrument. It is the Grantor's intent in creating this trust that all gifts made to this trust be complete and gifts of present interests for federal gift tax purposes, and that the assets of this trust, including any life insurance proceeds, be excluded from his gross estate for federal estate tax purposes. All provisions of this trust shall be construed in such a manner as best to effect these intents.

B. The Grantor transfers to the Trustee the property listed in Schedule A, to be held and administered according to the terms of this trust. The Grantor and anyone else may transfer additional property, whether or not such property is listed on Schedule A, to the Trustee at any time, whether during the Grantor's lifetime or after his death, to be held and administered according to the trust's terms. The Trustee may refuse to accept any gift to a trust hereunder if the Trustee deems it to be in the best interests of the trust and its beneficiaries, and the Trustee may accept it subject to one (1) or more conditions imposed by the donor on the Trustee, if the Trustee deems it to be in the best interests of the trust and the beneficiaries. No condition imposed on a gift and accepted by the Trustee may in any way alter, amend, or change the rights of a beneficiary with respect to any prior gifts. The Grantor retains no right, title, or interest in any trust property.

Placing the policy into an insurance trust is important because the general principle is that proceeds of a life insurance death benefit are included in the taxable estate of the decedent. This is true whether the death benefits are payable to the estate of the insured[7] or anyone else, as long as the insured exercised any "incidents of ownership" over the policy.[8] Furthermore, under I.R.C. §2035,

---

7. 26 U.S.C. §2042(a).
8. 26 U.S.C. §2042(b).

the proceeds of a policy can be included in the insured's estate if, at any point within three years of death, the insured exercised any "incidents of ownership" over the policy.[9]

To ensure that the death benefits are *not* part of the taxable estate of the insured, the trust must be drafted so that the insured has no "incidents of ownership" over the policy within. In addition, if the grantor is transferring the policy to the trust from his or her own name, the grantor must survive at least three years from the date of the transfer. If the policy is purchased initially in the name of the trust, surviving three years is unnecessary since the insured never actually owned the policy.

Although "incidents of ownership" is not defined by the Code, understanding the term is critical to drafting a proper life insurance trust. The grantor should not have *any* power or authority over the trust assets that could constitute an incident of ownership. Although it is difficult to present an exhaustive list of powers that could be considered incidents of ownership, the following powers have been held to constitute such and thus should NOT be afforded to the grantor of an irrevocable life insurance trust:

- The power to assign the policy;[10]
- The power to borrow money, using the policy as collateral (or to otherwise pledge the policy);[11]
- The power to change beneficiaries of the policy;[12] or
- The power to modify or revoke the trust.[13]

If the grantor is the insured (as is common), one must be careful not to give the insured powers that would cause the trust assets to be considered part of his taxable estate. That is, the grantor must not be afforded powers that are tantamount to retaining a life interest[14] or that cause the trust to be considered revocable.[15] These rules are discussed in more detail in chapter 4.

The rules are much less stringent for the beneficiaries of the trust, even if the spouse of the insured is a beneficiary. A trust may allow the spouse or any other beneficiary benefits from the trust (including the right to receive all of

---

9. 26 U.S.C. §2035(a).
10. Commissioner v. Estate of Noel, 380 U.S. 678 (1965).
11. Nelson v. Commissioner, 101 F2d 568 (8th Cir. 1939).
12. Cook v. Commissioner, 66 F2d 995 (3rd Cir. 1933).
13. Commissioner v. Estate of Karagheusian, 233 F2d 197 (2d Cir. 1956).
14. *See* 26 U.S.C. §2036.
15. *See* 26 U.S.C. §2038.

the trust income) and may allow him or her to control the trust without it being considered part of the insured's taxable estate. It will not be considered part of the spouse's taxable estate either unless his or her power is so broad that it is considered a general power of appointment.[16]

> *Example:* *Stanley and Meredith are married and each wish to purchase term life insurance policies with $2,000,000 death benefits. They want to establish life insurance trusts to ensure that the death benefits are not subject to estate taxation. They each want the maximum control possible over the trusts.*
>
> *Therefore, they establish two irrevocable life insurance trusts. The first trust is called* The Stanley ILIT *and the second one is called* The Meredith ILIT. *Stanley is the trustee of Meridith's ILIT and Meredith is the trustee of Stanley's ILIT. As trustees, each has the authority to spend trust assets for the "health, education, maintenance and support" of the couple's children. In addition, each is entitled to all income generated by the other trust. The trust also provides that the spouse/trustee can use trust assets for his or her own benefit, but only with the consent of a co-trustee or successor trustee named by the trust.*
>
> *In this way, each spouse can derive substantial benefit from the other spouse's trust, including the proceeds of the death benefit from the insurance policy of the first spouse to die. However, the trust assets will not be part of the taxable estate of either spouse.*
>
> *A typical provision that allows the spouse of the insured to enjoy the trust assets may be as follows:*
>
> *The trustee shall hold and administer all trust assets. During the lifetime of the grantor, the trustee may use some or all of the trust's income and principal, as necessary, to pay premiums on policies of life insurance on the life of the grantor, adding to principal any income not so used. In addition, subject to the restrictions set forth in later provisions of this trust, the trustee may distribute to the grantor's husband and/or the grantor's children, or may spend on their behalf, so much of the trust principal and income (including all or none) as the trustee deems appropriate for their health, education, maintenance and support. However, the trustee may not use any trust income or principal in a manner that would give the grantor any pecuniary ben-*

---

16. *See* 26 U.S.C. § 2041(b)(1).

efit, or pay for any debt or obligation for which the grantor would otherwise be liable. In addition, the consent of the successor trustee or any serving trustee other than the husband of the grantor, shall be necessary for the trustee to use trust assets for the benefit of the grantor's husband.

After the death of the grantor, the trustee shall continue to hold and administer all trust assets, including the proceeds of any life insurance policies paid as a result of the death of the grantor. During the lifetime of the grantor's husband, the trustee shall pay to him (or apply for his benefit) all of the net income of the trust, in quarterly or more frequent installments. In addition, the grantor's husband may withdraw no more than 5% of the trust's principal each year, at his discretion.[17] The trustee may also pay additional principal for the benefit of the grantor's husband or children to the extent that the trustee deems necessary for their health, education, maintenance and support. However, the consent of the successor trustee or any serving trustee other than the husband of the grantor, shall be necessary for the trustee to use trust assets for the benefit of the grantor's husband.

Upon the death of the second to die of the grantor and the grantor's husband, the trustee shall distribute the trust assets ... [insert final distribution plan in accordance with the clients' wishes].

Gift Tax Issues in Paying Premiums

Once a life insurance policy is owned by a life insurance trust, premiums paid by the grantor are classified as gifts to the trust. Since a gift to a trust is not generally a gift of a "present interest," it is not inherently eligible for the gift tax annual exclusion.[18] Therefore, any gift to the trust would count against the lifetime gift tax exclusion of the grantor.

To avoid having to use the grantor's lifetime gift tax exemption, the ILIT may grant "Crummey" withdrawal powers (discussed earlier, in chapter 3).

---

17. If the withdrawal power were larger than this, then when it lapses each year (i.e., when it's not exercised), it would be considered a taxable gift back to the trust. The IRC allows a lapsed withdrawal to not be considered a gift as long as it is less than the greater of $5,000 or 5% of the trust assets. *See* 26 U.S.C. § 2514(e).

18. *See* 26 U.S.C. § 2503(b)(1).

That is, every beneficiary of the trust (usually, the grantor's children) should have the right to withdraw his or her proportionate share of each contribution. This should prevent any adverse gift tax consequences, as long as the amount of the yearly contributions do not exceed the amount of the annual gift tax exemption ($13,000, as of 2011) times the number of trust beneficiaries. A married grantor can "gift split" with his or her spouse, thus doubling the annual exclusion amount, by checking the "gift splitting" box on the federal Form 709 (gift tax return).[19]

Withdrawal powers should be given to all current beneficiaries of the insurance trust. If the life insurance policy names future beneficiaries as well, they can also be given withdrawal rights.[20]

To ensure that the withdrawal powers are effective, it is best for the client to gift the cash to the trust assets and for the trust to use the gifted cash to pay the premiums for the insurance policies it holds. If the client pays the premiums directly, it is hard to argue that the withdrawal power was anything more than an empty formality.

Practice Tip: Because gifts to a life insurance trust will generally be used to pay the premiums, it is important that the holders of the withdrawal rights not actually exercise these rights. If they do so, there may not be assets available to pay the premiums, which may cause the policy to lapse. If the client does not trust a particular beneficiary to abstain from exercising his withdrawal right, the grantor should consider not giving that beneficiary a withdrawal power. It is possible to "cherry pick" which trust beneficiaries receive the withdrawal power. However, this must be decided at the outset, as the grantor cannot retain the power to change trust beneficiaries and still have the policy's death benefits be considered outside of his taxable estate.[21]

Creditor Protection

Life insurance policies benefit from favorable creditor protection rules, regardless of whether they are held in trust or by the client himself. Many states

---

19. 26 U.S.C. §2513.

20. See chapter 3 for a discussion of whom should be afforded withdrawal powers. *See also*, http://findarticles.com/p/articles/mi_hb6367/is_n7_71/ai_n28687905.

21. 26 U.S.C. §2038.

exempt the death benefits from creditors of the insured,[22] although some states do this only if the beneficiary is a close relative of the insured[23] and/or impose other policy driven conditions on the exemption of the proceeds.[24] The cash value in whole life policies is also protected under the laws of many states and under federal bankruptcy law, although only to a limited extent. Federal law protects up to $11,525 in cash value from creditors in a bankruptcy proceeding, subject to a variety of conditions.[25] Some states provide alternate or additional protections for the cash value of life insurance policies.[26]

Because of these protections, trusts are not as important a creditor protection device in the case of life insurance policies as they are in the cases of other assets. Still, ILITs can be effective creditor protection devices in that:

1) Placing the policy in an ILIT can protect the entire cash value of the policy, as opposed to the limits discussed above.
2) Placing the policy in an ILIT can protect the trust assets (including the death benefits) from the creditors of the beneficiaries, while the above referenced rules protect the assets only from the creditors of the owner/insured.

This can be accomplished much in the same manner as with any trust, as discussed in chapter 6. It is important, however, that the ILIT not allow the grantor access to the cash value. Otherwise, even if is not in the taxable estate of the grantor, it will likely be vulnerable to the grantor's creditors.

Benefits Protection

While the principal concern of clients with large estates may be ensuring that the life insurance death benefits are not part of their taxable estates, an equally important goal for poorer clients may be to remove the assets from their names for purposes of benefits eligibility. This is especially true for elderly clients who may be worried about Medicaid planning. Preserving the eligibility of the beneficiaries for government assistance may also be of importance to the clients. In that vein, the strategies discussed in chapter 8 are generally equally available to life insurance trusts.

---

22. *See, e.g.*, Fla Stat. Ann. §222.13.
23. *See, e.g.*, Hawaii Rev. Stat. §431:10-232(a).
24. *See, e.g.*, NY CLS Ins §3212.
25. 11 U.S.C. §522(d)(8).
26. *See, e.g.*, S.C. Code Ann. §15-41-30(8), Wis. Stat. Ann. §815.18(f).

However, there is an important factor that clients who are paying life insurance premiums must consider if they are also engaged in Medicaid planning. Clients engaged in Medicaid planning typically try to "impoverish" themselves to the point of having little or no spare income above living expenses. Maintenance of life insurance may require the payment of expensive premiums. Therefore, the client should arrange to have another source (such as the client's children or a different Medicaid trust) pay the premiums.

> *Example: Sarah is 69 years old. She has a whole life insurance policy that requires payment of $700 per month in premiums. Until now, she has lived off of her social security and pension checks and used her $400,000 in cash assets to generate enough income to pay her life insurance premiums. Now, for Medicaid planning purposes, she would like to transfer the $400,000 in cash assets to a Medicaid planning trust and her policy to a life insurance trust. If she keeps an income interest in the Medicaid planning trust, the income it earns will be considered an available resource to her if she needs Medicaid assistance. Instead, the Medicaid planning trust should provide that its income (and principal, for that matter) can be used to pay the premiums for a life insurance policy on the grantor's life. The life insurance policy may be placed in a separate life insurance trust or in the same trust.[27] As long as the grantor has no beneficial interest in either asset, this should not be a problem from an estate tax or Medicaid planning standpoint.*

Grantor Trust Status

Under the Internal Revenue Code, any trust is considered a "grantor trust" if, without the consent of an adverse party, any trust income may be "applied to the payment of premiums on policies of insurance on the life of the grantor or the grantor's spouse."[28] Therefore, most life insurance trusts are inherently grantor trusts. This means that any income earned by the trust will be considered income of the grantor. For income tax purposes, the trust is disregarded.

---

27. Whether they should be kept in the same trust or in different trusts depends on whether separate goals or legal considerations apply to the cash assets as opposed to the insurance policy.

28. 26 U.S.C. §677(a)(3).

In most cases, this is not a problem. In fact, it is often an advantage. Holding a life insurance policy has the advantage that any dividends/cash value withdrawn up to the total amount of the premiums paid will not be considered income.[29] Cash value of a policy held in grantor trust will receive the same benefits, even if the policy is not part of the grantor's assets or estate for any other purpose.

> *Example: Rick purchased a life insurance policy in 2000. Each year, he paid $3,000 in premiums. In 2012, Rick withdraws $30,000 from the cash value of the trust. This is not subject to income taxation, as the amount withdrawn is still less than the amount contributed as premiums.*

> *Assume that Rick had, in 2011, transferred the policy to an ILIT. In 2012, the trustee withdraws $30,000 for the benefit of Rick's children. Assuming that the ILIT is a grantor trust (as is usually the case), for income tax purposes, it is as though Rick had personally withdrawn the $30,000. Therefore, it is thus free of income tax.*

There are cases, however, where it will make sense to have the ILIT work as a non-grantor trust. This is often the case when:

1) The grantor has already withdrawn more than the amount of the total premiums paid; and
2) The grantor is taxed at a high rate because of high income.

> *Example: Deborah is 55 years old and earns $400,000 per year as a partner at a big Washington law firm. She owns a high priced whole life policy that costs $20,000 each year in premiums. She uses this policy primarily as an investment. The policy earns a high dividend while simultaneously serving as protection for her family. Deborah routinely withdraws cash value to pay for day-to-day expenses. In all, she has withdrawn more than the total amounts of all premiums she has paid. There is currently over $100,000 in cash value. Any further monies withdrawn from the policy will be subject to income taxation. Because Deborah is in the top federal income tax bracket she will pay top level federal income tax if anything is withdrawn if this trust is a grantor trust. On the other hand, if the trust is a non-grantor trust, the trust will pay its own income tax. Although trusts pay relatively high fed-*

---

29. 26 U.S.C. §72(e)(5)(A).

eral income tax rates, the total income tax will still be lower than it would be if it were considered Deborah's income.

If one wishes to create an ILIT as a non-grantor trust, one must get around Section 677(a)(3) (discussed above). One may do so by requiring the consent of an "adverse party" before the trust may pay life insurance premiums on the life of the grantor (or his spouse). As discussed in chapter 5, any trust beneficiary is typically an "adverse party" under Section 672(a). For example, in a trust where the trust beneficiaries are the grantor's children, the trust might provide:

> During the life of the grantor, the trustee may use trust assets to pay for life insurance policies held by the trust; provided, however, that the consent of at least one child of the grantor or another party who is considered an "adverse party" under Section 672(a) of the Internal Revenue Code shall be required before the trustee may make any such expenditure.

Other provisions of the trust, of course, also must comply with the "grantor trust" rules of Sections 671–679 (discussed in chapter 5) in order to avoid being considered a grantor trust.

ILIT Holding Whole Life Policies vs. Term Policies

As discussed, holding a life insurance policy in an ILIT has many advantages for estate tax planning, Medicaid planning, creditor protection, etc. The main disadvantage of an ILIT is flexibility. The grantor may not be the beneficiary of an ILIT and preserve most of the above discussed benefits.

Because of these factors, the type of insurance must be considered when deciding whether to recommend a life insurance trust. As a reminder, whole life policies tend to have relatively small death benefits (since the premiums are so high) but convenience and versatility may be at a premium, as the client may view the cash value as an investment that should be accessible in the event of a need. Term policies, on the other hand, tend to have high death benefits (because premiums are low and because they are relied on to protect family members in the event of the death of the insured and the loss of income and services that may be caused by such death). Flexibility during the life of the insured is almost irrelevant when it comes to term policies because the policies have no cash value that would need to be accessible.

For a client with an estate large enough to be subject to estate tax, placing a term policy with a large death benefit is usually a good strategy. If the client has a smaller estate or if the policy is a whole life policy, the inconvenience and decrease in flexibility that the trust may cause might outweigh the benefits of the ILIT.

In either case, it is important to discuss this balance between the benefits and loss of flexibility inherent in the ILIT strategy with the client prior to making a recommendation.

> *Example: Gerald and Michelle are married. They are each 49 years old and have a combined $5,000,000 in gross assets. Each spouse is purchasing a $2,000,000 term life insurance policy on his/her life. Because of the extent of their assets, it makes sense to have the death benefits outside of their estates. Furthermore, since the policies are term policies, as long as the insured is living, flexibility is not necessary. Even after one spouse's death, given the size of their estate, it is unlikely that one spouse will have desperate need for the assets in the other spouse's trust. There is no compelling reason to allow the surviving spouse unfettered access to the principal of the deceased spouse's trust. This is a classic case where an ILIT would be advisable.*

> *Example: John and Joanna are 34 and 32 years old respectively. They each purchase whole life insurance policies with $250,000 in death benefits. The monthly premiums for the policies total about $750. The two intend to use these policies primarily as a method of forcing themselves to save for their future. Other assets they own (including their residence) total about $500,000. In this case, placing the policies into an ILIT is probably not the best strategy. Their estates are not likely to be subject to estate tax in any case. The decease in flexibility in handling the policies' cash values that the ILIT will cause is likely not compensated for by any marginal estate tax or creditor protection benefits the trust may provide.*

Ethical Issues — Referrals from Brokers

Working with life insurance brokers is an important component of the job for many estate planning legal professionals. When properly structured, both parties can benefit substantially from this relationship. Estate planning attorneys can refer clients to insurance brokers when they have clients who are uninsured or under insured. Insurance brokers can refer clients to estate planning attorneys for advice as to how to best incorporate life insurance policies into their estate plan or to prepare a life insurance trust. Since life insurance and legal estate planning services are often essential components of a comprehensive estate plan, working together to service clients can create a truly symbiotic relationship between brokers and estate planning attorneys.

There are, however, some important ethical concerns that must be taken into account when estate planning attorneys deal with insurance brokers.

Confidentiality

That a life insurance broker refers a client to you does not inherently mean that you may disclose the client's confidences to the broker. On the contrary, unless the client specifically waives confidentiality, a legal professional may not discuss confidential information with anyone outside the law firm.[30] So, while insurance brokers who refer clients to you for the preparation of insurance trusts, wills, etc., may be interested in following the client's progress, it is critical that you obtain the client's permission before you discuss the client's information and/or plans with the insurance broker.

The best way to do this is through a formal waiver. However, a less formal communication, such as a letter or email that can be documented as having been signed or sent by the client, should generally suffice. The communication should make clear that only you, and not the life insurance agent represent the client in a legal capacity and that your responsibility is to the client and not the agent. Even after the client does consent to your discussing his estate plan with the life insurance agent, you should limit your discussions of the client's confidential information to only that information that is necessary and appropriate to help the agent assist the client with maximum effectiveness.

Referral Fees

Legal ethics rules stipulate that attorneys may not pay referral fees, especially to non-lawyers.[31] In a world where the legal services market is becoming more and more competitive, the temptation is great for attorneys to offer insurance agents referral fees for directing clients toward one's own practice. This is an unethical practice and must be avoided. Sharing the legal fee with an insurance agent is likewise unethical, even if the client knows about and con-

---

30. *See* Model Rules of Professional Conduct Rule 1.6.
31. *See* Model Rules of Professional Conduct Rule 7.2(b).

sents to the arrangement.[32] While attorneys can certainly refer clients to agents who refer business to the attorneys, there should be no money changing hands in the course of the referrals.

Reciprocal Advice Arrangements

Another issue to watch out for as estate planning legal professionals is that life insurance agents may request (or expect) that, in exchange for referring you a client, you help sell the client a product that the agent is trying to sell.

> *Example: Life insurance agent Steve calls Attorney Jane and says, "Listen, Jane, I just finished a meeting with Mr. and Mrs. Smith. They have a pretty serious estate and definitely need some life insurance. I'm trying to sell them a whole life policy, but they seem to be most interested on only term policies. I'd really like to sell them a whole life policy. First, these guys need to have insurance in place at their deaths to help pay the estate tax. Term policies will likely expire while they're alive. Second, of course, I stand to make a lot more money selling them high premium whole life policies. Now Jane, I really want to recommend that the Smiths come to you for an ILIT and an estate plan, but I also really need some help in selling them a whole life policy. Can I count on you to steer them in the right direction if I refer them to you?"*

This situation is more of a gray area than the referral fee and fee splitting rules discussed above. Nevertheless, a legal professional must be cognizant of the attorney's duty of loyalty to the client, which requires a legal professional to give "straightforward advice expressing the lawyer's honest assessment" of the situation.[33] An attorney may certainly not try to convince a client to purchase a product that the attorney does not believe to be in the best interest of the client simply to get a referral or to keep the insurance agent happy. The attorney must make a good faith independent analysis and recommend only the product that he or she believes to be in the best interest of the client. Of course, if the attorney does, in good faith, believe the product to be in the best interest of the client, the attorney can help "sell" the product to the client. However,

---

32. *See* Model Rules of Professional Conduct Rule 5.4.
33. Model Rules of Professional Conduct Rule 2.1, comment 1.

the attorney should not seek or accept any financial incentive from the agent to sell an insurance policy to the client.[34]

Review Questions

1) Describe two differences between a term life insurance policy and a whole life policy.

2) Which type of policy typically is advisable for younger clients with families to protect? Why?

3) What are the three parties involved in every life insurance contract (other than the life insurance company)? What are their roles?

4) What is an "insurable interest" and why is it important to life insurance contracts?

5) What is the reason behind the rule requiring that the purchaser of a life insurance policy have an insurable interest with the insured?

6) When are life insurance death benefits exempt from income taxation?

7) When and to what extent are life insurance death benefits subject to income taxation?

8) How can a life insurance trust aid in estate tax planning?

9) What types of powers should a grantor *not* have over a life insurance trust that is established for estate tax purposes?

10) What is the "three year" rule with respect to life insurance policies?

11) Why are payments of life insurance premiums for policies held by ILITs *not* generally eligible for the gift tax annual exclusion?

12) What can be done to avoid the problem raised by question 11?

13) Why are creditor protection issues not as relevant to a life insurance trust as they are to many other types of trusts?

14) Notwithstanding your answer to question 13, why is an ILIT nevertheless often a useful creditor protection device?

15) Why is a life insurance trust typically a grantor trust?

16) When would you want an ILIT to be a non-grantor trust?

17) What can one do to ensure that an ILIT is not a grantor trust?

---

34. *See* Model Rules of Professional Conduct Rule 1.8(f); *see also* comment 11 to Rule 1.8.

18) Why does it often make more sense to hold a term policy in an ILIT as opposed to holding a whole life policy in an ILIT?

19) Describe an ethical concern to be kept in mind when discussing a mutual client with a life insurance agent.

20) Discuss two important financial ethical concerns when dealing with a life insurance agent and a mutual client.

CHAPTER 11

COMMON TRUST TERMS

Naming Trustees and Successor Trustees

A trust instrument must designate at least the initial trustee of the trust. The trustee is the person who will hold legal title over the trust assets. The trustee will have the authority to manage and (in most cases) distribute trust assets. The trustee will be able to sign on behalf of the trust and his or her consent will be necessary for virtually anything to be done with the trust assets.

Obviously, it is important for clients to appoint trustees that have the client's confidence and trust. As discussed in other chapters, some trust purposes will allow the client to name his or her spouse as trustee, while other strategies require that a third party be named as trustee. For the latter, a common strategy is to name the clients' children or other relatives as trustee.

A child can usually be named as trustee even if the child is also a beneficiary. However, to ensure that "checks and balances" are established to protect the other children (and the trustee-child from allegations of unfairness), it is often a good idea to name multiple children as co-trustees or to name an outside party as co-trustee with the child.

The trust should also name one or more successor trustee(s), who will take over should the trustee be unable to continue serving as trustee. Otherwise, the beneficiaries may have to undergo the complex, time consuming and expensive process of having a court name a trustee. A trustee designation provision with successor trustees named might look something like this:

> The Grantor's children, Adam Smith and Bertha Smith, shall serve as co-trustees of this trust and of any trust created hereunder. If, at any time and for any reason, either of them is unwilling or unable to serve or continue to serve as co-trustee, then the other shall serve as sole trustee. If, at any time and for any reason, neither of them is willing and able to serve or to continue to serve as trustee, then the Grantor's sister, Michelle Smith, shall serve as successor trustee, and she shall serve without bond. If, at any time and for any reason, she is unwilling or un-

able to serve or continue to serve as co-trustee, then the adult trust beneficiaries shall, by majority vote, elect a successor trustee (who may or
may not be one of them).

If two trustees are named, the default rule will be that both trustees will
have to act together on behalf of the trust. If there are more than two trustees,
a majority should be able to act on behalf of a trust.[1] As with most default
rules, these can be changed by the trust instrument.

It is also possible that some banks or title companies dealing with the trust
will want to see *all* the trustees sign before they are satisfied that the trustees
have the authority to act on behalf of the trust.

Practice Tip: Clients tend to want to treat all of their children equally. Therefore, the natural tendency is for clients to ask that all of their children be
named as trustee of their trusts. For clients with several children, this can
prove quite unwieldy. Although technically possible, naming many trustees
will cause bureaucratic headaches in trying to administer the trust assets.
Clients should be made aware that having one or two trustees will simplify
administration of the trust.

Another option is to name a professional trustee, such as a bank or trust
company. The specific company can be named or a provision can direct the beneficiaries (or some other party) to hire a professional trustee.

The advantage of hiring a professional trust company is that you are virtually guaranteed responsible and conservative management of the trust resources.
The trust assets will not be risked or wasted by impetuous family members.
In addition, no family member will be burdened with the responsibility of
controlling other relatives' lives with the attendant pressure to make distributions from other family members.

There are, however, three important disadvantages to hiring a professional
trust company. The first is their fees. Trust company fees are typically based on
the value of the trust account, on a sliding scale.[2] The fee is likely to be at least
one percent of the trust's value per year, especially for a trust without a lot of
money in it. Since the trust company may, in some years, do little more than
hold the assets in an account, this can seem like a waste.

---

1. *See* Uniform Trust Code Section 703 (http://www.law.upenn.edu/bll/archives/ulc/uta/
2005final.htm).

2. *See, e.g.,* http://www.covenanttrust.com/about/feeschedulerlt.aspx.

Second, the trust company may be more hesitant to make distributions than a family member. They may require that beneficiaries in need of a distribution go through time consuming and inconvenient procedures before obtaining a distribution. Professional trustees are naturally worried about liability and may err on the side of withholding distributions when in doubt. They are unlikely to be swayed by emotional appeals of beneficiaries and are likely to interpret the trust's terms strictly and not in favor of the beneficiaries. Of course, this can also be an advantage, depending on the desires of the client.

Third, professional trustees are not likely to be flexible to allow significant changes in the client's estate plan. As discussed in the chapters that dealt with Medicaid planning, it is sometimes advisable to undo an estate plan and start from scratch. Although this may not technically be allowed by irrevocable trust terms, it can often be done nonetheless as long as the key parties agree. Professional trustees are less likely to be cooperative in this regard.

> *Example:* Meredith establishes an irrevocable Medicaid trust for the benefit of her children. She funds it with $300,000 and appoints First Bank & Trust Co. as the trustee. One year later, Meredith is required to enter a nursing home. Because of the five year period of ineligibility, Meredith will not be eligible for Medicaid for four more years. If the trust returns the money to Meredith, some of the $300,000 could be saved by some more complex Medicaid eligibility legal strategies. However, a professional trustee is less likely to be amenable to the undoing of an irrevocable trust (contrary to its terms) than would a family member.

If a trustee is also a potential trust beneficiary, it is also important that the trustee not be given powers that are considered a "general power of appointment." If the trustee/beneficiary is given too much power over the trust assets, it may be considered his or hers for purposes of taxation (income and estate[3]), benefits eligibility and the trust assets may be vulnerable to his or her creditors.

The simplest manner in which to avoid giving the trustee/beneficiary a general power of appointment is to require the consent of another person before distributions are made from the trust.[4] This person can be a co-trustee or a "trust protector" (discussed below). If the trustee requires the consent of such

---

3. 26 U.S.C. §2041.
4. 26 U.S.C. §2041(b)(1)(C).

a third party before making a distribution, he or she does not have the control necessary to be considered a general power of appointment.

The trustee can, however, safely have the discretion to distribute assets to every other trust beneficiary. This is true even if there are no limits on such discretion. As long as the ability to distribute trust assets to his or her *self* is limited (and not subject to his or her discretion alone), there is no general power of appointment.[5]

A trust provision that avoids a general power of appointment in this regard may read as follows:

> During the lifetime of the grantor, the trustee may distribute assets from the trust principal or income to the extent that she deems necessary and appropriate, in her sole discretion, to any of the trust beneficiaries; provided, however, that the trustee may not make any distribution of principal or income from this trust to herself or that would displace any legal obligation or satisfy any of her creditors without the consent of at least one other adult trust beneficiary.

Another way to avoid giving a trustee a general power of appointment for estate tax purposes is to limit the discretion of the trustee to make distributions by an "ascertainable standard." The Code explicitly states that a power of appointment subject to a limitation that it can only be exercised for the purposes of "health, education, support, or maintenance" of a beneficiary (even though the trustee may also be a beneficiary) is not a general power of appointment.[6]

In fact, the statutory language is not meant to be a limitation. The discretion of the trustee can be broader than that and still be considered an "ascertainable standard." For example, trusts allowing distributions for the "comfortable support, medical care or other purposes which seem wise to my trustees"[7] and allowing distributions "as necessary for her maintenance, comfort and happiness"[8] were both considered powers limited by an ascertainable standard.

> *Example: Gerald establishes a trust, naming his son, George as sole trustee. The trust gives the trustee the power to distribute trust assets for the "health, education, maintenance and support of the children of the grantor, to the extent that the trustee deems advisable, in his*

---

5. *See* Rev. Rul. 76-368.

6. 26 U.S.C. §2041(b)(1)(A).

7. Woodberry v. Bunker, 359 Mass. 239 (1971).

8. *See* Brantingham v. United States, 631 F.2d 542 (7th Cir. 1980).

*sole discretion." George does not have a general power of appointment,
for estate tax purposes, over the trust assets.*

While this latter method of avoiding a general power of appointment will
work for estate tax purpose, it may not work for creditor protection and will
almost certainly not work for purposes of benefits planning. If a trustee/ben-
eficiary has the power to distribute assets to himself, the trust assets would
likely be vulnerable to his creditors, especially if those creditors provided him
with goods or services that the trust would have the authority to pay for. The
trust assets would also likely be considered an "available resource" for government benefits eligibility.

Practice Tip: If a particular child of the client is likely to be vulnerable to
creditors and/or to require government benefits, it might be best to recommend that someone else serve as trustee. In any case, many people who
have debts or other economic problems are wary of having control over
significant assets. So, such a child may not want to serve as trustee in any
case.

The Trust Protector (or Trust Advisor)

Naming a trust protector or trust advisor can be an excellent way for a client
to split trust control among different people. This can help institute checks
and balances in the management of the trust. A trust protector or advisor can
be granted any authority chosen by the grantor. There are a few common roles
that a trust protector or advisor may have.

A limited role that the client may want to vest in a third party is the right
to direct trust investments.

*Example: Georgina establishes an irrevocable trust for the benefit of
her children. She trusts her son, Don, completely to be her trustee.
However, she is aware that Don has very limited investment experience and she wants to ensure that there is some oversight over Don's
investment decisions. So, Georgina decides to appoint her sister, Lacy,
to oversee the investment decisions. A provision establishing this relationship may read as follows:*

A. Don, who is the son of the grantor, shall serve as trustee of this trust.

> B. *Lacy, who is the sister of the grantor, shall serve as trust advisor hereunder. As trust advisor, Lacy shall be consulted and shall be required to give her consent, before trust assets may be invested in any specific security. In addition, no less than once ever three months, the trustee shall consult with the trust advisor regarding the investment portfolio held by the trust. The trustee shall make a good faith effort to follow the advice of the trust protector in this regard. However, the written consent of the trust advisor shall not be necessary for the trustee to transact business on behalf of the trust.*[9]

Trust "protectors" may also have a supervisory role over the trustee. For example, a trust protector may be vested with the authority to remove and replace a trustee or to appoint an additional co-trustee. The role of the trust protector can be defined however the client wishes. An example of an alternative trust protector provision would be:

> Jane Smith shall serve as trust protector hereunder. As trust protector, Jane Smith shall have the authority to remove and/or replace any acting trustee. In addition, she shall have the authority to name a co-trustee to commence serving along with the existing trustee. However, she may not name herself as trustee, nor may she name any person over which she has substantial control (such as an immediate family member or work subordinate) as trustee of this trust or any trust created hereunder.

Of course, like the trustee, the trust protector should be given powers that would constitute a general power of appointment.

Trustees' Duties and Authorities

State law provides the default rules for the duties and authorities that a trustee has with regard to the trust. Although these responsibilities and powers can and do vary from state to state, the list of duties and authorities granted by statute is fairly consistent in most states. As a representative sample, we will choose the state of Kansas (though, of course, the practitioner should become familiar with the rules of his or her home state in this regard).

---

9. This provision is included to ensure that banks and brokerage firms do not require two signatures before any action can be taken on behalf of the trust.

The Kansas rules state the following with respect to trustees' rights and responsibilities:

- The trustee has the responsibility to "administer the trust in good faith, in accordance with its terms and purposes and the interests of the beneficiaries."[10]
- The trustee has a "duty of loyalty towards the trust and the trust beneficiaries." This duty limits the types of transactions that trustee can engage in with the trust and provides measures to ensure that all dealings between the trustee and the trust pass a minimum level of fairness and disclosure.[11]
- The trustee has the responsibility to act with "impartiality" as between multiple beneficiaries of the trust.[12]
- The trustee is required to exercise prudence in administering the trust and must "exercise reasonable care, skill, and caution" in carrying out his or her responsibilities as trustee.[13]
- The trustee may only incur costs to the trust that are reasonable in "relation to the trust property, the purposes of the trust, and the skills of the trustee."[14]
- The trustee must use his or her "special skills and expertise" on behalf of the trust (if applicable).[15]
- Trustees may delegate trustee power to other people, with some limitations.[16]
- The trustee must comply with directions from the grantor or other person when those directions are allowed by the trust agreement.[17]
- Trustees may "control" and "protect" trust property.[18]
- A trustee must keep "adequate records" of the trust's dealings.[19]

---

10. Kan. Stat. Ann. § 58a-801.
11. Kan. Stat. Ann. § 58a-802.
12. Kan. Stat. Ann. § 58a-803.
13. Kan. Stat. Ann. § 58a-804.
14. Kan. Stat. Ann. § 58a-805.
15. Kan. Stat. Ann. § 58a-806.
16. Kan. Stat. Ann. § 58a-807.
17. Kan. Stat. Ann. § 58a-808.
18. Kan. Stat. Ann. § 58a-809.
19. Kan. Stat. Ann. § 58a-810.

- A trustee may (and shall) take the steps necessary to enforce claims the trust has against other parties and to defend the trust against claims of other parties.[20]
- A trustee is empowered to collect property from parties from whom such is owed.[21]
- A trustee must keep the beneficiaries reasonably informed as to the status of the trust assets and respond to beneficiaries' requests for information within reasonable (statutorily defined) time periods.[22]
- A trustee may exercise any powers on behalf of the trust that are "appropriate to achieve the proper investment, management, and distribution of the trust property."[23]
- The trustee may exercise a variety of specific powers enumerated by statute.[24]
- The trustee must distribute the trust assets after termination in accordance with the trust agreement.[25]

To ensure that the trustees have wide latitude to act in the best interests of the trust, many trusts have standard provisions that provide for many specific powers being vested in the trustee. An example of such a provision is as follows:

> In addition to any powers conferred by law, the Trustee is empowered, solely in the Trustee's fiduciary capacity:
>
> A. To hold and retain all or any property received from any source, without regard to diversification, risk, or the Trustee's personal interest in such property in any other capacity, and to keep all or part of the trust property at any place within the United States or abroad.
>
> B. To invest and reinvest the trust funds (or leave them temporarily un-invested), in any type of property and every kind of investment, including (but not limited to) corporate obligations of every kind, preferred or common stocks (including those in any corporate Trustee), securities of any regulated investment trust, common trust funds (including those maintained by any corporate Trustee), partnership interests, and United States bonds redeemable at par in payment of federal estate tax liabilities (for which the Trustee shall not be liable to anyone for losses resulting from the good faith purchase of these bonds).

---

20. Kan. Stat. Ann. §58a-811.
21. Kan. Stat. Ann. §58a-812.
22. Kan. Stat. Ann. §58a-813.
23. Kan. Stat. Ann. §58a-813(a)(1)(B).
24. Kan. Stat. Ann. §58a-816.
25. Kan. Stat. Ann. §58a-817.

C. To participate in the operation of any business or other enterprise, and to incorporate, dissolve, or otherwise change the form of such business.

D. To deposit trust funds in any commercial savings or savings and loan accounts.

E. To borrow money for any reasonable trust purpose and upon such terms, including (but not limited to) interest rates, security, and loan duration, as the Trustee deems advisable and to mortgage or otherwise encumber trust property as collateral for such borrowing under any reasonable commercial terms.

F. To lend trust funds to such persons and on such terms, including (but not limited to) interest rates, security, and loan duration, as the Trustee deems advisable.

G. To sell or otherwise dispose of trust assets, including (but not limited to) trust real property, for cash or credit, at public or private sale, and with such warranties or indemnifications as the Trustee deems advisable.

H. To improve, develop, manage, lease, or abandon any trust assets, as the Trustee deems advisable.

I. To hold property in the name of any Trustee or any custodian or nominee, without disclosing this trust, but the Trustee is responsible for the acts of any custodian or nominee so used.

J. To pay and advance money for the trust's protection and for all expenses, losses, and liabilities sustained in its administration.

K. To prosecute or defend any action for the protection of the trust, the Trustee in the performance of the Trustee's duties, or both, and to pay, contest, or settle any claim by or against the trust or the Trustee in the performance of the Trustee's duties.

L. To employ persons, even if they are associated with the Trustee, to advise or assist the Trustee in the performance of the Trustee's duties.

M. To distribute trust assets in kind or in cash, without the consent of any beneficiary.

N. To execute and deliver any instruments necessary or useful in the exercise of any of these powers.

Practice Tip: It is not necessary to discuss each individual authority of the trustee with your client. It is safe to assume that most clients want their trustees to have broad discretion over the trust assets. However, it does pay, at some point during discussions with the client, to ask if there are any specific authorities that it is important for the trustee to have. It is much easier to add a provision to grant the trustee a specific power at the time that the trust is being drafted than to wonder later whether the trustee has the authority to do something on behalf of the trust.

Trustee Fees

Trustees are entitled to reimbursement for their reasonable expenses borne on behalf of the trust. In addition, unless stated otherwise by the trust instrument, trustees are entitled to reasonable trustee fees. Some states set standard trustee fees that will control in the absence of a contrary provision in the agreement.[26] Other states provide no such rule and allow the trustee to be compensated based on the reasonable value of his or her time spent on trust business.

If a grantor wishes to prohibit trustee fees (as is common when one child of several is being named as trustee—the client may wish to avoid favoring one child by allowing him or her trustee fees in addition to his or her regular share of the trust), the trust should specifically state that no trustee fees will be allowed under the trust.

Reasonable trustee fees are a tax deductible expense of the trust. If trustee fees are taken after the death of the grantor, trustee fees may be taken as an estate tax deduction (where the trust assets are part of the grantor's taxable estate) or as an income tax deduction for the income earned after death (or in whatever combination the executors and/or trustees decide). However, keep in mind that trustee fees are considered taxable income to the trustees. Therefore, whether to take a trustee fee is often based on a calculation motivated by tax considerations.

> *Example: Brenda created the* Brenda Revocable Trust *during her lifetime. She names her sons, Brett and Jeremy, as trustees. They are also the sole trust beneficiaries after Brenda's death. After Benda's death, $1,000,000 in assets is held by the trust. Under local law, Brett and Jeremy would each be entitled to a $25,000 trustee fee.*
>
> *Since they are going to be splitting the money equally anyway, the question of whether to take the fee is solely a tax issue. If Brenda's es-*

---

26. *See, e.g.,* N.Y. S.C.P.A. § 2309.

tate is large enough so that her estate is subject to a 35% federal es-tate tax plus a state estate tax, it probably makes sense to pay out the trustee fees since the income to Brett and Jeremy will likely be taxed at a lower rate than the estate tax rates. On the other hand, if Brenda's estate is small enough so that it is not subject to federal estate tax, it might make sense for Brett and Jeremy to refuse their trustee fees and take the entire trust as a post-death distribution from the trust, which is free from income tax.

Provisions to Protect the Trustee(s)

As discussed above, trustees are subject to some strict requirements under state rules. In addition, where a court asserts jurisdiction over a trust (such as after the death of the testator, in the case of a testamentary trust), it may impose onerous reporting and bond requirements on the trustee. Filing and reporting requirements can be time consuming and bond requirements can be expensive.

These requirements are meant to protect the beneficiaries. However, if the grantor trusts the trustee to act in the best interests of the beneficiaries with or without court oversight, the grantor may want to exempt the trustee from such requirements.

Typical provisions designed to exempt the trustees from such requirements and to increase trustees' flexibility in trust administration include:

A. Any Trustee may, from time to time, delegate to any other Trustee by written instrument any or all of such Trustee's powers (except those, if any, not exercisable by such other Trustee). Such delegation may be temporary or permanent, and if temporary, may be for any duration of time or until any event specified by the delegating Trustee. Any person dealing in good faith with any Trustee may rely without inquiry upon the Trustee's certificate with respect to any delegation.

B. No Trustee shall be required to provide surety or other security on a bond.

C. No Trustee shall be required to obtain the order of any court to exercise any power or discretion under this trust.

D. No Trustee shall be required to file any accounting with any public official.

E. The Trustee is authorized to employ and rely on advice given by investment counsel, to delegate discretionary authority to investment counsel and to pay investment counsel reasonable compensation for services rendered. The Trustee may, but need not, favor retention of assets originally owned by the Grantor. The Trustee shall also not be under any duty to diversify investments, regardless of any principle of law requiring diversification, and he may retain and acquire property that does not produce income, as well as investments that are risky or speculative, so long as prudent procedures are followed in selecting and retaining the investments and the investments constitute a prudent percentage of the trust or estate.

F. The Trustee may enter into transactions on behalf of the Grantor's estate or trust in which that fiduciary is personally interested, so long as the terms of such transaction are fair to the estate or trust. For example, a Trustee may purchase estate or trust property without court approval.

G. Any Trustee may resign at any time without court approval and whether or not a successor has been appointed. In the event that a successor Trustee has not been designated in this instrument, any Trustee shall have the right to appoint, by an instrument in writing, a successor Trustee, such appointment to take effect upon the death, resignation or incapacity of the appointing Trustee. If the office of trustee is vacant, and no successor takes over pursuant to any other provision of this instrument, a successor Trustee may be appointed by a majority of the Grantor's adult descendants.

H. No Trustee shall be liable for any diminution in trust assets due to poor investments in the absence of gross negligence of bad faith.

Of course, the draftsman (with input from the client) may pick and choose from among these provisions and may alter them as appropriate.

Choice of Law and Forum

Like any other contract, a trust agreement can determine for itself which state will have jurisdiction over it. In addition, they can choose the law under which it will be governed. This is especially important where the beneficiaries live in a different state from the grantor or where, for whatever reason, the grantor is establishing a trust in a state in which she does not reside (such as a domestic asset protection trust).

The choice of law/forum provision is drafted in a trust similarly to that of any other contract. For example:

This trust and all trusts created hereunder shall be governed under the laws of the state of Nevada. Furthermore, if any dispute arises hereunder, the courts of the state of Nevada shall have sole jurisdiction over this trust of all parties' interests herein.

Severability

A severability clause seeks to ensure that if one clause in the trust is struck down as being illegal or against public policy, the rest of the trust will be unaffected. As with many other clauses in this chapter, this is a typical provision in many contracts.

In the event that any provision hereunder is invalidated by any court of competent jurisdiction, the remaining provision of this agreement shall be unaffected and shall remain in full force and effect.

Perpetuities Savings Clause

The rule against perpetuities is a rule that dates back to British common law that is designed to prevent the dictates of grantors from controlling property ad infinitum. Most states (though not all) have this rule or some variant thereof in effect.[27]

The basic rule (which has been modified by some states) states that a contingent future interest (which includes most trust interests) must vest, if at all, within twenty-one years after the death of a life in being when the future interest is created. The application of this rule can be quite complex. Essentially, this means that the trust, by its terms, must end within 21 years of the death of the last beneficiary. Some seemingly innocuous trust provisions may actually violate the rule against perpetuities.

Example: The Smith Family Trust *states: "Upon the death of the grantor, the assets will be held in trust for the benefit of the grantor's children and grandchildren. At the time that the youngest grandchild of the grantor reaches thirty (30) years of age, the trust will be terminated and the trust assets shall be distributed to the issue of the grantor, in equal shares, per stirpes." It is possible that a grandchild of the grantor will be born after the execution of the trust when the rest of*

---

27. *See, e.g.,* Michigan's version of the Rule Against Perpetuities, MCLS § 554.51.

the beneficiaries are dead and the trust will last for an additional 30 years. Although that scenario is farfetched, it is possible. Therefore, the trust provision violates the original version of the rule against perpetuities.

Because of the complex and antiquated nature of the rule, rather than worry about conforming the ultimate distribution provisions to the requirements of the rule against perpetuities, it is often simpler just to put a standard "perpetuities savings clause" into the trust. Such a provision may appear as follows:

> Notwithstanding any other provision hereunder, this trust shall terminate no later than twenty-one (21) years after the death of the last trust beneficiary who is alive at the time of the execution of this trust agreement. If the trust is terminated in this manner, all of the trust assets shall be distributed to the issue of the grantor, in equal shares, per stirpes.

Technical Corrections

Although irrevocable trusts cannot be amended, account should be made for the possibility of having to make technical corrections in the trust instrument. Typographical errors occur and are generally harmless. However, some can change the meaning of a provision and some can even unintentionally disinherit or expand the benefits of some beneficiaries.

A simple provision can be included in the trust to allow the trustees to make such necessary corrections. The provision may read as follows:

> In the event that any technical correction is required to any provision hereunder, then the acting trustee(s) are empowered to make such correction; so long as such change does not interfere with the intents of the grantor in establishing this trust, as those intents are set forth hereunder.

Any such technical correction should be in writing, signed by the acting trustee and notarized. An attached statement from the grantor, also signed and notarized, indicating that the correction is consistent with his or her intent in creating the trust, helps solidify the change. However, this is not absolutely necessary.

Review Questions

1) Explain one reason why it is important to name a successor trustee in a trust agreement.

2) Name one advantage and one disadvantage of naming multiple co-trustees for a trust.

3) What is a professional trustee and how are they generally compensated?

4) Name one advantage and one disadvantage of naming a professional trustee for a trust.

5) What is an "ascertainable standard"?

6) Why is it often important to limit a trustee's discretion by an ascertainable standard?

7) What is the role of a trust protector or trust advisor?

8) Give one example of a scenario in which a client would be interested in appointing a trust protector.

9) If trustee authorities are set forth by statute, why should one nevertheless give the trustee specific authorities in a trust agreement?

10) Why might it be advisable to limit the liabilities and duties of the trustee?

11) Under the default rule, is a trustee entitled to take a fee from a trust for managing it? In what way can this be altered by the agreement?

12) How would tax considerations affect the decision as to whether to take a trustee fee?

13) What are the functions of choice of law and choice of forum provisions?

14) What is a severability provision and what purpose does it serve?

15) What is the purpose of the rule against perpetuities?

16) What is the most efficient way of protecting a trust against failure based on the rule against perpetuities?

17) Why is it important to give the trustee (or another party) the power to make technical corrections to a trust instrument?

CHAPTER 12

CHARITABLE TRUSTS

Charitable trusts are distinguished from ordinary trusts primarily in that, while other trusts benefit specific individuals (or specific classes of people), charitable trusts benefit society at large or a needy subdivision of society at large. To be considered a charitable trust, a trust must meet the general requirements for trusts discussed in chapter 1 and must be organized "exclusively for religious, charitable, scientific, testing for public safety, literary, or educational purposes."[1]

To qualify as a charitable trust, no benefit from the trust may inure for the benefit of any specific individual named by the trust.[2] This applies whether that individual is the creator of the trust, an administrator of the trust or a member of the charitable class that the trust seeks to benefit. That is not to say that the trust cannot, in the end, support an individual. However, such individual or small group cannot be named by the trust initially.

Example: Tom has a poor neighbor named Jerry. Jerry has a wife and five children and no steady source of income since he lost his job last year. To help his neighbor, Tom establishes The Jerry Trust, *which states that the trust assets can only be used to pay necessary support expenses for the support of Jerry and his family. This trust does not qualify as a charitable trust.*

Example: Tom establishes a trust whose assets can be used "for the support of poor families that have been severely impacted by recent job loss." This trust can qualify as a charitable trust. If it uses all of its assets in a given year for the benefit of Jerry's family, it still can qualify as a charitable trust, as long as the beneficiaries are not specified at the outset.

---

1. 26 U.S.C. §501(c)(3) (some additional possible purposes are also enumerated by the statute; but the list in this text is cut short for the sake of brevity).

2. *See* Sebastian-Lathe Co. v. Johnson, 110 F. Supp. 245 (S.D.N.Y. 1952).

It should be noted that the trust can even specify that an individual is to be the ultimate beneficiary of the trust, as long as that individual is not identified by the trust instrument.

> **Example:** *Georgina sets aside $100,000 in trust "to pay for the college education of any one young adult from a disadvantaged background who would otherwise be unable to afford college; such beneficiary to be chosen by my trustee." Although this will inure to the benefit of an individual, since the individual is not identified by the trust instrument, the trust can qualify as a charitable trust.*[3]

Charitable Purpose

A charitable trust must contain language that demonstrates the intent that it serve as a charitable trust. Therefore, any charitable trust should specify, in the document, the charitable purposes for which the trust assets may be used.[4]

The purposes that are considered charitable for this purpose are fairly broadly defined. Charitable purposes include:

- Relief of poverty;
- Advancing education;
- Working to improve health of people; including medical research; and
- Advancing religious institutions.

The charitable purpose of advancing "education" may include politically biased or partisan forms of "education," even if the message being disseminated is an unpopular one.[5] However, a trust that advances an illegal or immoral cause (as determined by the court) or that advocates illegal activities or promulgates a message that is against public policy will not receive the benefits of a charitable trust.[6] In addition, trusts may not engage in "substantial" lobbying activities or engage in any political campaign and maintain its tax exempt status.[7]

The simplest type of charitable trust, which avoids the hassle of setting up charitable giving oversight mechanisms and greatly eases governance and re-

---

3. *See* Chapman's Estate, 39 Pa. D. & C.2d 701 (1965).

4. *See* Lorens v. Catholic Health Care Partners, 356 F. Supp. 2d 827 (N.D. Ohio 2005).

5. *See* In re Estate of Breeden, 208 Cal. App. 3d 981 (1989) (teaching people the benefits of socialism was considered a charitable purpose).

6. Girard Trust Co. v. Commissioner, 122 F.2d 108 (3d Cir. 1941).

7. http://www.irs.gov/charities/charitable/article/0,,id=120703,00.html.

porting requirements, is simply a trust that, by its terms, may only distribute its assets to other tax exempt, 501(c)(3) organizations.

> *Example:* Gil earns $1,000,000 on a single massive transaction during 2011. Because most of that money is in the highest tax bracket, he wants to contribute $500,000 to charity during the year 2011. He figures that he has certain charities that he wants to contribute to in any case, and so he might as well do so when he can get the biggest "bang" for his tax deductible buck. At this point, Gil knows that he wants to support the ability of poor people to afford educational services, but he does not know specifically to which charity or charities he would like to contribute these assets.

> Therefore, Gil establishes a charitable trust. The trust is only empowered to "distribute assets to organizations that are tax exempt under Section 501(c)(3) of the Internal Revenue Code and whose primary purpose is to assist poor people in affording educational services." The manner and timetable in which these distributions are made are left to the discretion of the trustee. In this way, Gil can take a tax deduction now (assuming his trust receives tax exempt status) and his gift is not subject to gift or estate tax implications. The ultimate organization recipients of the $500,000 (and income generated by the trust assets) can be determined later by the trustees. In fact, Gil can maintain some control over the assets, as long as they must be distributed ultimately to tax exempt charitable organizations.

Benefits of a Charitable Trust

There are various minor benefits available to charitable trusts apart from the tax advantages in many states. For example, charitable trusts have traditionally been exempt from the rule against perpetuities.[8] However, the key advantages of charitable trusts are tax related.

First, assets transferred to a charitable trust are exempt from gift and estate taxation.[9] Thus, assets can be transferred during one's lifetime to a charitable trust or posthumously held in a charitable trust without any gift or estate tax consequences.

---

8. *See, e.g.,* Texas Property Code—Section 112.036.
9. 26 U.S.C. § 2055.

Second, contributions to a charitable trust can be income tax deductible if the trust applies for and receives tax exempt status from the IRS. Application for tax exempt status is done by filing a form 1023 (Application for Recognition of Exemption Under Section 501(c)(3) of the Internal Revenue Code) and the IRS has put out Publication 557, which describes in detail the requirements necessary to obtain tax exempt status.[10]

Construing Charitable Intent

Because charitable trusts often last for many years, charitable trusts sometimes outlive their original purpose. In addition, changed circumstances may make the intent moot, irrelevant or impossible to fulfill. In such cases, the "cy pres" rule dictates that courts will allow the charitable trust to continue and its assets to be used in a manner that is as close to the original charitable intent as possible.

> *Example: In 1950, Sandy sets aside $1,000,000 in a charitable trust to study ways to develop a polio vaccine to be used in the United States. A few years later, polio is eradicated by a vaccine that has been developed independently of the trust. At the time, the trust still contains $600,000 in assets. Under the cy pres rule, a court can allow the trust assets to be used to research vaccines or cures for similar diseases with the trust assets.[11]*

> *Example: During the 1850s, Francis Jackson executed a will that set aside a charitable gift to further causes that would end slavery in the United States. He died in 1861. In 1863, slavery was abolished by the emancipation proclamation. In 1867, the Supreme Court of Massachusetts ruled that the trust assets can be used for similar causes, such as the advancement of the welfare of former slaves and African Americans in general.[12]*

Changes in laws and societal attitudes may also render a once "charitable" purpose illegal or against public policy. In such a case, the court may apply the cy pres doctrine and change the purpose of the trust. However, if the grantor's intent clearly will be frustrated by application of the cy pres rule, the

---

10. http://www.irs.gov/pub/irs-pdf/p557.pdf.
11. *See* In re Scott's Will, 8 N.Y.2d 419 (1960).
12. Jackson v. Phillips, 96 Mass. 539 (1867).

court may have no choice but to have the trust "fail" and be dissolved. In such case, all tax advantages of the trust will be eliminated and the trust assets will be distributed to the grantor or the grantor's heirs, under the grantor's will or the rules of intestacy.

> *Example: In 1948, Gil left $10,000 in a charitable trust for a public park in which only white people will be allowed. Because of subsequent court cases and civil rights legislation, such a public park can no longer be administered. Since it was clear from the document that the intent of the grantor was restricted to a "whites only" park (eliminating the possibility of changing the beneficiaries under the cy pres rule) the charitable trust fails.*[13]

Where the language of a trust indicates intent that the trust be held and used for charitable purposes but the language itself is ambiguous or faulty, courts will broadly construe the charitable intent. Furthermore, courts will strive to construe the trust in a manner that will serve to best achieve the intended charitable purpose and to attain the tax benefits afforded to charitable trusts.[14]

> *Example: Christine, in her will, sets aside $50,000 to be held "by my trustees and to be distributed to charitable causes in accordance with what my desires would have been had I been alive, as known to my trustees based on their interactions with me during my lifetime." Although this charitable bequest is very vague and could reasonably be construed as allowing the trustee to distribute assets to causes that are not tax exempt under Section 501(c)(3), a court would have the discretion to rule that, since the intent was clearly charitable, the entire bequest is considered a charitable bequest and the ensuing trust is a charitable trust.*[15]

Likewise, if the trust identifies a general charitable cause but doesn't specifically state that the trust funds must be used for charitable purposes, the court can construe the trust as being intended to satisfy charitable purposes and thus uphold the trust's status as a charitable trust.

---

13. *See* Evans v. Abney, 396 U.S. 435 (1970).

14. *See* N.Y. E.P.T.L. § 8-1.1(a) ("[No] disposition of property for religious, charitable, educational or benevolent purposes, otherwise valid under the laws of this state, is invalid by reason of the indefiniteness or uncertainty of the persons designated as beneficiaries.").

15. In re Estate of Carper, 67 A.D.2d 333 (4th Dept. 1979).

Example: George *gives assets to "my trustee for charitable and/or ed-*
ucational purposes in such manner as he shall deem fit and proper."
Even though the gift specifies both charitable and "educational" pur-
poses (which need not necessarily be charitable), the court looked at
the general charitable intent of the grantor and interpreted the trust
as a charitable trust.[16]

Administration of Charitable Trusts

As with all trusts, charitable trusts are administered by the trustee(s). As
long as the trust assets must be distributed to charity, there is no real limitation on who the trustee can be. Even the grantor can retain control over the
investments and distribution decisions of the charitable trust while maintaining the trust's status as a charitable trust.[17] However, if it is important that the
assets in the charitable trust be outside of the grantor's taxable estate (as it
often is for clients wealthy enough to establish charitable trusts), then care
must be exercised not to allow the grantor enough control over the trust assets
to bring it back into his or her taxable estate[18] (as discussed in chapter 4).

Split Interest Trusts

The general principle of split interest trusts is that they do not qualify as
charitable trusts. That is, if a trust has both charitable beneficiaries and non-
charitable beneficiaries, the trust will not be considered a charitable trust.

Example: Bob *sets up a trust for "the benefit of my daughter, Brenda*
and the United Way charitable organization." The trust gives the
trustee the authority to spend trust assets for either beneficiary's ben-
efit. This is not a charitable trust. If Bob contributes money to the
trust, this will be subject to gift tax and contributions to the trust are
not income tax deductible to any extent.[19] *Instead, if the trust later*
gives trust assets to the United Way (a 501(c)(3) organization), it can

---

16. In Re Estate of Bush, 475 N.Y.S.2d 311 (Lewis Cty. Surr. Ct. 1984).
17. *See* Private Letter Ruling 200445023.
18. 26 U.S.C. § 2038.
19. *See* I.R.S. Technical Advice Memorandum 200341002.

take a charitable deduction for the value of the contribution on the trust's income tax return.

There are, however, exceptions to this split interest rule. Qualifying "charitable remainder trusts" and "charitable lead trusts" are two types of charitable trusts that can partially qualify as charitable trusts even though they have both charitable and non-charitable beneficiaries.

Both types of trusts split the trust interests by time. In a charitable remainder trust, prior to a certain point in time (which could be a specific number of years or the occurrence of an event, such as the death of the grantor), the trust beneficiaries are private (often the grantor or his or her family). After the point in time, the trust beneficiaries switch to qualifying tax exempt charities. In a charitable lead trust, the charitable interest comes first, while the trust reverts to private beneficiaries after the event occurs.

In both cases, the value of the *charitable interest* placed in trust counts as a charitable contribution, which may be eligible for an income tax charitable deduction. In addition, the value of the charitable interest in the contribution is not subject to gift tax.[20]

Charitable Remainder Trusts

The charitable remainder trust starts with an interest being retained by the grantor or his or her family (or any private parties) and ends with a charitable interest.[21] This device is typically used when a client wants an income tax deduction now, but wants to enjoy the benefit of the monetary flow from the trust for a number of years, or even for the remainder of his life.

> **Example:** *Jerry, who is 63 years old and works as a personal injury attorney, wins a large civil judgment in early 2011. Based on the judgment, he earns a legal fee of $1,000,000, which far exceeds the amount of money that he has ever earned in an entire year. Jerry does not need all of this money during 2011 and he realizes that the $1,000,000 will be heavily taxed at the federal and state levels. Therefore, he establishes a charitable remainder trust and contributes $800,000 to the trust. The trust states that each year, the trust must distribute $50,000*

---

20. 26 U.S.C. § 2552.
21. *See* 26 U.S.C. § 664, which establishes the rules for a charitable remainder trust.

to Jerry, for the remainder of Jerry's life. After Jerry's death, the trustee is directed to distribute the trust assets to tax exempt charitable organizations of the trustee's choosing. This is a charitable lead trust. As discussed below, Jerry may take an income tax charitable deduction for the present value of the charitable remainder interest. He will, in effect, be preserving much of the money for his own use during his lifetime, while receiving a significant income tax deduction upon the contribution in 2011.

The determination of the value of the charitable remainder interest in any contribution to a charitable remainder trust is a complex matter. It depends on a variety of factors, which include:

1) The value of the contribution.

2) The term of the non-charitable interest. If the term is a specific number of years, this is easy. If the non-charitable interest is based on the life of a beneficiary or beneficiaries, the anticipated term must be calculated based on their life expectancies. Life expectancies are published by the IRS and are updated on a yearly basis.[22]

3) The payout rate of the non-charitable interest; i.e., how much will be paid each year to the non-charitable beneficiaries over the course of the pre-charitable term.

4) The applicable federal interest rate. This is the most complex element of the calculation. The future interest of the charity must be determined by assuming an interest rate that is equal to 120% of the federal midterm interest rate.[23] The IRS publishes the rate (also known as the "Section 7520" rate) on its website.[24]

Detailing how to figure out the value of the charitable future interest is beyond the scope of this text. Fortunately, there are free online tools that can do the legwork for you once you provide the basic relevant information.[25]

Example: Take Jerry's case, above. Based on his age (63) (and thus his life expectancy under federal tables), the amount of the contribution ($800,000), the amount of the distributions called for by the char-

---

22. I.R.S. Publication 590.
23. 26 U.S.C. §5720.
24. http://www.irs.gov/businesses/small/article/0,,id=112482,00.html.
25. *See, e.g* http://www.danbury.org/lfs/Remcalc.htm.

itable remainder trust ($50,000 per year) and the applicable Section 7520 rates as of March, 2011 (3.0%), the value of the charitable future interest is $283,096. Therefore, if Jerry makes the $800,000 contribution in March, 2011, he will be able to take a deduction of $283,096, which is over 40% of the contribution.

In the above example, the client was named as the non-charitable (remainder) beneficiary of the charitable lead trust. This is fine for income tax purposes. However, if estate tax is a concern (whether it depends on the extent of the grantor's assets), then this is not the ideal drafting strategy. If the grantor retains a beneficial interest in the trust as in the example, the entire value of the trust may be included in his gross estate for estate tax purposes.[26]

Instead, if estate tax is a factor, a better strategy might be to have the client's spouse and/or children named as the non-charitable (remainder) beneficiaries. The trust can even be drafted so as to give the trustee[27] discretion to distribute the assets once among multiple possible beneficiaries during the non-charitable term. The only thing that must be established by the trust is the amount to be distributed each year.

Distribution Plans from a Charitable Remainder Trust

There are two distinct manners in which distribution plans from charitable lead trusts can operate.

An "annuity trust" pays the present interest holder a fixed sum every year until the interest expires. For example, an annuity trust may pay the present interest beneficiary $50,000 per year. A charitable remainder trust that calls for annuity payments to the non-charitable beneficiaries is called a "charitable remainder annuity trust" and is often referred to by its initials, "CRAT."

A "unitrust" pays the present interest holders, each year, a specified percentage of the trust's value. This means that the non-charitable distributions can decrease each year as the trust corpus becomes smaller. On the other hand, if the trust is able to earn more income than it has to distribute, the trust cor-

---

26. *See* 26 U.S.C. § 2036.
27. The trustee should be someone other than the grantor. If it were the grantor, it would likely be part of the client's estate under § 2038 if the client dies during the trust term.

pus will grow and the amount paid out each year will increase. Such a trust is referred to as a "charitable remainder unitrust" and is often referred as a "CRUT."

Example: Doug established a charitable remainder trust that specifies a term of twenty years. The trust states, "During the term of the trust, the trustee shall distribute to Doug's children, in equal shares, an amount equal to $50,000, each year. Such distribution shall be made once annually on or about January 1 of each year. At the end of the twenty year term, the trust assets shall be distributed to charity." This is a charitable remainder annuity trust.

Example: Same as above, except that instead of designating $50,000 per year to the non-charitable beneficiaries each year, the trust designates "an annuity amount equal to FIVE PERCENT (5.0%) of the initial net fair market value of all property transferred to the trust" to be paid to the non-charitable beneficiaries each year. This is also a charitable remainder annuity trust since the amount of the annuity is fixed and is ascertainable at the outset of the trust's existence.

Example: Doug established a charitable remainder trust that specifies a term of twenty years. The trust states, "During the term of the trust, the trustee shall distribute to Doug's children, in equal shares, an amount equal to five percent (5%) of the trust's fair market value, as of the date of the distribution." This is a charitable remainder unitrust.

Charitable Lead Trust

The charitable lead trust is also a split interest trust that is similar to the charitable remainder trust. Instead of the non-charitable interest being up front and the charitable interest taking over after a given period of time, the opposite occurs. The trust designates an annual payment to charitable beneficiaries for a specified period of time (or it can be measured by the life of an individual). After the term, the interest reverts to non-charitable beneficiaries (usually the grantor or his or her heirs).

As with the charitable remainder trust, the amount distributed to charity each year can be a fixed sum (annuity trust) or a percentage of the trust assets (unitrust). A charitable lead trust that distributes an annuity to charity is called a charitable lead annuity trust ("CLAT") while a charitable lead trust that distributes a fixed percentage of the trust to charity is a charitable lead unitrust ("CLUT").

In other respects, the charitable lead trust works in the same manner as the charitable remainder trust. The value of the charitable interest (and thus the amount of the charitable income and gift tax deduction that can be taken upon a contribution) depends on the present value of the charitable interest and is calculated in the same manner as discussed above.

> *Example:* Joanne establishes The Joanne Charitable Lead Annuity Trust, *which she funds with a $1,000,000 initial gift. The trust's term is 15 years and the annual payment to charity is $50,000. Based on applicable interest rates as of March 2011, the charitable (lead) interest is worth $656,549.61. Therefore, that amount can be taken by Joanne as an income tax charitable deduction and is not subject to gift tax.*

Practice Tip: Choosing the type of split interest charitable trust involves an analysis of the client's needs and goals. For clients who earn large incomes and don't need additional income for the next number of years, a charitable lead trust is often best. The client can give assets to the charitable lead trust, take a deduction, and preserve the remainder interest for his or her children. For clients that need the steady income but may not feel as much of an impetus to leave assets for his or her children (the children may be taken care of from other sources or the client may not have children), a charitable remainder trust works well as it gives the client the present enjoyment of the trust assets while postponing the charitable interest into the future. Clients may be presented with both choices, but the legal professional must be prepared to make a recommendation based on the circumstances of the individual client.

Features and Provisions Common to Both Types of Split Interest Trusts

Both types of split interest charitable trusts are funded by a one time contribution. Since the value of the contributions and the value of both the charitable and non-charitable interests must be established at the outset, no additional contributions can be made. If the client wishes to repeat the strategy year after year (or even multiple times in the same year), a new split interest charitable trust should be established for each instance.

Both types of trusts can be grantor or non-grantor trusts. Even in a charitable lead trust, where most or all of the income is being distributed to charity each year, the income earned by the trust is taxable income. Keep in mind that the money being paid to charity each year was already accounted for in the charitable deduction taken based on the charitable interest in the initial contribution. It would therefore be anomalous to allow a second deduction for the charitable gifts being paid based on the annuity.

If the charitable trust is a grantor trust, all income earned by the trust is taxable directly to the grantor, as with any grantor trust. If the trust is a non-grantor trust, the trust will have to pay its own income tax or distribute and allocate the trust income to the beneficiaries of the present interest.

If the trust is a charitable remainder trust and is not a grantor trust, the trust may pay its own income tax or it may distribute the income to the present interest beneficiaries. As discussed in chapter 5, if there are beneficiaries in low tax brackets, allocating income to them may decrease the tax burden on the family as a whole.

A charitable lead trust, on the other hand, may not distribute anything to anyone but the charitable beneficiary during its term. Therefore, the trust income is going to have to be taxed either to the grantor or to the trust itself. If it is taxed to the grantor, the grantor will have to pay the tax from his or her funds. If it is taxed to the trust, it will decrease the principal that will be available to the remainder beneficiaries.

Ultimately, the decision as to whether to make a charitable lead trust a grantor trust or non-grantor trust depends on whether the trust or the grantor is likely to pay more income tax. If the grantor has a high income, a grantor trust's income will be taxed based on the marginal rate paid by the grantor. In such as case, it may make sense to establish a non-grantor trust. Otherwise, a grantor trust may be the better strategy.

Keep in mind that a charitable lead trust in which the grantor retains the remainder interest may inherently be considered a grantor trust under Section 673 of the Internal Revenue Code.[28] Therefore, if the client wants a non-grantor trust, she may not be able to be a remainder beneficiary of the trust.

Other provisions discussed elsewhere in this text that help protect the interests of the beneficiaries, to appoint trustees and trust protectors, to choose the forum and applicable law, etc., can generally be applied to charitable trusts as well.

---

28. 26 U.S.C. §673 ("The grantor shall be treated as the owner of any portion of a trust in which he has a reversionary interest in either the corpus or the income therefrom, if, as of the inception of that portion of the trust, the value of such interest exceeds 5 percent of the value of such portion.").

Annual Filing Requirements

Charitable trusts that have received tax exempt status must file a Form 990 to report their income and expenses.[29] Split interest charitable trusts must file the standard annual 1041 to report the trust's income. In addition, many states have specific requirements that certain forms be filed annually to allow the state to supervise the handling of the charitable trusts.[30]

Pooled Charitable Funds

Contributing assets to a pooled charitable fund is a viable alternative for clients who want to delay the naming of the ultimate end user recipients of their charitable contributions but do not want to go though the hassle and expense of establishing a private charitable trust. Instead of the individual establishing a separate charitable trust, the individual simply contributes the money to a charitable fund that has been established by a brokerage firm. Pooled charitable funds such as the Fidelity Donor Advised Charitable Gift Fund[31] hold contributions of many clients in one large charitable trust.

Typically, each donor establishes a separate account and contributes assets to this account. From that point, save for the brokerage fees and commissions, no distributions can be made from that account except to § 501(c)(3) charities. The client who funded the account is given the authority to advise (though not necessarily to direct) the ultimate disposition of the assets in the account, provided that they are made to § 501(c)(3) charities.

The client can take the income tax charitable deduction immediately upon the contribution while retaining some control over the charities that will eventually receive the contribution. The client, however, has to cede some control over the assets and the distributions themselves must be made by the brokerage firm at which the account is held.

Practice Tip: The pooled charitable fund will often be adequate for clients who come in initially seeking the establishment of a charitable trust. Clients are often unaware of this simple option that allows them to enjoy a chari-

---

29. http://www.irs.gov/pub/irs-pdf/f990.pdf.

30. *See, e.g.,* http://www.ag.ny.gov/bureaus/charities2/pdfs/CHAR001-RT.pdf.

31. http://www.fidelitycharitableservices.com/charity-giving-help/solutions/donor-advised.shtml.

table deduction now and be active in the allocation of their contributions to charities later.

Review Questions

1) What purposes may a trust have and be considered a charitable trust?

2) What limitations are there on the types of "education" that must be supplied by a trust that is a charitable education trust?

3) How can a trust be considered a charitable trust even when it does not specify its charitable purposes?

4) Can a trust that ultimately benefits a single person still be a charitable trust? Explain how.

5) What are the key advantages that charitable trusts have over other trusts?

6) What is the "cy pres" rule and how does it impact charitable trusts?

7) What happens to a trust whose goals are no longer consistent with public policy?

8) When will a court "reform" a trust to make it into a charitable trust? Why is this authority of the court important to the trust?

9) Aside from specific exceptions in the Internal Revenue Code, what is the general rule regarding trusts that have both charitable and non-charitable beneficiaries?

10) What are the two major exceptions to the split interest rule?

11) Explain the difference between a charitable lead trust and a charitable remainder trust.

12) Briefly describe how the charitable deduction is ascertained when a contribution is made to a charitable lead trust or a charitable remainder trust.

13) What is the difference between an annuity trust and a unitrust?

14) Why must a charitable lead trust pay income tax on its income even if all of its income is to be given to charity?

15) When would it be advisable to make a charitable lead trust a grantor trust?

16) What two types of federal annual filing requirements may exist with respect to a charitable trust?

17) Describe one advantage of contributing money to a pooled charitable fund over establishing a charitable trust.

18) Describe one advantage of establishing a charitable trust over contributing money to a pooled charitable fund.

Appendix A

Sample Completed Trusts

Sample Trust #1

Sample Revocable Trust with:

- Estate tax planning for client
- Credit shelter trust/Marital trust division
- Disclaimer Option on First Death
- Medicaid Eligibility Planning in the Credit Shelter Trust
- Unlimited Flexibility in QTIP for surviving spouse
- Creditor protection subtrusts for benefit of two of three individual children

THE DARREN WALTERS REVOCABLE TRUST

This Trust Agreement is made effective as of the _____ day of _____, 201__, by and between DARREN WALTERS, currently residing at 187 Main Street, Anywhere, Wisconsin (hereinafter sometimes referred to at the "Grantor" and sometimes referred to as the "Trustees" or "Trustee") and his wife, STEPHANIE WALTERS, also currently residing at 187 Main Street, Anywhere, Wisconsin (hereinafter referred to as the "Trustees" or "Trustee") on the following terms and conditions:

ARTICLE I
Purposes and Funding the Trust

The Grantor creates this trust as a means by which assets are to be held and administered in accordance with the terms and conditions set forth in this instrument. The Grantor hereby transfers to the Trustees the sum of ten dollars ($10) in cash. In addition to the initial transfer by the Grantor of the sum of ten dollars ($10) in cash, the Grantor and anyone else may transfer additional property to the Trustees at any time. All assets received by the Trustees shall be managed and distributed in accordance with this Agreement. It is the Grantor's intent in creating this trust to transfer assets into this trust for the use and benefit of a class of people, as described herein.

ARTICLE II
During the Lifetime of the Grantor

As long as the Grantor is living, the Trustee shall hold, manage, invest and reinvest the Trust Estate (if any requires such management and investment) and shall collect the income, if any, therefrom and shall dispose of the net income and principal as follows:

A. The Trustee shall pay to or apply for the benefit of the Grantor, or to or for the benefit of such person or persons (and in such proportions) as the Grantor may from time to time designate, all the net income from this Trust.

B. The Trustee may pay to or apply for the benefit of the Grantor, or to or for the benefit of such person or persons as the Grantor may from time to time designate, such sums from the principal of this Trust as in the Trustee's sole discretion shall be necessary or advisable from time to time for the medical care, comfortable maintenance and welfare of the Grantor or the Grantor's designee, taking into consideration to the extent the Trustee deems advisable, any other income or resources of the Grantor or the Grantor's designee known to the Trustees.

C. The Grantor may at any time and from time to time, withdraw all or any part of the principal of this Trust, free of trust, by delivering an instrument in writing duly signed by the Grantor to the Trustee, describing the property or portion thereof desired to be withdrawn. Upon receipt of such instrument, the Trustee shall thereupon convey and deliver to the Grantor, free of trust, the property described in such instrument.

ARTICLE III
Grantor's Powers

A. The Grantor may, during his lifetime: (1) withdraw property from this Trust in any amount and at any time; (2) add other property to the Trust; (3) change the beneficiaries, their respective shares and the plan of distribution; (4) amend this Trust Agreement in any other respect; (5) revoke this Trust in its entirety or any provision therein; provided, however, the duties or responsibilities of the Trustee shall not be enlarged without the Trustee's consent.

B. Unless sooner terminated, the trust shall become irrevocable upon the death of the Grantor and shall be administered and distributed as set forth hereinafter.

ARTICLE IV
After the Death of the Grantor

A. Upon the death of the Grantor, if the Grantor is survived by his wife, then the trust assets that can pass free of federal and state estate tax by reason of the unified credit, estate tax exclusion amount and/or any other estate tax exemption (taking into account other assets that are part of the Grantor's taxable estate that pass outside of this Trust) shall continue to be held in a "credit shelter trust" ("Trust B") the terms and conditions for which are set forth hereinafter in ARTICLE VI. The remainder of the Trust assets shall be held in a "marital trust" ("Trust A") for the benefit of the Grantor's wife, the terms and conditions for which are set forth hereinafter in ARTICLE V.

B. Upon the death of the Grantor, if the Grantor's wife (or her legal representative) makes a qualified disclaimer (as defined in Section 2518 of the Internal Revenue Code, as amended) on some or all of the bequest earmarked for the marital trust (Trust A) established under Paragraph B and administered under ARTICLE V, then the amount so disclaimed shall be added to the Credit Shelter trust (Trust B) created pursuant to Paragraph A above, and administered under ARTICLE VI, to be held, administered and distributed by the Trustees in accordance with the provisions of ARTICLE VI. This provision shall be applicable even if the disclaimer would result in federal or state estate tax.

ARTICLE V
Marital Trust — Trust A

The "marital trust" established under ARTICLE V shall be held, administered and distributed as follows:

A. It is the intent of the grantor that this trust shall qualify for the estate tax marital deduction under Section 2056 of the Internal Revenue Code. Any provision of this ARTICLE that would negate the eligibility of this trust for the marital deduction shall be null and void. All provisions hereunder shall be construed in accordance with this intent.

B. During the lifetime of the Grantor's wife, the Trustee shall pay to her all of this trust's net income in convenient installments, but at least annually.

C. The Trustee may not hold property that does not produce income in this trust without the consent of the Grantor's wife.

D. During the lifetime of the Grantor's wife, the Trustee shall pay to her as much of the Trust principal as she shall from time to time demand, at any time and for any reason.

E. Upon the later death of the Grantor's wife, the Trustee shall distribute any remaining trust income to the Grantor's wife's estate and the remaining principal in accordance with ARTICLE VII.

ARTICLE VI
Credit Shelter Trust — Trust B

The "credit shelter trust" established under ARTICLE V shall be held, administered and distributed as follows:

A. During the lifetime of the Grantor's wife, the trustee shall pay to or apply for the benefit of the Grantor's wife, all of the net income of the Trust.

B. As long as the Grantor's wife is living, the Grantor's wife shall have the right to live in any residential real property owned by the Trust. If any residential real property owned by the Trust is sold, the Trust may provide her with alternative residential housing of equivalent quality. The trust may accomplish this either by purchasing alternative residential property and allowing the Grantor's wife to reside in such property rent-free (but subject to the provisions of Paragraph E of this ARTICLE), or by leasing alternative housing for the Grantor's wife and paying the rent for the Grantor's wife for the rest of her life. However, the trust may not pay for the Grantor's wife's residence in any nursing home or similar long term care facility that provides enhanced medical or care services for its residents. In addition, if the Trust owns real property, the Grantor's wife shall have the right to live in any such residential real property owned by the Trust.

C. All property taxes, carrying charges, maintenance, expenses, etc. relating to real property owned by the Trust shall be the responsibility of the Grantor's wife, so long as she resides in such real property.

D. In addition, the Trustee may pay to, or spend on behalf of the Grantor's children, as much of the remaining trust principal as the trustees deem necessary and appropriate for their health, education, maintenance and support. However, no assets may be spent from this trust under this paragraph for the benefit of any child of the Grantor without the consent of at least one other child of the Grantor.

E. Upon the later death of the Grantor's wife, the Trustee shall distribute any remaining trust principal in accordance with ARTICLE VII.

ARTICLE VII
Upon the death of the second to die of the Grantor and his Wife

Upon the death of the second to die of the Grantor and his wife, the remaining trust assets (including those assets in the marital and credit shelter trusts administered under ARTICLE V and ARTICLE VI, respectively) shall be divided as follows:

A. ONE THIRD (1/3) shall be distributed to the Grantor's son, JOHN WALTERS, if he is living, or, if he is not living, to his issue, in equal shares, per stirpes.

B. ONE THIRD (1/3) shall be held in a trust for the benefit of the Grantor's son, MICHAEL WALTERS in accordance with the terms and conditions set forth hereinafter in ARTICLE VIII. If MICHAEL WALTERS is not living, then this share shall be distributed to his issue, in equal shares, per stirpes.

C. ONE THIRD (1/3) shall be held in a trust for the benefit of the Grantor's daughter, MICHELLE WALTERS SMITH in accordance with the terms and conditions set forth hereinafter in ARTICLE IX. If MICHELLE WALTERS SMITH is not living, then this share shall be distributed to her issue, in equal shares, per stirpes or if she has no issue then among the other beneficiaries under this Paragraph.

ARTICLE VIII
Trust for the Benefit of MICHAEL WALTERS

A trust for the benefit of MICHAEL WALTERS created under Paragraph B of ARTICLE VII shall be held, administered and distributed as follows.

A. During the lifetime of MICHAEL WALTERS, the trustee shall distribute to MICHAEL WALTERS, in quarterly or more frequent installments, all of the next income of the trust.

B. In addition, the trustee may, in his or her sole discretion, distribute to MICHAEL WALTERS as much of the trust principal as he deems appropriate for the health, education, maintenance and support of MICHAEL WALTERS. The trustee may, but need not, take into account other resources available to MICHAEL WALTERS when making this determination.

C. Upon the death of MICHAEL WALTERS, the trust assets shall be distributed to whomever among the issue of the Grantor that MICHAEL WALTERS shall appoint said assets by a Will that specifically references this limited power of appointment. In default of appointment, the trust assets shall be distributed to the issue of MICHAEL WALTERS, in equal shares, per stirpes.

ARTICLE IX
Trust for the Benefit of MICHELLE WALTERS SMITH

A trust for the benefit of MICHELLE WALTERS SMITH created under Paragraph C of ARTICLE VII shall be held, administered and distributed as follows.

A. During the lifetime of MICHELLE WALTERS SMITH, the trustee shall distribute to MICHELLE WALTERS SMITH, in quarterly or more frequent installments, all of the next income of the trust.

B. In addition, the trustee may, in his or her sole discretion, distribute MICHELLE WALTERS SMITH as much of the trust principal as he deems appropriate for the health, education, maintenance and support of MICHELLE WALTERS SMITH. The trustee may, but need not, take into account other resources available to MICHELLE WALTERS SMITH when making this determination.

C. Upon the death of MICHELLE WALTERS SMITH, the trust assets shall be distributed to whomever among the issue of the Grantor that MICHELLE WALTERS SMITH shall appoint said assets by a Will that specifically references this limited power of appointment. In default of appointment, the trust assets shall be distributed to the issue of MICHELLE WALTERS SMITH, in equal shares, per stirpes, or, if she has no issue, then to the issue of the Grantor, in equal shares, per stirpes.

ARTICLE X
Spendthrift Clause

To the extent permitted by law, the beneficiaries' interests will not be subject to their liabilities or creditor claims or to assignment or anticipation.

ARTICLE XI
Interests Vesting to a Beneficiary under the age of Twenty-one (21) Years

If any Trust principal or income shall vest in absolute ownership in a minor, the Trustee shall have the authority to: 1. Hold and manage the property and defer payment or distribution of all or a part of the property to that minor until that minor reaches the age of twenty-one (21) years; 2. Distribute part or all of the property to a custodian or guardian for the minor under the laws of the jurisdiction where the minor resides, and 3. Directly apply part or all of the property for the minor's health, education, support (in his/her accustomed manner of living) or maintenance costs.

ARTICLE XII
Merger, Consolidation, and Division

For convenience of administration or investment, the Trustee of any trusts created hereunder may:

A. Invest the assets of multiple trusts in a single fund, assigning them undivided interests in such common fund, dividing the income proportionately and accounting for them separately;

B. Merge or consolidate any trust created hereunder together with any other trusts having the same trustee and substantially the same dispositive provisions; and

C. Divide any trust created hereunder into two (2) or more separate trusts, each such trust to contain a fractional share of the assets of the trust before such division.

ARTICLE XIII
Trustee's Powers

The Trustee is exclusively empowered to do the following, exclusively in the Trustee's fiduciary capacity:

A. To hold and retain all or any property received from any source, without regard to diversification, risk, productivity, or the Trustee's personal interest in such property in any other capacity, and to keep all or part of the trust property at any place within the United States or abroad.

B. To invest and reinvest the trust funds (or leave them temporarily uninvested), in any type of property and every kind of investment, including (but not limited to) corporate obligations of every kind, preferred or common stocks, securities of any regulated investment trust, and partnership interests.

C. To participate in the operation of any business or other enterprise, and to incorporate, dissolve, or otherwise change the form of such business.

D. To deposit trust funds in any commercial savings or savings and loan accounts.

E. To borrow money for any reasonable trust purpose and upon such terms, including (but not limited to) interest rates, security, and loan duration, as the trustee deems advisable. The Trustee may secure the repayment of any or all amounts so borrowed by mortgage or pledge of any property, whether real property or personal property, as the Trustee deems advisable. The Trustee may also arrange for the mortgaging of trust property, whether through a private lender or through any bank or other financial institution.

F. To lend trust funds to such persons and on such terms, including (but not limited to) interest rates, security, and loan duration, as the Trustee deems advisable; provided, however, that the Trustee may not lend money to the Grantor's estate without receiving adequate security and an adequate rate of interest.

G. To sell or otherwise dispose of trust assets, including (but not limited to) trust real property, for cash or credit, at public or private sale, and with such warranties or indemnifications as the Trustee deems advisable.

H. To buy assets of any type from any person on such terms, including (but not limited to), cash or credit, interest rates, and security, as the Trustee deems advisable; provided, however, that the Trustee may not buy assets from the Grantor's estate other than at their fair market value.

I. To improve, develop, manage or abandon any trust assets, as the Trustee deems advisable.

J. To hold property in the name of any trustee or any custodian or nominee, without disclosing this trust; but the Trustee is responsible for the acts of any custodian or nominee so used.

K. To pay and advance money for the trust's protection and for all expenses, losses, and liabilities sustained in its administration.

L. To prosecute or defend any action for the protection of the trust, the Trustee in the performance of the Trustee's duties, or both, and to pay, contest, or settle any claim by or against the trust or the Trustee in the performance of the Trustee's duties.

M. To employ persons, even if they are associated with the Trustee, to advise or assist the Trustee in the performance of the Trustee's duties.

N. To determine what is principal or income and what items shall be charged or credited to either.

O. To distribute trust assets in kind or in cash.

P. To execute and deliver any instruments necessary or useful in the exercise of any of these powers.

Q. To rent or lease out any real property held by the trust to any tenant upon such terms as the Trustee, in his or her sole discretion, determines to be in the best interest of the Trust.

R. To assign or delegate, for convenience purposes, the authority to perform administrative tasks in connection with the Trust, to any person that the Trustee deems appropriate.

ARTICLE XIV
The Trustees

A. As long as both the Grantor and his wife are living, the Grantor, DAR-REN WALTERS and his wife, STEPHANIE WALTERS, shall serve as Co-Trustees of this trust and they shall serve without bond. Each trustee shall have the authority to act as sole Trustee for any purpose. If, for any reason, either of them is unable or unwilling to serve or to continue to serve, then the other shall serve as sole Trustee, and shall serve without bond. If neither is able and willing to serve or to continue to serve as Trustee, then the Grantor's son, JOHN WALTERS shall serve as Trustee of this trust, and shall serve without bond. If he is unable or unwilling to serve or to continue to serve, then the Grantor's son, MICHAEL WALTERS, shall serve as successor trustee, and he shall serve without bond.

B. Subject to the provisions of Paragraph C of this Article, after the Grantor's death, the Grantor's wife, STEPHANIE WALTERS, shall serve as sole trustee of all trusts created hereunder. If she is unable or unwilling to serve or to continue to serve as Trustee, then the Grantor's son, JOHN WALTERS shall serve as Trustee of this trust and all trusts created hereunder, and he shall serve without bond. If he is unable or unwilling to serve or to continue to serve, then the Grantor's son, MICHAEL WALTERS, shall serve as successor trustee, and he shall serve without bond.

C. JOHN WALTERS shall serve as trustee of the trust for the benefit of MICHAEL WALTERS created under Paragraph C of ARTICLE VII and administered under ARTICLE VIII. If, for any reason, he is unable or unwilling to serve or to continue to serve, then MICHAEL WALTERS shall have the authority to name a successor trustee; provided, however, that such successor trustee must not be a "related or subordinate party" to MICHAEL WALTERS, as defined under Section 672(c) of the Internal Revenue Code. In addition, as long as JOHN WALTERS is not serving as trustee, MICHAEL WALTERS shall have the authority to remove and replace any then serving trustee, though no more frequently than once every year, so long as any trustee that he appoints must not be a "related or subordinate party" to MICHAEL WALTERS, as defined under Section 672(c) of the Internal Revenue Code. All trustees serving under this Paragraph shall serve without bond.

D. JOHN WALTERS shall serve as trustee of the trust for the benefit of MICHELLE WALTERS SMITH created under Paragraph C of ARTICLE VII and administered under ARTICLE VIII. If, for any reason, he is unable or unwilling to serve or to continue to serve, then JOHN WALTERS shall have the authority to name a successor trustee; provided, however, that such successor trustee must not be a "related or subordinate party" to MICHELLE WALTERS SMITH, as defined under Section 672(c) of the Internal Revenue Code. In addition, as long as JOHN WALTERS is not serving as trustee, MICHELLE WALTERS SMITH shall have the authority to remove and replace any then serving trustee, though no more frequently than once every year, so long as any trustee that he appoints must not be a "related or subordinate party" to MICHELLE WALTERS SMITH, as defined under Section 672(c) of the Internal Revenue Code. All trustees serving under this Paragraph shall serve without bond.

E. Notwithstanding the above Trustee designation provisions, in the event that trust principal from the credit shelter trust (Trust B) is to be paid to or expended for the benefit of the Grantor's wife, then the Grantor's wife shall not participate in any such distribution or in the decision to make such distribution. In such event, only the successor Trustees shall participate in the decision to make such distribution. The Grantor's wife may, however, in her capacity as beneficiary and Trustee, participate in the distribution of Trust income to herself (in accordance with the provisions of ARTICLE VI). Furthermore, with respect to the credit shelter trust (Trust B), in no event shall the Grantor's wife, acting in her capacity as beneficiary or Trustee, possess any power or authority, if the possession of such power or authority would be deemed to be a General Power of Appointment under Sections 2041 and 2514 of the Internal Revenue Code.

F. No Trustee shall be required to obtain the order of any court to exercise any power or discretion under this trust. In addition, no Trustee shall be required to file any accounting with any public official.

G. Any Co-Trustee may delegate any or all Trustee duties and powers to any other Co-Trustee, provided that such authority may be revoked by the delegating trustee. Furthermore, any Trustee may delegate any and all trust administrative duties to any other party, provided that such delegation may be revoked by the delegating Trustee.

ARTICLE XV
Miscellaneous

A. This declaration of trust shall be governed by and construed according to the laws of the State of Wisconsin.

B. Whenever the context of this trust requires, the masculine gender includes the feminine and neuter, and vice versa, and the singular number includes the plural, and vice versa.

C. Except as otherwise provided herein, all payments of principal and income payable, or to become payable, to the beneficiary of any trust created hereunder shall not be subject to anticipation, assignment, pledge, sale or transfer in any manner, nor shall any said beneficiary have the power to anticipate or encumber such interest, nor shall such interest, while in the possession of the Trustee, be liable for, or subject to, the debts, contracts, obligations, liabilities or torts of any beneficiary.

D. If any provision of this trust instrument should be invalid or unenforceable, the remaining provisions shall continue to be fully effective.

E. Notwithstanding any contrary provision of this trust, the principal of any trust created hereunder shall vest absolutely in interest not later than twenty-one years after the death of the last survivor of the Grantor and any beneficiary who is living at the time of the creation of this trust. Immediately prior to the expiration of twenty-one years after the death of the last survivor of the above group, the principal of each trust that has not previously vested shall become payable to the issue of the Grantor and his wife, per stirpes.

F. If this trust or any trust created hereunder is the beneficiary of an IRA or any qualified tax-deferred retirement plan account, then the Trustee shall have the authority to take whatever steps are required so that the minimum required distribution amounts from such account are to be measured based on the life expectancy of an individual beneficiary of such trust. This shall include (but not be limited to) the authority to establish new sub-trusts that benefit individual beneficiaries. Any such steps shall be allowed so long as they are not contrary to the purposes of the trust as set forth hereunder.

G. In the event that any technical corrections must be made to this trust document, then any acting trustee shall have the authority to make such technical corrections; provided, however, that the corrections must be consistent with the Grantor's intentions in creating this trust, as set forth in this trust instrument, with regard to the beneficiaries of the trust, the uses and purposes of the trust, the distribution plan of the trust, etc.

IN WITNESS WHEREOF, the Grantor has executed this agreement, effective as of the above referenced date.

[notarized signatures of Darren Walters and Stephanie Walters]

Sample Trust #2

Sample Medicaid Planning Trust with:

- Lifetime Medicaid and Creditor Protection
- Grantor Trust Provision
- Posthumous estate tax planning
- Credit shelter trust/ Marital trust division
- Qualified Domestic Trust for foreign spouse

THE WHITE IRREVOCABLE TRUST

This Trust Agreement is made effective as of the _____ day of _____, 20___, by and between DOUG WHITE and LINDA WHITE, husband and wife, both currently residing at _____ (the "Grantors" or "Grantor"), and WARREN WHITE, who is the son of the Grantors, currently residing at _____, (hereinafter referred to as the "Trustee") on the following terms and conditions:

ARTICLE I
Purposes and Funding the Trust

A. The Grantors create this trust as a means by which assets are to be held and administered in accordance with the terms and conditions set forth in this instrument. The Grantors hereby transfer to the Trustee the sum of ten dollars ($10) in cash. In addition to the initial transfer by the Grantors of the sum of ten dollars ($10) in cash, the Grantors and anyone else may transfer additional property to the Trustee at any time. All assets received by the Trustee shall be managed and distributed in accordance with this Agreement. It is the Grantors' intent in creating this Trust to irrevocably transfer assets into this Trust for the use and benefit of a class of people, as described herein.

B. Specifically, this Trust is established as a vehicle into which residential real estate (along with other assets as may be contributed to the Trust from time to time) can be transferred for a class of beneficiaries, as described herein.

C. Unless specified otherwise at the time of the gift, one-half (1/2) of any gift to this trust given by either of the Grantors shall be presumed to be given by each Grantor.

ARTICLE II
Irrevocability

This Trust and all interests in it are irrevocable, and the Grantors have no power to alter, amend, revoke, or terminate any trust provision or interest, whether under this trust or under any statute or other rule of law.

ARTICLE III
Spendthrift Clause

To the extent permitted by law, the beneficiaries' interests will not be subject to their liabilities or creditor claims or to assignment or anticipation.

ARTICLE IV
During the Lifetime of the Grantors

A. As long as both Grantors are living, each Grantor shall have the right to live in one-half of any residential real property owned by the Trust. If only one grantor is living, then he or she shall have the right to live in all such residential real property.

B. As long as either Grantor is living, each Grantor shall have the right to disallow the sale of any residential real property owned by the Trust by a letter in writing signed by the Grantor and delivered to the Trustee.

C. If any residential real property owned by the Trust is sold, the Trust may (but is not obligated to) purchase alternative residential real property. If it does so, then each Grantor shall have a right to live in any one-half (1/2) of such residential real property (or, if one Grantor is living, then he or she shall have the right to live in such real property). Alternatively, the Trust may (but is not obligated to) utilize some or all of the trust income to pay for the Grantors' rent at a suitable alternative location. This right of the Trustee shall not include the right to pay for care for the Grantor(s) at any nursing home or any facility or residence that provides enhanced care services to its residents.

D. All property taxes, carrying charges, maintenance, expenses, etc. relating to real property owned by the Trust shall be the responsibility of the Grantor(s), so long as at least one Grantor resides in such real property.

E. In addition, the Trustee may pay to, or spend on behalf of the trust beneficiaries, as much of the remaining trust principal and income, as the Trustee deems appropriate for their health, education, maintenance and support, after taking into account, to the extent the trustee deems advisable, the other resources available to them.

F. Any distribution made by the trustee under Paragraph E of this ARTI-CLE shall require the consent of one person who is not receiving the distribution and who does not have a legal obligation to support the person receiving the distribution.

G. Each grantor shall have the authority, without the consent of any other party and in a non-fiduciary capacity, to remove trust assets that he or she contributed from the trust by substituting other assets of reasonably equivalent value.

H. It is the intent of the Grantors that, for income and capital gains tax purposes, each Grantor shall be treated as owner of the assets in the trust that he or she contributed under Section 675 of the Internal Revenue Code and that this trust be treated as a "grantor trust" under that section, for purposes of calculating income tax and capital gains tax under the Internal Revenue Code; particularly with respect to the provisions of Section 121 of the Code. All provisions in this trust shall be interpreted in accordance with this intent.

ARTICLE V
After the Death of the First Grantor

A. Upon the death of the first-to-die of the Grantors, the Trust assets that were contributed by the surviving Grantor shall continue to be held in trust under the terms and conditions set forth above in ARTICLE IV.

B. Upon the death of the first-to-die of the Grantors, the Trust assets that were contributed by the deceased Grantor shall be distributed to whomever among the issue of the Grantors that the deceased Grantor shall appoint these assets by a Will that specifically references this special power of appointment. The assets not appointed pursuant to this power of appointment shall continue to be held, managed and distributed as follows:

B1. The amount of such trust assets that can pass free of federal and state estate tax by reason of the unified credit, estate tax exclusion amount and/or any other estate tax exemption (taking into account other assets that are part of the deceased Grantor's taxable estate that pass outside of this Trust) shall continue to be held in a **credit shelter trust**, the terms and conditions for which are set forth hereinafter in ARTICLE VI.

B2. The remainder of such assets shall be held in a **marital trust** the terms and conditions for which are set forth hereinafter in ARTICLE VII. However, if the surviving spouse is not a citizen of the United States at the time of the death of the first spouse, then this share shall instead be held in a **qualified domestic trust**, the terms and conditions for which are set forth hereinafter in ARTICLE VIII.

ARTICLE VI
Credit Shelter Trust

The credit shelter trust established under Paragraph B1 of ARTICLE V shall be held, administered and distributed as follows:

A. The Trustee shall pay to or apply for the benefit of the surviving Grantor, all of the net income of the trust.

B. As long as the surviving Grantor is living, the surviving Grantor shall have the right to live in any residential real property owned by the Trust.

C. As long the surviving Grantor is living, the surviving Grantor shall have the right to disallow the sale of any residential real property owned by the Trust by a letter in writing signed by the surviving Grantor and delivered to the Trustee.

D. As long as the surviving Grantor is living, if any residential real property owned by the Trust is sold, the Trust may (but is not required to) provide him or her with alternative residential housing of equivalent quality. The Trust may accomplish this either by purchasing alternative residential property and allowing the surviving Grantor to reside in such property rent-free (but subject to the provisions of Paragraph D of this ARTICLE), or by leasing alternative housing for the surviving Grantor and paying the rent for the surviving Grantor from the trust income for the rest of his or her life. This right of the Trustee shall not include the right to pay for care for the Grantor at any nursing home or any facility or residence that provides enhanced care services to its residents.

E. All property taxes, carrying charges, maintenance, expenses, etc. relating to real property owned by the Trust shall be the responsibility of the surviving Grantor, so long as he or she resides in such real property.

F. In addition, the Trustee may pay to, or spend on behalf of the Grantors' children as much of the remaining trust assets, including trust income and trust principal, as the trustee deems appropriate. However, the Trustee may not make any distributions from this trust to himself without the consent of at least one other child of the Grantors.

G. Upon the death of the surviving Grantor, the Trustee shall distribute all remaining trust assets to the Grantors' children, in equal shares, per stirpes.

ARTICLE VII
Marital Trust

A marital trust established under Paragraph B2 of ARTICLE V shall be held, administered and distributed as follows:

A. During the lifetime of the surviving Grantor, the Trustee shall pay to him or her all of this trust's net income in convenient installments, but at least annually.

B. The Trustee may not hold property that does not produce income in this trust without the consent of the surviving Grantor.

C. As long as the surviving Grantor is living, the surviving Grantor shall have the right to live in any residential real property owned by the Trust.

D. As long the surviving Grantor is living, the surviving Grantor shall have the right to disallow the sale of any residential real property owned by the Trust by a letter in writing signed by the surviving Grantor and delivered to the Trustee.

E. As long the surviving Grantor is living, if any residential real property owned by the Trust is sold, the Trust may provide him or her with alternative residential housing of equivalent quality. The Trust may accomplish this either by purchasing alternative residential property and allowing the surviving Grantor to reside in such property rent-free (but subject to the provisions of Paragraph G of this ARTICLE), or by leasing alternative housing for the surviving Grantor and paying the rent with the trust income for the surviving Grantor for the rest of his or her life

F. The rights contained in Paragraphs C through E are specifically intended to fulfill the requirements necessary to be considered a "qualifying income interest for life" under section 2056(b)(7)(B)(ii)(I) of the Internal Revenue Code. If that section would require any further rights in any residential real property owned by the Trust for the marital deduction to be preserved, the surviving Grantor is hereby granted whatever power and authority is necessary for that purpose.

G. All property taxes, carrying charges, maintenance, expenses, etc. relating to real property owned by the Trust shall be the responsibility of the surviving Grantor, so long as he or she resides in such real property.

H. It is the Grantors' intent that the Trust created under this paragraph shall qualify for the federal estate tax marital deduction, and all provisions of this instrument shall be construed consistent with this intent. It is expressly provided that the grant of rights, powers, privileges, and authority to the Trustee in connection with the imposition of duties upon the Trustee by any provision of this Trust or by any statute relating thereto, shall not be effective if it would disqualify the marital deduction as established in this Trust. The Trustee shall not, in the exercise of its discretion, make any determination inconsistent with the foregoing.

I. Upon the later death of the surviving Grantor, the Trustee shall distribute any remaining trust principal to the Grantors' children, in equal shares, per stirpes.

ARTICLE VIII
Qualified Domestic Trust

A Qualified Domestic Trust established under Paragraph B2 of ARTICLE V shall be held, administered and distributed as follows:

A. These provisions are intended to insure that the gift to this trust upon the death of the first Grantor shall meet all requirements as a **Qualified Domestic Trust** as defined in Section 2056A of the Internal Revenue Code (or in any successor provision), in order to permit the Trustee (and/or the Executor of the deceased Grantor's estate who is preparing the estate's estate tax return) to qualify such bequest for the marital deduction. The Trustee is authorized to amend the provisions of this trust, as required, in order to qualify it at the time of the Grantor's death as a Qualified Domestic Trust as defined in IRC Section 2056A. All provisions of this ARTICLE shall be construed in such a manner as best to effect these intents:

B. The Trustee is authorized in its absolute discretion to determine whether to elect under Section 2056A of the Internal Revenue Code or any successor provision to qualify this bequest as a Qualified Domestic Trust (QDOT) in order to qualify for the federal estate tax marital deduction.

C. To the extent not inconsistent with the terms of Paragraph D of this ARTICLE and to the extent not inconsistent with the purposes of this Trust as set forth in Paragraph A of this ARTICLE, the income and principal of this trust shall be held and distributed under the provisions set forth in ARTICLE VII (the Marital Trust). However, no term referenced in that ARTICLE shall apply is such term would cause the assets being distributed to this Trust to be ineligible for the marital deduction.

D. The Trustee shall comply with the requirements for security arrangements for qualified domestic trusts as set forth in Treas. Reg. section 20.2056A 2(d)(1)(i) or (ii), and or any subsequent regulations, summarized as follows:

(1) TRUST IN EXCESS OF $2 MILLION. If the fair market value of the assets passing to the trust (determined without reduction for any indebtedness thereon) exceeds $2 million on the relevant valuation date, then the Trustee must at all times during the term of the Trust either satisfy the U.S. Bank as Trustee requirement (see Treas. Reg. section 20.2056A 2(d)(1)(i)(A)), or furnish a bond that satisfies the requirements of Treas. Reg. section 20.2056A 2(d)(1)(i)(B), or furnish an irrevocable letter of credit that satisfies the requirements of Treas. Reg. section 20.2056A 2(d)(1)(i)(C), (hereinafter referred to as the U.S. Bank, Bond, or Letter of Credit Requirement). The Trustee

may alternate between any of the security arrangements described in the preceding sentence provided that, at all times during the term of the trust, one of the arrangements is operative. If the Trustee elects to furnish a bond or letter of credit as security, then in the event the Internal Revenue Service draws on the instrument in accordance with its terms, neither the U.S. Trustee nor any other person will seek a return of any part of the remittance until after April 15th of the calendar year following the year in which the bond or letter of credit is drawn upon.

(2) TRUST OF $2 MILLION OR LESS. If the fair market value of the assets passing to the trust (determined without reduction for any indebtedness) is $2 million or less on the relevant valuation date, then the Trustee must comply with either the U.S. Bank, Bond, or Letter of Credit Requirement only if more than 35% of the fair market value of the trust assets, determined annually on the last day of the taxable year of the trust, consists of real property located outside the United States. For purposes of determining whether more than 35% of the trust assets consist of foreign real property, Treas. Reg. section 20.2056A 2(d)(1)(ii)(B) applies.

(3) DETERMINATION OF VALUE. For purposes of determining whether the fair market value of the trust assets exceeds $2 million, the Trustee is authorized to make the election under Treas. Reg. section 20.2056A 2(d)(1)(iv)(A) with respect to real property used as the Grantor's spouse's personal residence.

(4) AMOUNT OF BOND OR LETTER OF CREDIT. For purposes of determining the amount of the bond or letter of credit, the Trustee is authorized to make the election under Treas. Reg. section 20.2056A 2(d)(1)(iv)(B) with respect to real property used as the spouse's personal residence.

(5) ANNUAL STATEMENTS. The Trustee is directed to file any annual statements required under Treas Reg. section 20.2056A 2(d)(3).

(6) GENERAL CONDUCT. Notwithstanding anything contained herein to the contrary, the U.S. Trustee is hereby authorized to enter into alternative plans or arrangements with the Internal Revenue Service pursuant to Treas. Reg. section 20.2056A 2(d)(4) to assure collection of the deferred estate tax, in lieu of the provisions contained herein.

(7) REFERENCES TO REGULATIONS. All references to "Treas. Reg." in this document shall be references to regulations published under 26 CFR as in effect on the date of execution of this document, or, in

the event that any such regulation is amended or superseded thereafter, to the regulation (or any successor regulation) as so amended.

E. Upon the death of the surviving Grantor, the Trustee shall distribute any remaining trust principal to the Grantors' children, in equal shares, per stirpes.

ARTICLE IX
Upon the death of the Second Grantor

Upon the death of the second-to-die of the Grantors, the trust assets contributed by the second-to-die of the Grantors shall be distributed to whomever among the issue of the second-to-die of the Grantors shall appoint said assets by a Will that specifically references this special power of appointment. All such trust assets not distributed in accordance with the exercise of such appointment shall be distributed to the Grantors' children, in equal shares, per stirpes.

ARTICLE X
Interests Vesting to a Beneficiary under the age of Twenty-one (21) Years

If any Trust principal or income shall vest in absolute ownership in a minor, the Trustee shall have the authority to: 1. Hold and manage the property and defer payment or distribution of all or a part of the property to that minor until that minor reaches the age of twenty-one (21) years; 2. Distribute part or all of the property to a custodian or guardian for the minor under the laws of the jurisdiction where the minor resides, and 3. Directly apply part or all of the property for the minor's health, education, support (in his/her accustomed manner of living) or maintenance costs.

ARTICLE XI
Trustee's Powers

A. The Trustee is exclusively empowered to do the following, exclusively in the Trustee's fiduciary capacity:

1. To hold and retain all or any property received from any source, without regard to diversification, risk, productivity, or the Trustee's personal interest in such property in any other capacity, and to keep all or part of the trust property at any place within the United States or abroad.

2. To invest and reinvest the trust funds (or leave them temporarily uninvested), in any type of property and every kind of investment, including (but not limited to) corporate obligations of every kind, preferred or common stocks, securities of any regulated investment trust, and partnership interests.

3. To participate in the operation of any business or other enterprise, and to incorporate, dissolve, or otherwise change the form of such business.

4. To deposit trust funds in any commercial savings or savings and loan accounts.

5. To borrow money for any reasonable trust purpose and upon such terms, including (but not limited to) interest rates, security, and loan duration, as the trustee deems advisable. The Trustee may secure the repayment of any or all amounts so borrowed by mortgage or pledge of any property, whether real property or personal property, as the Trustee deems advisable. The Trustee may also arrange for the mortgaging of trust property, whether through a private lender or through any bank or other financial institution.

6. To lend trust funds to such persons and on such terms, including (but not limited to) interest rates, security, and loan duration, as the Trustee deems advisable; provided, however, that the Trustee may not lend money to the Grantor's estate without receiving adequate security and an adequate rate of interest.

7. To sell or otherwise dispose of trust assets, including (but not limited to) trust real property, for cash or credit, at public or private sale, and with such warranties or indemnifications as the Trustee deems advisable.

8. To buy assets of any type from any person on such terms, including (but not limited to), cash or credit, interest rates, and security, as the Trustee deems advisable; provided, however, that the Trustee may not buy assets from the Grantor's estate other than at their fair market value.

9. To improve, develop, manage or abandon any trust assets, as the Trustee deems advisable.

10. To hold property in the name of any trustee or any custodian or nominee, without disclosing this trust; but the Trustee is responsible for the acts of any custodian or nominee so used.

11. To pay and advance money for the trust's protection and for all expenses, losses, and liabilities sustained in its administration.

12. To prosecute or defend any action for the protection of the trust, the Trustee in the performance of the Trustee's duties, or both, and to pay, contest, or settle any claim by or against the trust or the Trustee in the performance of the Trustee's duties.

13. To employ persons, even if they are associated with the Trustee, to advise or assist the Trustee in the performance of the Trustee's duties.

14. To determine what is principal or income and what items shall be charged or credited to either.

15. To distribute trust assets in kind or in cash.

16. To execute and deliver any instruments necessary or useful in the exercise of any of these powers.

17. To rent or lease out any real property held by the trust to any tenant upon such terms as the Trustee, in his or her sole discretion, determines to be in the best interest of the Trust.

18. To assign or delegate, for convenience purposes, the authority to perform administrative tasks in connection with the Trust, to any person that the Trustee deems appropriate.

B. In making any payment to a minor or disabled beneficiary, the Trustee may expend such payments for the benefit of such beneficiary or make such payments to such beneficiary, or to his or her parent, guardian, personal representative, or the person with whom he or she resides, without having to look to the proper application of those payments. This paragraph does not limit the Trustee's powers and must be construed to enable the Trustee to give each beneficiary the fullest possible benefit and enjoyment of all of the trust income and principal to which he or she is entitled.

ARTICLE XII
The Trustee

A. WARREN WHITE, who is the son of the Grantors, shall serve as Trustee of this trust of all trusts created hereunder, and he shall serve without bond. If, for any reason, he is unable or unwilling to serve or to continue to serve, then REBECCA WHITE, who is the daughter of the Grantors, shall serve as successor Trustee, and she shall serve without bond. If, for any reason, she is unable or unwilling to serve or to continue to serve, then the children of the Grantors shall, by majority vote, name a successor trustee, and such trustee shall serve without bond.

B. Notwithstanding the above Trustee designation provisions, no acting trustee shall possess any power or authority, if the possession of such power or authority would be deemed to be a General Power of Appointment under Sections 2041 and 2514 of the Internal Revenue Code.

C. No Trustee shall be required to obtain the order of any court to exercise any power or discretion under this Trust.

D. Any Trustee may delegate any and all trust administrative duties to any third party, provided that such delegation may be revoked.

E. No Trustee shall be required to file any accounting with any public official.

F. No Trustee shall be liable for damage to, loss of, or mismanagement of, Trust assets in the absence of bad faith.

ARTICLE XIII
Miscellaneous

A. This declaration of trust shall be governed by and construed according to the laws of the State of _____.

B. Whenever the context of this trust requires, the masculine gender includes the feminine and neuter, and vice versa, and the singular number includes the plural, and vice versa.

C. Except as otherwise provided herein, all payments of principal and income payable, or to become payable, to the beneficiary of any trust created hereunder shall not be subject to anticipation, assignment, pledge, sale or transfer in any manner, nor shall any said beneficiary have the power to anticipate or encumber such interest, nor shall such interest, while in the possession of the Trustee, be liable for, or subject to, the debts, contracts, obligations, liabilities or torts of any beneficiary.

D. If any provision of this trust instrument should be invalid or unenforceable, the remaining provisions shall continue to be fully effective.

E. Notwithstanding any contrary provision of this trust, the principal of any trust created hereunder shall vest absolutely in interest not later than twenty-one years after the death of the last survivor of the Grantors and any beneficiary who is living at the time of the creation of this trust. Immediately prior to the expiration of twenty-one years after the death of the last survivor of the above group, the principal of each trust that has not previously vested shall become payable to the issue of the Grantors, per stirpes.

F. If this trust or any trust created hereunder is the beneficiary of an IRA or any qualified tax-deferred retirement plan account, then the Trustee shall have the authority to take whatever steps are required so that the minimum required distribution amounts from such account are to be measured based on the life expectancy of an individual beneficiary of such trust. This shall include (but not be limited to) the authority to establish new sub-trusts that benefit individual beneficiaries. Any such steps shall be allowed so long as they are not contrary to the purposes of the trust as set forth hereunder

G. In the event that any technical corrections must be made to this trust document, then any acting trustee shall have the authority to make such technical corrections; provided, however, that the corrections must be consistent with the Grantors' intentions in creating this trust, as set forth in this trust instrument, with regard to the beneficiaries of the trust, the uses and purposes of the trust, the distribution plan of the trust, etc.

IN WITNESS WHEREOF, the Grantor has executed this agreement, effective as of the above referenced date.

[notarized signatures of Grantor and Trustee]

Sample Trust #3

Sample Irrevocable Life Insurance Trust with:

- Spouse as trustee
- "Crummey" withdrawal rights provisions
- Contingent Marital Trust at first death
- Credit shelter trust at first death
- Individual Single Beneficiary trusts at second death

THE SAMANTHA McNEIL IRREVOCABLE LIFE INSURANCE TRUST

This trust agreement is effective as of _____, 2011, by SAMANTHA McNEIL, currently residing at _____ (the "Grantor"), and the Grantor's husband, JOSEPH McNEIL, also currently residing at _____ (the "Trustee") on the following terms and conditions:

ARTICLE I
Purposes and Funding the Trust

A. The Grantor creates this trust as a means by which assets, which may include one (1) or more policies of insurance on her life, may be held for the benefit of her family, on the terms and conditions set forth in this instrument. It is the Grantor's intent in creating this trust that all gifts made to this trust be complete and gifts of present interests for federal gift tax purposes, and that the assets of this trust, including any life insurance proceeds, be excluded from her gross estate for federal estate tax purposes. All provisions of this trust shall be construed in such a manner as best to effect these intents.

B. The Grantor transfers to the Trustee the property listed in Schedule A [omitted], to be held and administered according to the terms of this trust. The Grantor and anyone else may transfer additional property, whether or not such property is listed on Schedule A, to the Trustee at any time, whether during the Grantor's lifetime or after her death, to be held and administered according to the trust's terms. The Trustee may refuse to accept any gift to a trust hereunder if the Trustee deems it to be in the best interests of the trust and its beneficiaries, and the Trustee may accept it subject to one (1) or more conditions imposed by the donor on the Trustee, if the Trustee deems it to be in the best interests of the trust and the beneficiaries. No condition imposed on a gift and accepted by the Trustee may in any way alter, amend, or change the rights of a beneficiary with respect to any prior gifts. The Grantor retains no right, title, or interest in any trust property.

ARTICLE II
Irrevocability

This trust and all interests in it are irrevocable, and the Grantor has no power to alter, amend, revoke, or terminate any trust provision or interest, whether under this trust or under any statute or other rule of law.

ARTICLE III
Annual Demand Power

During the Grantor's life, the following demand powers shall exist with respect to contributions to the trust:

A. Immediately following any contribution to the trust, each of the Grantor's children, shall have the right to withdraw an amount equal to a pro rata share of each contribution to the trust (subject to the limitations in this article). Such pro rata portion will be the amount of the contribution, divided by the number of the beneficiaries of this right of withdrawal at the time of the contribution. If any such beneficiary demands and receives a distribution in excess of the amount authorized under this article, the Trustee shall immediately notify him or her in writing, requiring the prompt repayment of such excess amount. This demand power takes precedence over any other power or discretion granted the Trustee or any other person.

B. With respect to these demand powers, the following rules shall apply:

1. This demand power can be exercised by a written request delivered to the Trustee. If a beneficiary is unable to exercise such demand power because of a legal disability, any legally authorized personal representative, including (but not limited to) a parent, guardian, committee, or conservator, may make the demand on such beneficiary's behalf. In the event that no such legally authorized personal representative is available, then the Trustee may, acting as a fiduciary for the legally disabled beneficiary, exercise the demand power on the beneficiary's behalf. However, in no event can the Grantor make the demand for any beneficiary.

2. The Trustee must reasonably notify the person who would exercise the demand power granted under this Article of its existence and of any contributions made to the trust that are subject to the power.

3. The maximum amount that any beneficiary may withdraw with respect to all contributions made by the same donor during a single calendar year shall be the lesser of the total amount of such contributions and the amount of the federal gift tax annual exclusion in effect on the date of the earliest of such contributions. If requested by a married donor at the time of a contribution, the alternative limitation based on the gift tax annual exclusion shall be two (2) times the amount of the gift tax annual exclusion.

4. Each beneficiary's unexercised right to withdraw a contribution shall lapse after thirty (30) days following notification to the beneficiary of the contribution, provided, however, that in any calendar year the extent of the lapse of a right of withdrawal shall not exceed the greater of Five Thousand Dollars ($5,000.00) or five percent (5%) of the value of the trust assets from which such withdrawal could be satisfied. To the extent that a withdrawal power does not lapse on a particular December 31, the withdrawal power continues to be exercisable (whether or not a contribution was made in that year), in all later years, subject to the same lapse provisions.

5. The Trustee may satisfy a demand for a distribution by distributing cash, other assets, or fractional interests in other assets, as the Trustee deems appropriate. Without limiting the Trustee's power to select assets to satisfy a demand, the Grantor prefers that cash or tangible assets be distributed before life insurance policies and intangible assets, unless the Trustee decides that another selection is warranted.

6. "Contribution" means any cash or other assets transferred to the Trustee to be held as part of the trust funds and the payment of any premiums on life insurance policies owned (in whole or in part) by the trust. The amount of any contribution is its federal gift tax value, as determined by the Trustee at the time of the contribution.

7. After the calendar year in which the trust is created, a person who makes a contribution to any trust created under this instrument may, by a written instrument delivered to the Trustee at the time of such contribution and with respect solely to the contribution then being made, do one (1) or more of the following: (a) increase or decrease the amount subject to any person's demand power as to such new contribution; and (b) change the period during which any person's demand power as to such new contribution may be exercised. No such direction may in any way alter, amend or change such person's demand power with respect to any prior contributions.

ARTICLE IV
During the Grantor's Life

During the Grantor's life, the Trustee shall hold and administer all funds remaining after the exercise or lapse of all demand powers created under Article III, using some or all of the trust's net income and principal to pay premiums on policies of life insurance on the life of the Grantor, adding to principal any income not so used. In addition, subject to the restrictions set forth in later provisions of this trust, the Trustee may distribute to the Grantor's husband and/or children, or may spend on their behalf, so much of the trust principal and income (including all or none) as the Trustee deems necessary for their health, education, maintenance and support. However, the Trustee may not use any trust income or principal in a manner that would give the Grantor any pecuniary benefit, or pay for any debt or obligation for which the Grantor would otherwise be liable. In addition, the husband of the Grantor shall not participate in the decision to make any distribution under this Paragraph. Instead, the successor Trustees shall have the sole authority to make a distribution under this Paragraph.

ARTICLE V
After the Grantor's Death

Upon the Grantor's death, the Trustee will hold the trust funds, including any funds received on account of the Grantor's death, in trust as follows:

A. If the Grantor is survived by her husband, the Trustee shall hold the proceeds of any life insurance policies on the Grantor's life that are included in her gross estate for federal estate tax purposes, whether or not she died within three (3) years of transferring such policies to the trust, in a separate trust, for the exclusive lifetime benefit of the Grantor's husband. During the lifetime of the Grantor's husband, the Trustee will pay to him all of this trust's net income in convenient installments, but at least annually. The Trustee will also pay to him so much of this trust's principal (including all or none) as the Trustee deems necessary or advisable for his health, education, support and maintenance. The Trustee may not hold unproductive property in this trust without the consent of the Grantor's husband. It is the Grantor's intent that the trust created under this paragraph shall qualify for the federal estate tax marital deduction, and all provisions of this instrument shall be construed consistent with this intent. It is expressly provided that the grant of rights, powers, privileges, and authority to the Trustee in connection with the imposition of duties upon the Trustee by any provision of this Trust or by any statute relating thereto, shall not be effective if it would disqualify the marital deduction as established in this Trust. The Trustee shall not, in the exercise of its discretion, make any determination inconsistent with the foregoing. Upon the later death of the Grantor's husband, the Trustee shall distribute any remaining trust principal pursuant to paragraph C of this Article.

B. If the Grantor is survived by her husband, the Trustee will hold any trust funds not distributed pursuant to paragraph A, above, in trust (including any portion of the marital trust established under Paragraph A disclaimed by the Grantor's husband pursuant to Section 2518 of the Internal Revenue Code B i.e., a qualified disclaimer), and shall administer and distribute such funds as follows:

B.1. During the lifetime of the Grantor's husband, the Trustee shall pay to or for the benefit of the Grantor's husband, in quarterly or more frequent installments, all of the net income of the trust.

B.2. During the lifetime of the Grantor's husband, the Trustee may, in his or her sole discretion, also pay to or apply for the benefit of the Grantor's husband and/or children or may spend on their behalf, so much of the trust principal and income (including all or none) as the Trustee deems advisable; provided, however, that the husband of the Grantor shall not participate in the decision to make any distribution under this Paragraph. Instead, the successor Trustees shall have the sole authority to make a distribution under this Paragraph.

B.3. In addition to the above provisions, during the month of December of any calendar year, the Grantor's husband shall have the power to direct the Trustee to pay to her out of the trust's principal in each year, an amount not in excess of the greater of five thousand dollars ($5,000) or five percent (5%) of the aggregate value of the trust principal as determined at the end of each taxable year of the trust. This power is non-cumulative and can be exercised only by an instrument in writing signed by the Grantor's husband during the month of December and delivered that month to the Trustee in any calendar year of withdrawal.

B.4. Upon the death of the Grantor's husband, the Trustee shall divide the remaining trust principal and income in the same manner as is provided for in Paragraph C of this ARTICLE.

C. Upon the Grantor's death if her husband does not survive him, the Trustee shall divide and distribute the remaining trust principal among the children of the Grantor; provided, however, that the share any child of the Grantor under the age of thirty-five (35) shall be held in an individual single beneficiary trust for the benefit of such child under the terms and conditions set forth hereinafter in ARTICLE VI. If any of the Grantor's children do not survive the Grantor, then the share of such child shall be distributed to his or her issue, in equal shares, per stirpes, or, if he or she does not leave issue then living, then to the Grantor's issue, in equal shares, per stirpes.

ARTICLE VI
Individual Single Beneficiary Trusts

An individual trust that is maintained for the benefit of a single beneficiary shall be held, administered and distributed as follows:

A. The trustee shall pay to or apply for the benefit of the beneficiary, until distribution pursuant to Paragraph B, as much of the net income and/or principal from the trust as the trustee in his/her sole discretion shall determine, for the health, education, support (in his/her accustomed manner of living) or maintenance of said beneficiary, taking into consideration to the extent the trustee deems advisable, any other income or resources of said beneficiary known to the trustee.

B. Upon the beneficiary's attainment of age twenty-five (25) or if the beneficiary has already attained the age of twenty-five (25) prior to the Trust's creation, the trustee shall distribute to that beneficiary one-third (1/3) of the trust principal (and accumulated income). Upon the beneficiary's attainment of age thirty (30) or if the beneficiary has already attained the age of thirty (30) prior to the trust's creation, the trustee shall distribute to that beneficiary one-half (1/2) of the trust principal (and accumulated income). Upon the beneficiary's attainment of age thirty-five (35), the trustee shall terminate the trust and shall distribute outright to the beneficiary all of the remaining principal of the trust.

C. In the event that the beneficiary should die prior to the termination of the trust, the trust principal and income shall be distributed to whomever said beneficiary shall appoint said funds (by a will specifically referring to this power of appointment), or in default of appointment to the beneficiary's issue per stirpes, or if the beneficiary leaves no issue, to the grantor's other issue, per stirpes.

ARTICLE VII
Interests Vesting in a Minor

If, when any trust created by this instrument ends, any principal vests in absolute ownership in any minor beneficiary, the Trustee may, if the Trustee deems it appropriate to do so, hold such interest in trust until the beneficiary attains age twenty-one (21), paying so much (including all or none) of the trust's net income and principal to the beneficiary as the Trustee deems appropriate for the beneficiary's health, education, support, and maintenance, adding to principal any undistributed income. The Trustee may make such payments to the beneficiary, or to his or her parent, guardian, or the person with whom the beneficiary resides, without having to look to the proper application of those payments. The Trustee may also make any payments to a custodian (who may be the Trustee) under any applicable Uniform Transfers (or Gifts) to Minors Act. When the beneficiary attains age twenty-one (21), the Trustee will pay him or her all of the remaining trust funds and this trust will end. If the beneficiary dies before attaining age twenty-one (21), the Trustee will pay all of such funds to the beneficiary's estate. The authority conferred on the Trustee is a power only and will not operate to suspend absolute vesting of any property in such beneficiary.

ARTICLE VIII
Spendthrift Clause

To the extent permitted by law, the beneficiaries' interests will not be subject to their liabilities or creditor claims or to assignment or anticipation.

ARTICLE IX
Uneconomical Trusts

If, after the Grantor's death, any trust created under this instrument ever shall have a fair market value of twenty-five thousand dollars ($25,000) or less, the Trustee may terminate such trust and distribute the trust funds to the issue of the Grantor, in equal shares, per stirpes.

ARTICLE X
Merger, Consolidation, and Division

For convenience of administration or investment, the Trustee of any trusts created hereunder may:

A. Invest the assets of multiple trusts in a single fund, assigning them undivided interests in such common fund, dividing the income proportionately and accounting for them separately;

B. Merge or consolidate any trust created hereunder together with any other trusts having the same trustee and substantially the same dispositive provisions; and

C. Divide any trust created hereunder into two (2) or more separate trusts, each such trust to contain a fractional share of the assets of the trust before such division.

ARTICLE XI
Trustee's Powers

A. The Trustee is exclusively empowered to do the following, exclusively in the Trustee's fiduciary capacity:

1. To hold and retain all or any property received from any source, without regard to diversification, risk, productivity, or the Trustee's personal interest in such property in any other capacity, and to keep all or part of the trust property at any place within the United States or abroad.

2. To invest and reinvest the trust funds (or leave them temporarily uninvested), in any type of property and every kind of investment, including (but not limited to) corporate obligations of every kind, preferred or common stocks, securities of any regulated investment trust, and partnership interests.

3. To participate in the operation of any business or other enterprise, and to incorporate, dissolve, or otherwise change the form of such business.

4. To deposit trust funds in any commercial savings or savings and loan accounts.

5. To borrow money (and mortgage, pledge or encumber any trust real or personal property to secure such loan) for any reasonable trust purpose and upon any such terms, including (but not limited to) interest rates, security, and loan duration, as the trustee deems advisable.

6. To lend trust funds to such persons and on such terms, including (but not limited to) interest rates, security, and loan duration, as the Trustee deems advisable; provided, however, that the trustee may not lend money to the Grantor's estate without receiving adequate security and an adequate rate of interest.

7. To sell or otherwise dispose of trust assets, including (but not limited to) trust real property, for cash or credit, at public or private sale, and with such warranties or indemnifications as the Trustee deems advisable.

8. To buy assets of any type from any person on such terms, including (but not limited to), cash or credit, interest rates, and security, as the Trustee deems advisable; provided, however, that the Trustee may not buy assets from the Grantor's estate other than at their fair market value.

9. To improve, develop, manage, lease, or abandon any trust assets, as the Trustee deems advisable.

10. To pay and advance money for the trust's protection and for all expenses, losses, and liabilities sustained in its administration.

11. To prosecute or defend any action for the protection of the trust, the Trustee in the performance of the Trustee's duties, or both, and to pay, contest, or settle any claim by or against the trust or the Trustee in the performance of the Trustee's duties.

12. To employ persons, even if they are associated with the Trustee, to advise or assist the Trustee in the performance of the Trustee's duties.

13. To determine what is principal or income and what items shall be charged or credited to either.

14. To distribute trust assets in kind or in cash.

15. To execute and deliver any instruments necessary or useful in the exercise of any of these powers.

B. During the administration of the Grantor's estate under applicable state law, the Trustee may use the trust funds, in the Trustee's discretion, to lend money to and buy assets from the Grantor's estate, on such terms and conditions as the Trustee deems to be in the best interests of the trust's beneficiaries. The Trustee will not, however, make grants to the Grantor's estate or otherwise distribute funds except through bona fide loans or purchases, it not being the Grantor's intention to make any persons who are not specifically so identified in this instrument, the beneficiaries of any trust created hereunder.

C. With respect to any life insurance policies held as part of the trust funds, the following special rules shall apply:

1. The Trustee may, in the Trustee's discretion, pay any premiums or other charges from trust income or principal. If the trust funds are inadequate to pay such premiums or charges, the Trustee may, in the Trustee's discretion, do one or more of the following: (a) use any automatic premium loan feature; (b) borrow against any policy cash reserves (whether or not on the policy for which premium or charges will be paid); or (c) elect any automatic non-forfeiture feature.

2. Any additional insurance policies, no matter how acquired (including, but not limited to acquisition by gift, conversion, reissue, consolidation), should be listed on Schedule A, but failure to do so does not affect the trust's policy ownership.

3. The Trustee may, in the Trustee's discretion, refuse to enter into or maintain any litigation, endorse policy payments, or take other action respecting any trust insurance policies, until the Trustee has been indemnified against all expenses and liabilities that, in the Trustee's judgment, may be involved in such action.

4. The Trustee need not inquire whether or not the Trustee or the trust has been designated the beneficiary of any insurance policy or other death benefit, and the Trustee need not act with respect to such policies until receipt of written notice that the Trustee or the trust is a beneficiary.

5. No Trustee shall participate in the exercise of any discretion (including any discretion that would constitute an "incident of ownership" within the meaning of IRC 2042) with respect to any policy of insurance on his or her life held hereunder.

D. In making any payment to a minor or disabled beneficiary, the Trustee may expend such payments for the benefit of such beneficiary or make such payments to such beneficiary, or to his or her parent, guardian, personal representative, or the person with whom he or she resides, without having to look to the proper application of those payments. This paragraph does not limit the Trustee's powers and must be construed to enable the Trustee to give each beneficiary the fullest possible benefit and enjoyment of all of the trust income and principal to which he or she is entitled.

ARTICLE XII
The Trustees

A. Subject to the limitations set forth in Paragraph D of this ARTICLE and those contained elsewhere in this instrument, JOSEPH McNEIL, who is the husband of the Grantor, shall serve as trustee of this trust and he shall serve without bond. If, for any reason, he is unable or unwilling to serve or to continue to serve, then the Grantor's two children, STUART McNEIL and TIFFANY McNEIL, shall serve as successor Co-Trustees, and they shall serve without bond. If, for any reason, either of them is unable or unwilling to serve or to continue to serve, then the other shall serve as sole Trustee, and shall serve without bond.

B. Subject to the limitation set forth in Paragraph C of this ARTICLE, Grantor's two children, STUART McNEIL and TIFFANY McNEIL, shall serve as Co-Trustees of all individual single beneficiary trusts administered under ARTICLE VI of this Trust Agreement, and they shall serve without bond. If, for any reason, one of them is unable or unwilling to serve or to continue to serve, then the other shall serve as sole Trustee, and he or she shall serve without bond.

C. Notwithstanding the Trustee designation set forth in Paragraph B of this ARTICLE, no child of the Grantor shall be eligible to serve as Trustee of any individual single beneficiary trust administered under ARTICLE VI unless he or she is age forty-five (45) years or older. Unless and until any trustee designated in Paragraph B reaches that age, the designated successor Trustee shall serve in his or her stead; or, if one of two designated Co-Trustees is under that age, then the other Co-Trustee shall serve as sole Trustee until such child reaches the age of forty-five (45) years. If no trustee is available for any individual single beneficiary trust by reason of this limitation, then the Grantor's brother, MICHAEL WILLIAMSON, shall serve as successor trustee of such trust, and he shall serve without bond.

D. Notwithstanding any other provision hereunder, in the event that Trust assets from the trust principal that are in excess of the greater of $5,000 or 5% of the aggregate value of the Trust principal, are, in any calendar year, to be paid to or applied for the benefit of any beneficiary under any provision hereunder, the Grantor's husband shall not participate in any such distribution or in the decision to make such distribution. In such event, only the successor Trustee shall participate in the decision to make such distribution. Furthermore, in no event shall the Grantor's husband or any other Trustee of any trust created hereunder, acting in his or her capacity as beneficiary or Trustee, possess any power or authority, if the possession of such power or authority would be deemed to be a General Power of Appointment under Sections 2041 and 2514 (or any similar or successor statute) of the Internal Revenue Code.

E. No Trustee shall be required to obtain the order of any court to exercise any power or discretion under this trust.

F. Any Trustee or Co-Trustee shall have the authority to delegate any trustee duty to any other Co-Trustee, provided that such delegation may be revoked at any time by the delegating trustee. Further, the Trustee(s) may delegate any and all trust administrative duties to any third party, provided that such delegation may be revoked.

G. No Trustee shall be required to file any accounting with any public official. The Trustee must, however, maintain accurate records concerning the trust. If requested by a Trust beneficiary, the Trustee shall furnish an annual accounting of the trust's condition, including receipts and disbursements, to each adult beneficiary of the current trust income. This required accounting may be satisfied by a copy of the trust's federal income tax return, if one is required.

ARTICLE XII
Miscellaneous

A. This declaration of trust shall be governed by and construed according to the laws of the State of _____.

B. Whenever the context of this trust requires, the masculine gender includes the feminine and neuter, and vice versa, and the singular number includes the plural, and vice versa.

C. Except as otherwise provided herein, all payments of principal and income payable, or to become payable, to the beneficiary of any trust created hereunder shall not be subject to anticipation, assignment, pledge, sale or transfer in any manner, nor shall any said beneficiary have the power to anticipate or encumber such interest, nor shall such interest, while in the possession of the Trustee, be liable for, or subject to, the debts, contracts, obligations, liabilities or torts of any beneficiary.

D. If any provision of this trust instrument should be invalid or unenforceable, the remaining provisions shall continue to be fully effective.

E. Notwithstanding any contrary provision of this trust, the principal of any trust created hereunder shall vest absolutely in interest not later than twenty-one years after the death of the last survivor of the Grantor and any beneficiary who is living at the time of the creation of this trust. Immediately prior to the expiration of twenty-one years after the death of the last survivor of the above group, the principal of each trust that has not previously vested shall become payable to the issue of the Grantor, per stirpes.

F. In the event that any technical corrections must be made to this trust document, the then acting trustee shall have the authority to make such technical corrections; provided, however, that the corrections must be consistent with the Grantors' intentions in creating this trust, as set forth in this trust instrument, with regard to the beneficiaries of the trust, the uses and purposes of the trust, the distribution plan of the trust, etc.

IN WITNESS WHEREOF, the Grantor has executed this agreement at _____ on the day and year first written above.

[notarized signatures of grantor and trustee]

Schedule A

[listing of the trust assets]

Appendix B

Selected Statutes

Selected Federal Income and Capital Gains Tax Statutes

26 U.S.C. §1: Tax Imposed

(h) Maximum capital gains rate

(1) In general

If a taxpayer has a net capital gain for any taxable year, the tax imposed by this section for such taxable year shall not exceed the sum of—

(A) a tax computed at the rates and in the same manner as if this subsection had not been enacted on the greater of—

(i) taxable income reduced by the net capital gain; or

(ii) the lesser of—

(I) the amount of taxable income taxed at a rate below 25 percent; or

(II) taxable income reduced by the adjusted net capital gain;

(B) 5 percent (0 percent in the case of taxable years beginning after 2007) of so much of the adjusted net capital gain (or, if less, taxable income) as does not exceed the excess (if any) of—

(i) the amount of taxable income which would (without regard to this paragraph) be taxed at a rate below 25 percent, over

(ii) the taxable income reduced by the adjusted net capital gain;

(C) 15 percent of the adjusted net capital gain (or, if less, taxable income) in excess of the amount on which a tax is determined under subparagraph (B);

(D) 25 percent of the excess (if any) of—

(i) the unrecaptured section 1250 gain (or, if less, the net capital gain (determined without regard to paragraph (11))), over

(ii) the excess (if any) of—

(I) the sum of the amount on which tax is determined under subparagraph (A) plus the net capital gain, over
(II) taxable income; and
(E) 28 percent of the amount of taxable income in excess of the sum of the amounts on which tax is determined under the preceding subparagraphs of this paragraph.

26 U.S.C. § 101: Certain Death Benefits

(a) Proceeds of life insurance contracts payable by reason of death

(1) General rule

Except as otherwise provided in paragraph (2), subsection (d), subsection (f), and subsection (j), gross income does not include amounts received (whether in a single sum or otherwise) under a life insurance contract, if such amounts are paid by reason of the death of the insured.

(2) Transfer for valuable consideration

In the case of a transfer for a valuable consideration, by assignment or otherwise, of a life insurance contract or any interest therein, the amount excluded from gross income by paragraph (1) shall not exceed an amount equal to the sum of the actual value of such consideration and the premiums and other amounts subsequently paid by the transferee. The preceding sentence shall not apply in the case of such a transfer—

(A) if such contract or interest therein has a basis for determining gain or loss in the hands of a transferee determined in whole or in part by reference to such basis of such contract or interest therein in the hands of the transferor, or
(B) if such transfer is to the insured, to a partner of the insured, to a partnership in which the insured is a partner, or to a corporation in which the insured is a shareholder or officer.
The term "other amounts" in the first sentence of this paragraph includes interest paid or accrued by the transferee on indebtedness with respect to such contract or any interest therein if such interest paid or accrued is not allowable as a deduction by reason of section 264 (a)(4).

...

(c) Interest

If any amount excluded from gross income by subsection (a) is held under an agreement to pay interest thereon, the interest payments shall be included in gross income.

26 U.S.C. § 102: Gifts and Inheritances

(a) General rule

Gross income does not include the value of property acquired by gift, bequest, devise, or inheritance.

(b) Income

Subsection (a) shall not exclude from gross income—

(1) the income from any property referred to in subsection (a); or
(2) where the gift, bequest, devise, or inheritance is of income from property, the amount of such income.

Where, under the terms of the gift, bequest, devise, or inheritance, the payment, crediting, or distribution thereof is to be made at intervals, then, to the extent that it is paid or credited or to be distributed out of income from property, it shall be treated for purposes of paragraph (2) as a gift, bequest, devise, or inheritance of income from property. Any amount included in the gross income of a beneficiary under subchapter J shall be treated for purposes of paragraph (2) as a gift, bequest, devise, or inheritance of income from property.

(c) Employee gifts

(1) In general

Subsection (a) shall not exclude from gross income any amount transferred by or for an employer to, or for the benefit of, an employee.

26 U.S.C. § 121: Exclusion of gain from sale of principal residence

(a) Exclusion

Gross income shall not include gain from the sale or exchange of property if, during the 5-year period ending on the date of the sale or exchange, such property has been owned and used by the taxpayer as the taxpayer's principal residence for periods aggregating 2 years or more.

(b) Limitations

(1) In general

The amount of gain excluded from gross income under subsection (a) with respect to any sale or exchange shall not exceed $250,000.

(2) Special rules for joint returns

In the case of a husband and wife who make a joint return for the taxable year of the sale or exchange of the property—

(A) $500,000 Limitation for certain joint returns

Paragraph (1) shall be applied by substituting "$500,000" for "$250,000" if—

    (i) either spouse meets the ownership requirements of subsection (a) with respect to such property;

    (ii) both spouses meet the use requirements of subsection (a) with respect to such property; and

    (iii) neither spouse is ineligible for the benefits of subsection (a) with respect to such property by reason of paragraph (3).

(B) Other joint returns

If such spouses do not meet the requirements of subparagraph (A), the limitation under paragraph (1) shall be the sum of the limitations under paragraph (1) to which each spouse would be entitled if such spouses had not been married. For purposes of the preceding sentence, each spouse shall be treated as owning the property during the period that either spouse owned the property.

(3) **Application to only 1 sale or exchange every 2 years**

(A) In general

Subsection (a) shall not apply to any sale or exchange by the taxpayer if, during the 2-year period ending on the date of such sale or exchange, there was any other sale or exchange by the taxpayer to which subsection (a) applied.

. . .

(4) **Special rule for certain sales by surviving spouses**

In the case of a sale or exchange of property by an unmarried individual whose spouse is deceased on the date of such sale, paragraph (1) shall be applied by substituting "$500,000" for "$250,000" if such sale occurs not later than 2 years after the date of death of such spouse and the requirements of paragraph (2)(A) were met immediately before such date of death.

(5) **Exclusion of gain allocated to nonqualified use**

    (A) **In general**

Subsection (a) shall not apply to so much of the gain from the sale or exchange of property as is allocated to periods of nonqualified use.

(B) **Gain allocated to periods of nonqualified use**

For purposes of subparagraph (A), gain shall be allocated to periods of nonqualified use based on the ratio which—

    (i) the aggregate periods of nonqualified use during the period such property was owned by the taxpayer, bears to

    (ii) the period such property was owned by the taxpayer.

(C) **Period of nonqualified use**

For purposes of this paragraph—

(i) In general The term "period of nonqualified use" means any period (other than the portion of any period preceding January 1, 2009) during which the property is not used as the principal residence of the taxpayer or the taxpayer's spouse or former spouse.

(ii) Exceptions The term "period of nonqualified use" does not include—

(I) any portion of the 5-year period described in subsection (a) which is after the last date that such property is used as the principal residence of the taxpayer or the taxpayer's spouse,

(II) any period (not to exceed an aggregate period of 10 years) during which the taxpayer or the taxpayer's spouse is serving on qualified official extended duty (as defined in subsection (d)(9)(C)) described in clause (i), (ii), or (iii) of subsection (d)(9)(A), and

(III) any other period of temporary absence (not to exceed an aggregate period of 2 years) due to change of employment, health conditions, or such other unforeseen circumstances as may be specified by the Secretary.

...

(c) Exclusion for taxpayers failing to meet certain requirements

(1) In general

In the case of a sale or exchange to which this subsection applies, the ownership and use requirements of subsection (a), and subsection (b)(3), shall not apply; but the dollar limitation under paragraph (1) or (2) of subsection (b), whichever is applicable, shall be equal to—

(A) the amount which bears the same ratio to such limitation (determined without regard to this paragraph) as

(B)

(i) the shorter of—

(I) the aggregate periods, during the 5-year period ending on the date of such sale or exchange, such property has been owned and used by the taxpayer as the taxpayer's principal residence; or

(II) the period after the date of the most recent prior sale or exchange by the taxpayer to which subsection (a) applied and before the date of such sale or exchange, bears to

(ii) 2 years.

...

Selected Federal Income Tax
Statutes Relating to Trusts

26 U.S.C. §641: Imposition of Tax

(a) Application of tax

The tax imposed by section 1 (e) shall apply to the taxable income of estates or of any kind of property held in trust, including—

> (1) income accumulated in trust for the benefit of unborn or unascertained persons or persons with contingent interests, and income accumulated or held for future distribution under the terms of the will or trust;
>
> (2) income which is to be distributed currently by the fiduciary to the beneficiaries, and income collected by a guardian of an infant which is to be held or distributed as the court may direct;
>
> (3) income received by estates of deceased persons during the period of administration or settlement of the estate; and
>
> (4) income which, in the discretion of the fiduciary, may be either distributed to the beneficiaries or accumulated.

...

(c) Special rules for taxation of electing small business trusts

(1) In general

For purposes of this chapter—

> (A) the portion of any electing small business trust which consists of stock in 1 or more S corporations shall be treated as a separate trust, and
>
> (B) the amount of the tax imposed by this chapter on such separate trust shall be determined with the modifications of paragraph (2).

(2) Modifications

> For purposes of paragraph (1), the modifications of this paragraph are the following:
>
> (A) Except as provided in section 1 (h), **the amount of the tax imposed by section 1 (e) shall be determined by using the highest rate of tax set forth in section 1 (e).**
>
> (B) The exemption amount under section 55 (d) shall be zero.
>
> (C) The only items of income, loss, deduction, or credit to be taken into account are the following:

(i) The items required to be taken into account under section 1366.

(ii) Any gain or loss from the disposition of stock in an S corporation.

(iii) To the extent provided in regulations, State or local income taxes or administrative expenses to the extent allocable to items described in clauses (i) and (ii).

(iv) Any interest expense paid or accrued on indebtedness incurred to acquire stock in an S corporation.

No deduction or credit shall be allowed for any amount not described in this paragraph, and no item described in this paragraph shall be apportioned to any beneficiary.

(D) No amount shall be allowed under paragraph (1) or (2) of section 1211 (b).

(3) Treatment of remainder of trust and distributions

For purposes of determining—

(A) the amount of the tax imposed by this chapter on the portion of any electing small business trust not treated as a separate trust under paragraph (1), and

(B) the distributable net income of the entire trust, the items referred to in paragraph (2)(C) shall be excluded. Except as provided in the preceding sentence, this subsection shall not affect the taxation of any distribution from the trust.

(4) Treatment of unused deductions where termination of separate trust

If a portion of an electing small business trust ceases to be treated as a separate trust under paragraph (1), any carryover or excess deduction of the separate trust which is referred to in section 642 (h) shall be taken into account by the entire trust.

(5) Electing small business trust

For purposes of this subsection, the term "electing small business trust" has the meaning given such term by section 1361 (e)(1).

26 U.S.C. §651: Deduction for trusts distributing current income only

(a) Deduction

In the case of any trust the terms of which—

(1) provide that all of its income is required to be distributed currently, and

(2) do not provide that any amounts are to be paid, permanently set aside, or used for the purposes specified in section 642 (c) (relating to

deduction for charitable, etc., purposes), there shall be allowed as a deduction in computing the taxable income of the trust the amount of the income for the taxable year which is required to be distributed currently. This section shall not apply in any taxable year in which the trust distributes amounts other than amounts of income described in paragraph (1).

(b) Limitation on deduction

If the amount of income required to be distributed currently exceeds the distributable net income of the trust for the taxable year, the deduction shall be limited to the amount of the distributable net income. For this purpose, the computation of distributable net income shall not include items of income which are not included in the gross income of the trust and the deductions allocable thereto.

26 U.S.C. §661: Deduction for estates and trusts accumulating income or distributing corpus

(a) Deduction

In any taxable year there shall be allowed as a deduction in computing the taxable income of an estate or trust (other than a trust to which subpart B applies), the sum of—
(1) any amount of income for such taxable year required to be distributed currently (including any amount required to be distributed which may be paid out of income or corpus to the extent such amount is paid out of income for such taxable year); and
(2) any other amounts properly paid or credited or required to be distributed for such taxable year; but such deduction shall not exceed the distributable net income of the estate or trust.

(b) Character of amounts distributed

The amount determined under subsection (a) shall be treated as consisting of the same proportion of each class of items entering into the computation of distributable net income of the estate or trust as the total of each class bears to the total distributable net income of the estate or trust in the absence of the allocation of different classes of income under the specific terms of the governing instrument. In the application of the preceding sentence, the items of deduction entering into the computation of distributable net income (including the deduction allowed under section 642 (c)) shall be allocated among the items of distributable net income in accordance with regulations prescribed by the Secretary.

(c) Limitation on deduction

No deduction shall be allowed under subsection (a) in respect of any portion of the amount allowed as a deduction under that subsection (without regard to this subsection) which is treated under subsection (b) as consisting of any item of distributable net income which is not included in the gross income of the estate or trust.

26 U.S.C. §664 Charitable remainder trusts

(a) General rule

Notwithstanding any other provision of this subchapter, the provisions of this section shall, in accordance with regulations prescribed by the Secretary, apply in the case of a charitable remainder annuity trust and a charitable remainder unitrust.

(b) Character of distributions

Amounts distributed by a charitable remainder annuity trust or by a charitable remainder unitrust shall be considered as having the following characteristics in the hands of a beneficiary to whom is paid the annuity described in subsection (d)(1)(A) or the payment described in subsection (d)(2)(A):

(1) First, as amounts of income (other than gains, and amounts treated as gains, from the sale or other disposition of capital assets) includible in gross income to the extent of such income of the trust for the year and such undistributed income of the trust for prior years;

(2) Second, as a capital gain to the extent of the capital gain of the trust for the year and the undistributed capital gain of the trust for prior years;

(3) Third, as other income to the extent of such income of the trust for the year and such undistributed income of the trust for prior years; and

(4) Fourth, as a distribution of trust corpus.

For purposes of this section, the trust shall determine the amount of its undistributed capital gain on a cumulative net basis.

(c) Taxation of trusts

(1) Income tax

A charitable remainder annuity trust and a charitable remainder unitrust shall, for any taxable year, not be subject to any tax imposed by this subtitle.

(2) Excise tax

(A) In general

In the case of a charitable remainder annuity trust or a charitable remainder unitrust which has unrelated business taxable income (within the meaning of section 512, determined as if part III of subchapter F applied to such trust) for a taxable year, there is hereby imposed on such trust or unitrust an excise tax equal to the amount of such unrelated business taxable income.

(B) **Certain rules to apply**

The tax imposed by subparagraph (A) shall be treated as imposed by chapter 42 for purposes of this title other than subchapter E of chapter 42.

(C) **Tax court proceedings**

For purposes of this paragraph, the references in section 6212 (c)(1) to section 4940 shall be deemed to include references to this paragraph.

(d) **Definitions**

(1) **Charitable remainder annuity trust**

For purposes of this section, a charitable remainder annuity trust is a trust—

(A) from which a sum certain (which is not less than 5 percent nor more than 50 percent of the initial net fair market value of all property placed in trust) is to be paid, not less often than annually, to one or more persons (at least one of which is not an organization described in section 170 (c) and, in the case of individuals, only to an individual who is living at the time of the creation of the trust) for a term of years (not in excess of 20 years) or for the life or lives of such individual or individuals,

(B) from which no amount other than the payments described in subparagraph (A) and other than qualified gratuitous transfers described in subparagraph (C) may be paid to or for the use of any person other than an organization described in section 170 (c),

(C) following the termination of the payments described in subparagraph (A), the remainder interest in the trust is to be transferred to, or for the use of, an organization described in section 170 (c) or is to be retained by the trust for such a use or, to the extent the remainder interest is in qualified employer securities (as defined in subsection (g)(4)), all or part of such securities are to be transferred to an employee stock ownership plan (as defined in section 4975 (e)(7)) in a qualified gratuitous transfer (as defined by subsection (g)), and

(D) the value (determined under section 7520) of such remainder interest is at least 10 percent of the initial net fair market value of all property placed in the trust.

(2) Charitable remainder unitrust

For purposes of this section, a charitable remainder unitrust is a trust—

(A) from which a fixed percentage (which is not less than 5 percent nor more than 50 percent) of the net fair market value of its assets, valued annually, is to be paid, not less often than annually, to one or more persons (at least one of which is not an organization described in section 170 (c) and, in the case of individuals, only to an individual who is living at the time of the creation of the trust) for a term of years (not in excess of 20 years) or for the life or lives of such individual or individuals,

(B) from which no amount other than the payments described in subparagraph (A) and other than qualified gratuitous transfers described in subparagraph (C) may be paid to or for the use of any person other than an organization described in section 170 (c),

(C) following the termination of the payments described in subparagraph (A), the remainder interest in the trust is to be transferred to, or for the use of, an organization described in section 170 (c) or is to be retained by the trust for such a use or, to the extent the remainder interest is in qualified employer securities (as defined in subsection (g)(4)), all or part of such securities are to be transferred to an employee stock ownership plan (as defined in section 4975 (e)(7)) in a qualified gratuitous transfer (as defined by subsection (g)), and

(D) with respect to each contribution of property to the trust, the value (determined under section 7520) of such remainder interest in such property is at least 10 percent of the net fair market value of such property as of the date such property is contributed to the trust.

. . .

Selected Grantor Trust Statutes

26 U.S.C. §671: Trust income, deductions, and credits attributable to grantors and others as substantial owners

Where it is specified in this subpart that the grantor or another person shall be treated as the owner of any portion of a trust, there shall then be included in computing the taxable income and credits of the grantor or the other person those items of income, deductions, and credits against tax of the trust which are attributable to that portion of the trust to the extent that such items would be taken into account under this chapter in computing taxable income or credits against the tax of an individual. Any remaining portion of the trust shall be subject to subparts A through D. No items of a trust shall be included in computing the taxable income and credits of the grantor or of any other person solely on the grounds of his dominion and control over the trust under section 61 (relating to definition of gross income) or any other provision of this title, except as specified in this subpart.

26 U.S.C. §672: Definitions and Rules

(a) Adverse party

For purposes of this subpart, the term "adverse party" means any person having a substantial beneficial interest in the trust which would be adversely affected by the exercise or nonexercise of the power which he possesses respecting the trust. A person having a general power of appointment over the trust property shall be deemed to have a beneficial interest in the trust.

(b) Nonadverse party

For purposes of this subpart, the term "nonadverse party" means any person who is not an adverse party.

(c) Related or subordinate party

For purposes of this subpart, the term "related or subordinate party" means any nonadverse party who is—

> (1) the grantor's spouse if living with the grantor;
> (2) any one of the following: The grantor's father, mother, issue, brother or sister; an employee of the grantor; a corporation or any employee of a corporation in which the stock holdings of the grantor and the trust are significant from the viewpoint of voting control; a subordinate employee of a corporation in which the grantor is an executive.
>
> For purposes of subsection (f) and sections 674 and 675, a related or subordinate party shall be presumed to be subservient to the grantor in respect of the exercise or nonexercise of the powers conferred on him unless such party is shown not to be subservient by a preponderance of the evidence.

(d) Rule where power is subject to condition precedent

A person shall be considered to have a power described in this subpart even though the exercise of the power is subject to a precedent giving of notice or takes effect only on the expiration of a certain period after the exercise of the power.

(e) Grantor treated as holding any power or interest of grantor's spouse

(1) In general

For purposes of this subpart, a grantor shall be treated as holding any power or interest held by—

(A) any individual who was the spouse of the grantor at the time of the creation of such power or interest, or

(B) any individual who became the spouse of the grantor after the creation of such power or interest, but only with respect to periods after such individual became the spouse of the grantor.

(2) Marital status

For purposes of paragraph (1)(A), an individual legally separated from his spouse under a decree of divorce or of separate maintenance shall not be considered as married.

...

26 U.S.C. § 673: Reversionary Interests

(a) General rule

The grantor shall be treated as the owner of any portion of a trust in which he has a reversionary interest in either the corpus or the income therefrom, if, as of the inception of that portion of the trust, the value of such interest exceeds 5 percent of the value of such portion.

(b) Reversionary interest taking effect at death of minor lineal descendant beneficiary

In the case of any beneficiary who—

(1) is a lineal descendant of the grantor, and

(2) holds all of the present interests in any portion of a trust,

the grantor shall not be treated under subsection (a) as the owner of such portion solely by reason of a reversionary interest in such portion which takes effect upon the death of such beneficiary before such beneficiary attains age 21.

(c) Special rule for determining value of reversionary interest

For purposes of subsection (a), the value of the grantor's reversionary interest shall be determined by assuming the maximum exercise of discretion in favor of the grantor.

(d) Postponement of date specified for reacquisition

Any postponement of the date specified for the reacquisition of possession or enjoyment of the reversionary interest shall be treated as a new transfer in trust commencing with the date on which the postponement is effective and terminating with the date prescribed by the postponement. However, income for any period shall not be included in the income of the grantor by reason of the preceding sentence if such income would not be so includible in the absence of such postponement.

26 U.S.C. §674: Power to control beneficial enjoyment

(a) General rule

The grantor shall be treated as the owner of any portion of a trust in respect of which the beneficial enjoyment of the corpus or the income therefrom is subject to a power of disposition, exercisable by the grantor or a nonadverse party, or both, without the approval or consent of any adverse party.

(b) Exceptions for certain powers

Subsection (a) shall not apply to the following powers regardless of by whom held:

(1) Power to apply income to support of a dependent

A power described in section 677 (b) to the extent that the grantor would not be subject to tax under that section.

(2) Power affecting beneficial enjoyment only after occurrence of event

A power, the exercise of which can only affect the beneficial enjoyment of the income for a period commencing after the occurrence of an event such that a grantor would not be treated as the owner under section673 if the power were a reversionary interest; but the grantor may be treated as the owner after the occurrence of the event unless the power is relinquished.

(3) Power exercisable only by will

A power exercisable only by will, other than a power in the grantor to appoint by will the income of the trust where the income is accumulated for such disposition by the grantor or may be so accumulated in the discretion of the grantor or a nonadverse party, or both, without the approval or consent of any adverse party.

(4) Power to allocate among charitable beneficiaries

A power to determine the beneficial enjoyment of the corpus or the income therefrom if the corpus or income is irrevocably payable for a purpose specified in section 170 (c) (relating to definition of charitable contributions) or to an employee stock ownership plan (as defined in section 4975 (e)(7)) in a qualified gratuitous transfer (as defined in section 664 (g)(1)).

(5) Power to distribute corpus

A power to distribute corpus either—

(A) to or for a beneficiary or beneficiaries or to or for a class of beneficiaries (whether or not income beneficiaries) provided that the power is limited by a reasonably definite standard which is set forth in the trust instrument; or

(B) to or for any current income beneficiary, provided that the distribution of corpus must be chargeable against the proportionate share of corpus held in trust for the payment of income to the beneficiary as if the corpus constituted a separate trust.

A power does not fall within the powers described in this paragraph if any person has a power to add to the beneficiary or beneficiaries or to a class of beneficiaries designated to receive the income or corpus, except where such action is to provide for afterborn or after-adopted children.

(6) Power to withhold income temporarily

A power to distribute or apply income to or for any current income beneficiary or to accumulate the income for him, provided that any accumulated income must ultimately be payable—

(A) to the beneficiary from whom distribution or application is withheld, to his estate, or to his appointees (or persons named as alternate takers in default of appointment) provided that such beneficiary possesses a power of appointment which does not exclude from the class of possible appointees any person other than the beneficiary, his estate, his creditors, or the creditors of his estate, or

(B) on termination of the trust, or in conjunction with a distribution of corpus which is augmented by such accumulated income, to the current income beneficiaries in shares which have been irrevocably specified in the trust instrument.

Accumulated income shall be considered so payable although it is provided that if any beneficiary does not survive a date of distribution which could reasonably have been expected to occur within the beneficiary's lifetime, the share of the deceased beneficiary is to be paid to his appointees or to one or more designated alternate takers (other than the grantor or the grantor's estate) whose shares have been irrevocably specified. A power does not fall within the powers described in this paragraph if any person has a power to add to the beneficiary or beneficiaries or to a class of beneficiaries designated to receive the income or corpus except where such action is to provide for after-born or after-adopted children.

(7) Power to withhold income during disability of a beneficiary

A power exercisable only during—

  (A) the existence of a legal disability of any current income beneficiary, or

  (B) the period during which any income beneficiary shall be under the age of 21 years, to distribute or apply income to or for such beneficiary or to accumulate and add the income to corpus. A power does not fall within the powers described in this paragraph if any person has a power to add to the beneficiary or beneficiaries or to a class of beneficiaries designated to receive the income or corpus, except where such action is to provide for after-born or after-adopted children.

(8) Power to allocate between corpus and income

A power to allocate receipts and disbursements as between corpus and income, even though expressed in broad language.

(c) Exception for certain powers of independent trustees

Subsection (a) shall not apply to a power solely exercisable (without the approval or consent of any other person) by a trustee or trustees, none of whom is the grantor, and no more than half of whom are related or subordinate parties who are subservient to the wishes of the grantor—

  (1) to distribute, apportion, or accumulate income to or for a beneficiary or beneficiaries, or to, for, or within a class of beneficiaries; or

  (2) to pay out corpus to or for a beneficiary or beneficiaries or to or for a class of beneficiaries (whether or not income beneficiaries).

A power does not fall within the powers described in this subsection if any person has a power to add to the beneficiary or beneficiaries or to a class of beneficiaries designated to receive the income or corpus, except where such action is to provide for after-born or after-adopted children. For periods during which an individual is the spouse of the grantor (within the meaning of section 672 (e)(2)), any reference in this subsection to the grantor shall be treated as including a reference to such individual.

(d) Power to allocate income if limited by a standard

Subsection (a) shall not apply to a power solely exercisable (without the approval or consent of any other person) by a trustee or trustees, none of whom is the grantor or spouse living with the grantor, to distribute, apportion, or accumulate income to or for a beneficiary or beneficiaries, or to, for, or within a class of beneficiaries, whether or not the conditions of paragraph (6) or (7) of subsection (b) are satisfied, if such power is limited by a reasonably definite external standard which is set forth in the trust instrument. A power does not fall within the powers described in this subsection if any person has a power to add to the beneficiary or beneficiaries or to a class of beneficiaries designated to receive the income or corpus except where such action is to provide for after-born or after-adopted children.

26 U.S.C. § 675: Administrative Powers

The grantor shall be treated as the owner of any portion of a trust in respect of which—

(1) Power to deal for less than adequate and full consideration

A power exercisable by the grantor or a nonadverse party, or both, without the approval or consent of any adverse party enables the grantor or any person to purchase, exchange, or otherwise deal with or dispose of the corpus or the income therefrom for less than an adequate consideration in money or money's worth.

(2) Power to borrow without adequate interest or security

A power exercisable by the grantor or a nonadverse party, or both, enables the grantor to borrow the corpus or income, directly or indirectly, without adequate interest or without adequate security except where a trustee (other than the grantor) is authorized under a general lending power to make loans to any person without regard to interest or security.

(3) Borrowing of the trust funds

The grantor has directly or indirectly borrowed the corpus or income and has not completely repaid the loan, including any interest, before the beginning of the taxable year. The preceding sentence shall not apply to a loan which provides for adequate interest and adequate security, if such loan is made by a trustee other than the grantor and other than a related or subordinate trustee subservient to the grantor. For periods during which an individual is the spouse of the grantor (within the meaning of section 672 (e)(2)), any reference in this paragraph to the grantor shall be treated as including a reference to such individual.

(4) General powers of administration

A power of administration is exercisable in a nonfiduciary capacity by any person without the approval or consent of any person in a fiduciary capacity. For purposes of this paragraph, the term "power of administration" means any one or more of the following powers:

(A) a power to vote or direct the voting of stock or other securities of a corporation in which the holdings of the grantor and the trust are significant from the viewpoint of voting control;

(B) a power to control the investment of the trust funds either by directing investments or reinvestments, or by vetoing proposed investments or reinvestments, to the extent that the trust funds consist of stocks or securities of corporations in which the holdings of the grantor and the trust are significant from the viewpoint of voting control; or

(C) a power to reacquire the trust corpus by substituting other property of an equivalent value.

26 U.S.C. §676: Power to Revoke

(a) General rule

The grantor shall be treated as the owner of any portion of a trust, whether or not he is treated as such owner under any other provision of this part, where at any time the power to revest in the grantor title to such portion is exercisable by the grantor or a non-adverse party, or both.

(b) Power affecting beneficial enjoyment only after occurrence of event

Subsection (a) shall not apply to a power the exercise of which can only affect the beneficial enjoyment of the income for a period commencing after the occurrence of an event such that a grantor would not be treated as the owner under section 673 if the power were a reversionary interest. But the grantor may be treated as the owner after the occurrence of such event unless the power is relinquished.

26 U.S.C. §677: Income for Benefit of Grantor

(a) General rule

The grantor shall be treated as the owner of any portion of a trust, whether or not he is treated as such owner under section 674, whose income without the approval or consent of any adverse party is, or, in the discretion of the grantor or a nonadverse party, or both, may be—

(1) distributed to the grantor or the grantor's spouse;

(2) held or accumulated for future distribution to the grantor or the grantor's spouse; or

(3) applied to the payment of premiums on policies of insurance on the life of the grantor or the grantor's spouse (except policies of insurance irrevocably payable for a purpose specified in section 170 (c) (relating to definition of charitable contributions)).

This subsection shall not apply to a power the exercise of which can only affect the beneficial enjoyment of the income for a period commencing after the occurrence of an event such that the grantor would not be treated as the owner under section 673 if the power were a reversionary interest; but the grantor may be treated as the owner after the occurrence of the event unless the power is relinquished.

(b) Obligations of support

Income of a trust shall not be considered taxable to the grantor under subsection (a) or any other provision of this chapter merely because such income in the discretion of another person, the trustee, or the grantor acting as trustee or co-trustee, may be applied or distributed for the support or maintenance of a beneficiary (other than the grantor's spouse) whom the grantor is legally obligated to support or maintain, except to the extent that such income is so applied or distributed. In cases where the amounts so applied or distributed are paid out of corpus or out of other than income for the taxable year, such amounts shall be considered to be an amount paid or credited within the meaning of paragraph (2) of section 661 (a) and shall be taxed to the grantor under section 662.

26 U.S.C. §678: Person other than grantor treated as substantial owner

(a) General rule

A person other than the grantor shall be treated as the owner of any portion of a trust with respect to which:

> (1) such person has a power exercisable solely by himself to vest the corpus or the income therefrom in himself, or
> (2) such person has previously partially released or otherwise modified such a power and after the release or modification retains such control as would, within the principles of sections 671 to 677, inclusive, subject to grantor of a trust to treatment as the owner thereof.

(b) Exception where grantor is taxable

Subsection (a) shall not apply with respect to a power over income, as originally granted or thereafter modified, if the grantor of the trust or a transferor (to whom section 679 applies) is otherwise treated as the owner under the provisions of this subpart other than this section.

(c) Obligations of support

Subsection (a) shall not apply to a power which enables such person, in the capacity of trustee or cotrustee, merely to apply the income of the trust to the support or maintenance of a person whom the holder of the power is obligated to support or maintain except to the extent that such income is so applied. In cases where the amounts so applied or distributed are paid out of corpus or out of other than income of the taxable year, such amounts shall be considered to be an amount paid or credited within the meaning of paragraph (2) of section 661 (a) and shall be taxed to the holder of the power under section 662.

(d) Effect of renunciation or disclaimer

Subsection (a) shall not apply with respect to a power which has been renounced or disclaimed within a reasonable time after the holder of the power first became aware of its existence.

(e) Cross reference

For provision under which beneficiary of trust is treated as owner of the portion of the trust which consists of stock in an S corporation, see section 1361 (d).

26 U.S.C. § 1014. Basis in property acquired from a decedent

(a) In general

Except as otherwise provided in this section, the basis of property in the hands of a person acquiring the property from a decedent or to whom the property passed from a decedent shall, if not sold, exchanged, or otherwise disposed of before the decedent's death by such person, be—

  (1) the fair market value of the property at the date of the decedent's death,
  (2) in the case of an election under either section 2032 or section 811(j) of the Internal Revenue Code of 1939 where the decedent died after October 21, 1942, its value at the applicable valuation date prescribed by those sections,
  (3) in the case of an election under section 2032A, its value determined under such section, or
  (4) to the extent of the applicability of the exclusion described in section 2031 (c), the basis in the hands of the decedent.

(b) Property acquired from the decedent

For purposes of subsection (a), the following property shall be considered to have been acquired from or to have passed from the decedent:

  (1) Property acquired by bequest, devise, or inheritance, or by the decedent's estate from the decedent;
  (2) Property transferred by the decedent during his lifetime in trust to pay the income for life to or on the order or direction of the decedent,

with the right reserved to the decedent at all times before his death to revoke the trust;

(3) In the case of decedents dying after December 31, 1951, property transferred by the decedent during his lifetime in trust to pay the income for life to or on the order or direction of the decedent with the right reserved to the decedent at all times before his death to make any change in the enjoyment thereof through the exercise of a power to alter, amend, or terminate the trust;

(4) Property passing without full and adequate consideration under a general power of appointment exercised by the decedent by will;

...

(10) Property includible in the gross estate of the decedent under section 2044 (relating to certain property for which marital deduction was previously allowed). In any such case, the last 3 sentences of paragraph (9) shall apply as if such property were described in the first sentence of paragraph (9).

26 U.S.C. § 1015. Basis in property acquired by gifts and transfers in trust.

(a) Gifts after December 31, 1920

If the property was acquired by gift after December 31, 1920, the basis shall be the same as it would be in the hands of the donor or the last preceding owner by whom it was not acquired by gift, except that if such basis (adjusted for the period before the date of the gift as provided in section 1016) is greater than the fair market value of the property at the time of the gift, then for the purpose of determining loss the basis shall be such fair market value. If the facts necessary to determine the basis in the hands of the donor or the last preceding owner are unknown to the donee, the Secretary shall, if possible, obtain such facts from such donor or last preceding owner, or any other person cognizant thereof. If the Secretary finds it impossible to obtain such facts, the basis in the hands of such donor or last preceding owner shall be the fair market value of such property as found by the Secretary as of the date or approximate date at which, according to the best information that the Secretary is able to obtain, such property was acquired by such donor or last preceding owner.

(b) Transfer in trust after December 31, 1920

If the property was acquired after December 31, 1920, by a transfer in trust (other than by a transfer in trust by a gift, bequest, or devise), the basis shall be the same as it would be in the hands of the grantor increased in the amount of gain or decreased in the amount of loss recognized to the grantor on such transfer under the law applicable to the year in which the transfer was made.

...

(e) **Gifts between spouses**

In the case of any property acquired by gift in a transfer described in section 1041 (a), the basis of such property in the hands of the transferee shall be determined under section 1041 (b)(2) and not this section.

26 U.S.C. § 1022. Treatment of property acquired from a decedent dying after December 31, 2009.

(a) **In general**

Except as otherwise provided in this section—

> (1) property acquired from a decedent dying after December 31, 2009, shall be treated for purposes of this subtitle as transferred by gift, and
> (2) the basis of the person acquiring property from such a decedent shall be the lesser of—
> > (A) the adjusted basis of the decedent, or
> > (B) the fair market value of the property at the date of the decedent's death.

...

(e) **Property acquired from the decedent**

For purposes of this section, the following property shall be considered to have been acquired from the decedent:

> (1) Property acquired by bequest, devise, or inheritance, or by the decedent's estate from the decedent.
> (2) Property transferred by the decedent during his lifetime—
> > (A) to a qualified revocable trust (as defined in section 645 (b)(1)), or
> > (B) to any other trust with respect to which the decedent reserved the right to make any change in the enjoyment thereof through the exercise of a power to alter, amend, or terminate the trust.
> (3) Any other property passing from the decedent by reason of death to the extent that such property passed without consideration.

Selected Federal Estate Tax Statutes

26 U.S.C. § 2031: Definition of Gross Estate

(a) General

The value of the gross estate of the decedent shall be determined by including to the extent provided for in this part, the value at the time of his death of all property, real or personal, tangible or intangible, wherever situated.

…

26 U.S.C. § 2035. Adjustments for certain gifts made within 3 years of decedent's death

(a) Inclusion of certain property in gross estate

If—

> (1) the decedent made a transfer (by trust or otherwise) of an interest in any property, or relinquished a power with respect to any property, during the 3-year period ending on the date of the decedent's death, and
> (2) the value of such property (or an interest therein) would have been included in the decedent's gross estate under section 2036, 2037, 2038, or 2042 if such transferred interest or relinquished power had been retained by the decedent on the date of his death, the value of the gross estate shall include the value of any property (or interest therein) which would have been so included.

(b) Inclusion of gift tax on gifts made during 3 years before decedent's death

The amount of the gross estate (determined without regard to this subsection) shall be increased by the amount of any tax paid under chapter 12 by the decedent or his estate on any gift made by the decedent or his spouse during the 3-year period ending on the date of the decedent's death.

…

26 U.S.C. § 2036. Transfers with retained life estate

(a) General rule

The value of the gross estate shall include the value of all property to the extent of any interest therein of which the decedent has at any time made a transfer (except in case of a bona fide sale for an adequate and full consideration in money or money's worth), by trust or otherwise, under which he has retained for his life or for any period not ascertainable without reference to his death or for any period which does not in fact end before his death—

(1) the possession or enjoyment of, or the right to the income from, the property, or

(2) the right, either alone or in conjunction with any person, to designate the persons who shall possess or enjoy the property or the income therefrom.

(b) Voting rights

(1) In general

For purposes of subsection (a)(1), the retention of the right to vote (directly or indirectly) shares of stock of a controlled corporation shall be considered to be a retention of the enjoyment of transferred property.

(2) Controlled corporation

For purposes of paragraph (1), a corporation shall be treated as a controlled corporation if, at any time after the transfer of the property and during the 3-year period ending on the date of the decedent's death, the decedent owned (with the application of section 318), or had the right (either alone or in conjunction with any person) to vote, stock possessing at least 20 percent of the total combined voting power of all classes of stock.

(3) Coordination with section 2035

For purposes of applying section 2035 with respect to paragraph (1), the relinquishment or cessation of voting rights shall be treated as a transfer of property made by the decedent.

...

26 U.S.C. § 2037. Transfers taking effect at death

(a) General rule

The value of the gross estate shall include the value of all property to the extent of any interest therein of which the decedent has at any time after September 7, 1916, made a transfer (except in case of a bona fide sale for an adequate and full consideration in money or money's worth), by trust or otherwise, if—

(1) possession or enjoyment of the property can, through ownership of such interest, be obtained only by surviving the decedent, and

(2) the decedent has retained a reversionary interest in the property (but in the case of a transfer made before October 8, 1949, only if such reversionary interest arose by the express terms of the instrument of transfer), and the value of such reversionary interest immediately before the death of the decedent exceeds 5 percent of the value of such property.

(b) Special rules

For purposes of this section, the term "reversionary interest" includes a possibility that property transferred by the decedent—

(1) may return to him or his estate, or

(2) may be subject to a power of disposition by him,

but such term does not include a possibility that the income alone from such property may return to him or become subject to a power of disposition by him. The value of a reversionary interest immediately before the death of the decedent shall be determined (without regard to the fact of the decedent's death) by usual methods of valuation, including the use of tables of mortality and actuarial principles, under regulations prescribed by the Secretary. In determining the value of a possibility that property may be subject to a power of disposition by the decedent, such possibility shall be valued as if it were a possibility that such property may return to the decedent or his estate. Notwithstanding the foregoing, an interest so transferred shall not be included in the decedent's gross estate under this section if possession or enjoyment of the property could have been obtained by any beneficiary during the decedent's life through the exercise of a general power of appointment (as defined in section 2041) which in fact was exercisable immediately before the decedent's death.

26 U.S.C. § 2038. Revocable Transfers

(a) In general

The value of the gross estate shall include the value of all property—

(1) Transfers after June 22, 1936

To the extent of any interest therein of which the decedent has at any time made a transfer (except in case of a bona fide sale for an adequate and full consideration in money or money's worth), by trust or otherwise, where the enjoyment thereof was subject at the date of his death to any change through the exercise of a power (in whatever capacity exercisable) by the decedent alone or by the decedent in conjunction with any other person (without regard to when or from what source the decedent acquired such power), to alter, amend, revoke, or terminate, or where any such power is relinquished during the 3 year period ending on the date of the decedent's death.

...

26 U.S.C. § 2041. Power of Appointment

(a) In general

The value of the gross estate shall include the value of all property—

(1) Powers of appointment created on or before October 21, 1942

To the extent of any property with respect to which a general power of appointment created on or before October 21, 1942, is exercised by the decedent—

(A) by will, or

(B) by a disposition which is of such nature that if it were a transfer of property owned by the decedent, such property would be includible in the decedent's gross estate under sections 2035 to 2038, inclusive;

but the failure to exercise such a power or the complete release of such a power shall not be deemed an exercise thereof. If a general power of appointment created on or before October 21, 1942, has been partially released so that it is no longer a general power of appointment, the exercise of such power shall not be deemed to be the exercise of a general power of appointment if—

(i) such partial release occurred before November 1, 1951, or

(ii) the donee of such power was under a legal disability to release such power on October 21, 1942, and such partial release occurred not later than 6 months after the termination of such legal disability.

...

(b) Definitions

For purposes of subsection (a)—

(1) General power of appointment

The term "general power of appointment" means a power which is exercisable in favor of the decedent, his estate, his creditors, or the creditors of his estate; except that—

(A) A power to consume, invade, or appropriate property for the benefit of the decedent which is limited by an ascertainable standard relating to the health, education, support, or maintenance of the decedent shall not be deemed a general power of appointment. (B) A power of appointment created on or before October 21, 1942, which is exercisable by the decedent only in conjunction with another person shall not be deemed a general power of appointment. (C) In the case of a power of appointment created after October 21, 1942, which is exercisable by the decedent only in conjunction with another person—

(i) If the power is not exercisable by the decedent except in conjunction with the creator of the power—such power shall not be deemed a general power of appointment.

(ii) If the power is not exercisable by the decedent except in conjunction with a person having a substantial interest in the property, subject to the power, which is adverse to exercise of the power in favor of the decedent—such power shall not be deemed a general power of appointment. For the purposes of this clause a person who, after the death of the decedent, may be possessed of a power of appointment (with respect to the property subject to the decedent's power) which he may exercise in his own favor shall be deemed as having an interest in the property and such interest shall be deemed adverse to such exercise of the decedent's power.

(iii) If (after the application of clauses (i) and (ii)) the power is a general power of appointment and is exercisable in favor of such other person—such power shall be deemed a general power of appointment only in respect of a fractional part of the property subject to such power, such part to be determined by dividing the value of such property by the number of such persons (including the decedent) in favor of whom such power is exercisable.

For purposes of clauses (ii) and (iii), a power shall be deemed to be exercisable in favor of a person if it is exercisable in favor of such person, his estate, his creditors, or the creditors of his estate.

(2) Lapse of power

The lapse of a power of appointment created after October 21, 1942, during the life of the individual possessing the power shall be considered a release of such power. The preceding sentence shall apply with respect to the lapse of powers during any calendar year only to the extent that the property, which could have been appointed by exercise of such lapsed powers, exceeded in value, at the time of such lapse, the greater of the following amounts:

(A) $5,000, or

(B) 5 percent of the aggregate value, at the time of such lapse, of the assets out of which, or the proceeds of which, the exercise of the lapsed powers could have been satisfied.

26 U.S.C. § 2042. Proceeds of Life Insurance

The value of the gross estate shall include the value of all property—

(1) Receivable by the executor

To the extent of the amount receivable by the executor as insurance under policies on the life of the decedent.

(2) Receivable by other beneficiaries

To the extent of the amount receivable by all other beneficiaries as insurance under policies on the life of the decedent with respect to which the decedent possessed at his death any of the incidents of ownership, exercisable either alone or in conjunction with any other person. For purposes of the preceding sentence, the term "incident of ownership" includes a reversionary interest (whether arising by the express terms of the policy or other instrument or by operation of law) only if the value of such reversionary interest exceeded 5 percent of the value of the policy immediately before the death of the decedent. As used in this paragraph, the term "reversionary interest" includes a possibility that the policy, or the proceeds of the policy, may return to the decedent or his estate, or may be subject to a power of disposition by him. The value of a reversionary interest at any time shall be determined (without regard to the fact of the decedent's death) by usual methods of valuation, including the use of tables of mortality and actuarial principles, pursuant to regulations prescribed by the Secretary. In determining the value of a possibility that the policy or proceeds thereof may be subject to a power of disposition by the decedent, such possibility shall be valued as if it were a possibility that such policy or proceeds may return to the decedent or his estate.

26 U.S.C. § 2056. Bequests, etc., to surviving spouse

(a) Allowance of marital deduction

For purposes of the tax imposed by section 2001, the value of the taxable estate shall, except as limited by subsection (b), be determined by deducting from the value of the gross estate an amount equal to the value of any interest in property which passes or has passed from the decedent to his surviving spouse, but only to the extent that such interest is included in determining the value of the gross estate.

(b) Limitation in the case of life estate or other terminable interest

(1) General rule

Where, on the lapse of time, on the occurrence of an event or contingency, or on the failure of an event or contingency to occur, an interest passing to the surviving spouse will terminate or fail, no deduction shall be allowed under this section with respect to such interest—

(A) if an interest in such property passes or has passed (for less than an adequate and full consideration in money or money's worth) from the decedent to any person other than such surviving spouse (or the estate of such spouse); and

(B) if by reason of such passing such person (or his heirs or assigns) may possess or enjoy any part of such property after such termination or failure of the interest so passing to the surviving spouse;

and no deduction shall be allowed with respect to such interest (even if such deduction is not disallowed under subparagraphs (A) and (B))—

(C) if such interest is to be acquired for the surviving spouse, pursuant to directions of the decedent, by his executor or by the trustee of a trust.

For purposes of this paragraph, an interest shall not be considered as an interest which will terminate or fail merely because it is the ownership of a bond, note, or similar contractual obligation, the discharge of which would not have the effect of an annuity for life or for a term.

. . .

(5) Life estate with power of appointment in surviving spouse

In the case of an interest in property passing from the decedent, if his surviving spouse is entitled for life to all the income from the entire interest, or all the income from a specific portion thereof, payable annually or at more frequent intervals, with power in the surviving spouse to appoint the entire interest, or such specific portion (exercisable in favor of such surviving spouse, or of the estate of such surviving spouse, or in favor of either, whether or not in each case the power is exercisable in favor of others), and with no power in any other person to appoint any part of the interest, or such specific portion, to any person other than the surviving spouse—

(A) the interest or such portion thereof so passing shall, for purposes of subsection (a), be considered as passing to the surviving spouse, and

(B) no part of the interest so passing shall, for purposes of paragraph (1)(A), be considered as passing to any person other than the surviving spouse.

This paragraph shall apply only if such power in the surviving spouse to appoint the entire interest, or such specific portion thereof, whether exercisable by will or during life, is exercisable by such spouse alone and in all events.

(6) Life insurance or annuity payments with power of appointment in surviving spouse

In the case of an interest in property passing from the decedent consisting of proceeds under a life insurance, endowment, or annuity contract, if under the terms of the contract such proceeds are payable in installments or are held by the insurer subject to an agreement to pay interest thereon (whether the proceeds, on the termination of any interest payments, are payable in a lump sum or in annual or more frequent installments), and such installment or interest payments are payable annually or at more frequent intervals, commencing not later than 13 months after the decedent's death, and all amounts, or a specific portion of all such amounts, payable during the life of the surviving spouse are payable only to such spouse, and such spouse has the power to appoint all amounts, or such specific portion, payable under such contract (exercisable in favor of such surviving spouse, or of the estate of such surviving spouse, or in favor of either, whether or not in each case the power is exercisable in favor of others), with no power in any other person to appoint such amounts to any person other than the surviving spouse—

(A) such amounts shall, for purposes of subsection (a), be considered as passing to the surviving spouse, and

(B) no part of such amounts shall, for purposes of paragraph (1)(A), be considered as passing to any person other than the surviving spouse.

This paragraph shall apply only if, under the terms of the contract, such power in the surviving spouse to appoint such amounts, whether exercisable by will or during life, is exercisable by such spouse alone and in all events.

(7) Election with respect to life estate for surviving spouse

(A) **In general**

In the case of qualified terminable interest property—

(i) for purposes of subsection (a), such property shall be treated as passing to the surviving spouse, and

(ii) for purposes of paragraph (1)(A), no part of such property shall be treated as passing to any person other than the surviving spouse.

(B) **Qualified terminable interest property defined**

For purposes of this paragraph—

(i) In general The term "qualified terminable interest property" means property—

(I) which passes from the decedent,

(II) in which the surviving spouse has a qualifying income interest for life, and

(III) to which an election under this paragraph applies.

(ii) Qualifying income interest for life The surviving spouse has a qualifying income interest for life if—

(I) the surviving spouse is entitled to all the income from the property, payable annually or at more frequent intervals, or has a usufruct interest for life in the property, and

(II) no person has a power to appoint any part of the property to any person other than the surviving spouse.

Subclause (II) shall not apply to a power exercisable only at or after the death of the surviving spouse. To the extent provided in regulations, an annuity shall be treated in a manner similar to an income interest in property (regardless of whether the property from which the annuity is payable can be separately identified).

(iii) Property includes interest therein The term "property" includes an interest in property.

(iv) Specific portion treated as separate property A specific portion of property shall be treated as separate property.

(v) Election An election under this paragraph with respect to any property shall be made by the executor on the return of tax imposed by section 2001. Such an election, once made, shall be irrevocable.

. . .

(d) Disallowance of marital deduction where surviving spouse not United States citizen

(1) In general

Except as provided in paragraph (2), if the surviving spouse of the decedent is not a citizen of the United States—

(A) no deduction shall be allowed under subsection (a), and

(B) section 2040 (b) shall not apply.

(2) Marital deduction allowed for certain transfers in trust

(A) In general

Paragraph (1) shall not apply to any property passing to the surviving spouse in a qualified domestic trust.

26 U.S.C. §2056A. Qualified domestic trust

(a) Qualified domestic trust defined

For purposes of this section and section 2056 (d), the term "qualified domestic trust" means, with respect to any decedent, any trust if—

(1) the trust instrument—

> (A) except as provided in regulations prescribed by the Secretary, requires that at least 1 trustee of the trust be an individual citizen of the United States or a domestic corporation, and
>
> (B) provides that no distribution (other than a distribution of income) may be made from the trust unless a trustee who is an individual citizen of the United States or a domestic corporation has the right to withhold from such distribution the tax imposed by this section on such distribution,

(2) such trust meets such requirements as the Secretary may by regulations prescribe to ensure the collection of any tax imposed by subsection (b), and

(3) an election under this section by the executor of the decedent applies to such trust.

...

Selected Federal Gift Tax Statutes

26 U.S.C. §2501. Imposition of Tax

(a) Taxable transfers

(1) General rule

A tax, computed as provided in section 2502, is hereby imposed for each calendar year on the transfer of property by gift during such calendar year by any individual resident or nonresident.

...

26 U.S.C. §2503. Taxable Gifts

(a) General definition

The term "taxable gifts" means the total amount of gifts made during the calendar year, less the deductions provided in subchapter C (section 2522 and following).

(b) **Exclusions from gifts**

   (1) **In general**
   In the case of gifts (other than gifts of future interests in property) made to any person by the donor during the calendar year, the first $10,000 of such gifts to such person shall not, for purposes of subsection (a), be included in the total amount of gifts made during such year. Where there has been a transfer to any person of a present interest in property, the possibility that such interest may be diminished by the exercise of a power shall be disregarded in applying this subsection, if no part of such interest will at any time pass to any other person.

   (2) **Inflation adjustment**
   In the case of gifts made in a calendar year after 1998, the $10,000 amount contained in paragraph (1) shall be increased by an amount equal to—
      (A) $10,000, multiplied by
      (B) the cost-of-living adjustment determined under section 1 (f)(3) for such calendar year by substituting "calendar year 1997" for "calendar year 1992" in subparagraph (B) thereof.
   If any amount as adjusted under the preceding sentence is not a multiple of $1,000, such amount shall be rounded to the next lowest multiple of $1,000.

(c) **Transfer for the benefit of minor**

No part of a gift to an individual who has not attained the age of 21 years on the date of such transfer shall be considered a gift of a future interest in property for purposes of subsection (b) if the property and the income therefrom—

   (1) may be expended by, or for the benefit of, the donee before his attaining the age of 21 years, and
   (2) will to the extent not so expended—
      (A) pass to the donee on his attaining the age of 21 years, and
      (B) in the event the donee dies before attaining the age of 21 years, be payable to the estate of the donee or as he may appoint under a general power of appointment as defined in section 2514 (c).

...

(e) **Exclusion for certain transfers for educational expenses or medical expenses**

   (1) **In general**

Any qualified transfer shall not be treated as a transfer of property by gift for purposes of this chapter.

(2) **Qualified transfer**

For purposes of this subsection, the term "qualified transfer" means any amount paid on behalf of an individual—

> (A) as tuition to an educational organization described in section 170 (b)(1)(A)(ii) for the education or training of such individual, or
>
> (B) to any person who provides medical care (as defined in section 213 (d)) with respect to such individual as payment for such medical care.

...

26 U.S.C. § 2505. Unified credit against gift tax.

(a) **General rule**

In the case of a citizen or resident of the United States, there shall be allowed as a credit against the tax imposed by section 2501 for each calendar year an amount equal to—

> (1) the amount of the tentative tax which would be determined under the rate schedule set forth in section 2502 (a)(2) if the amount with respect to which such tentative tax is to be computed were $1,000,000, reduced by
>
> (2) the sum of the amounts allowable as a credit to the individual under this section for all preceding calendar periods.

...

26 U.S.C. § 2511. Transfers in general.

(a) **Scope**

Subject to the limitations contained in this chapter, the tax imposed by section 2501 shall apply whether the transfer is in trust or otherwise, whether the gift is direct or indirect, and whether the property is real or personal, tangible or intangible; but in the case of a nonresident not a citizen of the United States, shall apply to a transfer only if the property is situated within the United States.

(b) **Intangible property**

For purposes of this chapter, in the case of a nonresident not a citizen of the United States who is excepted from the application of section 2501 (a)(2)—

(1) shares of stock issued by a domestic corporation, and

(2) debt obligations of—

(A) a United States person, or

(B) the United States, a State or any political subdivision thereof, or the District of Columbia,

which are owned and held by such nonresident shall be deemed to be property situated within the United States.

(c) Treatment of certain transfers in trust

Notwithstanding any other provision of this section and except as provided in regulations, a transfer in trust shall be treated as a transfer of property by gift, unless the trust is treated as wholly owned by the donor or the donor's spouse under subpart E of part I of subchapter J of chapter 1.

26 U.S.C. §2513. Gifts by husband or wife to third party.

(a) Considered as made one-half by each

(1) In general

A gift made by one spouse to any person other than his spouse shall, for the purposes of this chapter, be considered as made one-half by him and one-half by his spouse, but only if at the time of the gift each spouse is a citizen or resident of the United States. This paragraph shall not apply with respect to a gift by a spouse of an interest in property if he creates in his spouse a general power of appointment, as defined in section 2514 (c), over such interest. For purposes of this section, an individual shall be considered as the spouse of another individual only if he is married to such individual at the time of the gift and does not remarry during the remainder of the calendar year.

(2) Consent of both spouses

Paragraph (1) shall apply only if both spouses have signified (under the regulations provided for in subsection (b)) their consent to the application of paragraph (1) in the case of all such gifts made during the calendar year by either while married to the other.

(b) Manner and time of signifying consent

(1) Manner

A consent under this section shall be signified in such manner as is provided under regulations prescribed by the Secretary.

(2) Time

Such consent may be so signified at any time after the close of the calendar year in which the gift was made, subject to the following limitations—

(A) The consent may not be signified after the 15th day of April following the close of such year, unless before such 15th day no return has been filed for such year by either spouse, in which case the consent may not be signified after a return for such year is filed by either spouse.

(B) The consent may not be signified after a notice of deficiency with respect to the tax for such year has been sent to either spouse in accordance with section 6212 (a).

(c) **Revocation of consent**

Revocation of a consent previously signified shall be made in such manner as in provided under regulations prescribed by the Secretary, but the right to revoke a consent previously signified with respect to a calendar year—

(1) shall not exist after the 15th day of April following the close of such year if the consent was signified on or before such 15th day; and

(2) shall not exist if the consent was not signified until after such 15th day.

(d) **Joint and several liability for tax**

If the consent required by subsection (a)(2) is signified with respect to a gift made in any calendar year, the liability with respect to the entire tax imposed by this chapter of each spouse for such year shall be joint and several.

26 U.S.C. §2514. Powers of Appointment.

. . .

(b) **Powers created after October 21, 1942**

The exercise or release of a general power of appointment created after October 21, 1942, shall be deemed a transfer of property by the individual possessing such power.

(c) **Definition of general power of appointment**

For purposes of this section, the term "general power of appointment" means a power which is exercisable in favor of the individual possessing the power (hereafter in this subsection referred to as the "possessor"), his estate, his creditors, or the creditors of his estate; except that—

(1) A power to consume, invade, or appropriate property for the benefit of the possessor which is limited by an ascertainable standard re-

lating to the health, education, support, or maintenance of the possessor shall not be deemed a general power of appointment.

(2) A power of appointment created on or before October 21, 1942, which is exercisable by the possessor only in conjunction with another person shall not be deemed a general power of appointment.

(3) In the case of a power of appointment created after October 21, 1942, which is exercisable by the possessor only in conjunction with another person—

  (A) if the power is not exercisable by the possessor except in conjunction with the creator of the power—such power shall not be deemed a general power of appointment;

  (B) if the power is not exercisable by the possessor except in conjunction with a person having a substantial interest, in the property subject to the power, which is adverse to exercise of the power in favor of the possessor—such power shall not be deemed a general power of appointment. For the purposes of this subparagraph a person who, after the death of the possessor, may be possessed of a power of appointment (with respect to the property subject to the possessor's power) which he may exercise in his own favor shall be deemed as having an interest in the property and such interest shall be deemed adverse to such exercise of the possessor's power;

  (C) if (after the application of subparagraphs (A) and (B)) the power is a general power of appointment and is exercisable in favor of such other person—such power shall be deemed a general power of appointment only in respect of a fractional part of the property subject to such power, such part to be determined by dividing the value of such property by the number of such persons (including the possessor) in favor of whom such power is exercisable.

For purposes of subparagraphs (B) and (C), a power shall be deemed to be exercisable in favor of a person if it is exercisable in favor of such person, his estate, his creditors, or the creditors of his estate.

...

(e) **Lapse of power**

The lapse of a power of appointment created after October 21, 1942, during the life of the individual possessing the power shall be considered a release of such power. The rule of the preceding sentence shall apply with respect to the lapse of powers during any calendar year only to the extent that the property which could have been appointed by exercise of such lapsed powers exceeds in value the greater of the following amounts:

(1) $5,000, or

(2) 5 percent of the aggregate value of the assets out of which, or the proceeds of which, the exercise of the lapsed powers could be satisfied.

. . .

26 U.S.C. § 2518. Disclaimers.

(a) **General rule**

For purposes of this subtitle, if a person makes a qualified disclaimer with respect to any interest in property, this subtitle shall apply with respect to such interest as if the interest had never been transferred to such person.

(b) **Qualified disclaimer defined**

For purposes of subsection (a), the term "qualified disclaimer" means an irrevocable and unqualified refusal by a person to accept an interest in property but only if—

   (1) such refusal is in writing,

   (2) such writing is received by the transferor of the interest, his legal representative, or the holder of the legal title to the property to which the interest relates not later than the date which is 9 months after the later of—

      (A) the day on which the transfer creating the interest in such person is made, or

      (B) the day on which such person attains age 21,

   (3) such person has not accepted the interest or any of its benefits, and

   (4) as a result of such refusal, the interest passes without any direction on the part of the person making the disclaimer and passes either—

      (A) to the spouse of the decedent, or

      (B) to a person other than the person making the disclaimer.

(c) **Other rules**

For purposes of subsection (a)—

   (1) **Disclaimer of undivided portion of interest**
      A disclaimer with respect to an undivided portion of an interest which meets the requirements of the preceding sentence shall be treated as a qualified disclaimer of such portion of the interest.

   (2) **Powers**
   A power with respect to property shall be treated as an interest in such property.

   (3) **Certain transfers treated as disclaimers**

A written transfer of the transferor's entire interest in the property—
  (A) which meets requirements similar to the requirements of paragraphs (2) and (3) of subsection (b), and
  (B) which is to a person or persons who would have received the property had the transferor made a qualified disclaimer (within the meaning of subsection (b)),
  shall be treated as a qualified disclaimer.

26 U.S.C. §2522. Charitable and similar gifts.

(a) Citizens or residents

In computing taxable gifts for the calendar year, there shall be allowed as a deduction in the case of a citizen or resident the amount of all gifts made during such year to or for the use of—

  (1) the United States, any State, or any political subdivision thereof, or the District of Columbia, for exclusively public purposes;
  (2) a corporation, or trust, or community chest, fund, or foundation, organized and operated exclusively for religious, charitable, scientific, literary, or educational purposes, or to foster national or international amateur sports competition (but only if no part of its activities involve the provision of athletic facilities or equipment), including the encouragement of art and the prevention of cruelty to children or animals, no part of the net earnings of which inures to the benefit of any private shareholder or individual, which is not disqualified for tax exemption under section 501 (c)(3) by reason of attempting to influence legislation, and which does not participate in, or intervene in (including the publishing or distributing of statements), any political campaign on behalf of (or in opposition to) any candidate for public office;
  (3) a fraternal society, order, or association, operating under the lodge system, but only if such gifts are to be used exclusively for religious, charitable, scientific, literary, or educational purposes, including the encouragement of art and the prevention of cruelty to children or animals;
  (4) posts or organizations of war veterans, or auxiliary units or societies of any such posts or organizations, if such posts, organizations, units, or societies are organized in the United States or any of its possessions, and if no part of their net earnings insures to the benefit of any private shareholder or individual.

...

(c) Disallowance of deductions in certain cases

...

(5) Contributions to donor advised funds

A deduction otherwise allowed under subsection (a) for any contribution to a donor advised fund (as defined in section 4966 (d)(2)) shall only be allowed if—

(A) the sponsoring organization (as defined in section 4966 (d)(1)) with respect to such donor advised fund is not—

(i) described in paragraph (3) or (4) of subsection (a), or

(ii) a type III supporting organization (as defined in section 4943 (f)(5)(A)) which is not a functionally integrated type III supporting organization (as defined in section 4943 (f)(5)(B)), and

(B) the taxpayer obtains a contemporaneous written acknowledgment (determined under rules similar to the rules of section 170 (f)(8)(C)) from the sponsoring organization (as so defined) of such donor advised fund that such organization has exclusive legal control over the assets contributed.

...

26 U.S.C. § 2522. Gifts to spouse.

(a) Allowance of deduction

Where a donor transfers during the calendar year by gift an interest in property to a donee who at the time of the gift is the donor's spouse, there shall be allowed as a deduction in computing taxable gifts for the calendar year an amount with respect to such interest equal to its value.

...

Selected Federal Medicaid Statute

26 U.S.C. § 1396p. Liens, adjustments and recoveries, and transfers of assets.

(a) Imposition of lien against property of an individual on account of medical assistance rendered to him under a State plan

(1) No lien may be imposed against the property of any individual prior to his death on account of medical assistance paid or to be paid on his behalf under the State plan, except—

(A) pursuant to the judgment of a court on account of benefits incorrectly paid on behalf of such individual, or

(B) in the case of the real property of an individual—

> (i) who is an inpatient in a nursing facility, intermediate care facility for the mentally retarded, or other medical institution, if such individual is required, as a condition of receiving services in such institution under the State plan, to spend for costs of medical care all but a minimal amount of his income required for personal needs, and

> (ii) with respect to whom the State determines, after notice and opportunity for a hearing (in accordance with procedures established by the State), that he cannot reasonably be expected to be discharged from the medical institution and to return home, except as provided in paragraph (2).

(2) No lien may be imposed under paragraph (1)(B) on such individual's home if—

(A) the spouse of such individual,

(B) such individual's child who is under age 21, or (with respect to States eligible to participate in the State program established under subchapter XVI of this chapter) is blind or permanently and totally disabled, or (with respect to States which are not eligible to participate in such program) is blind or disabled as defined in section 1382c of this title, or

(C) a sibling of such individual (who has an equity interest in such home and who was residing in such individual's home for a period of at least one year immediately before the date of the individual's admission to the medical institution), is lawfully residing in such home.

(3) Any lien imposed with respect to an individual pursuant to paragraph (1)(B) shall dissolve upon that individual's discharge from the medical institution and return home.

(b) **Adjustment or recovery of medical assistance correctly paid under a State plan**

(1) No adjustment or recovery of any medical assistance correctly paid on behalf of an individual under the State plan may be made, except that the State shall seek adjustment or recovery of any medical assistance correctly paid on behalf of an individual under the State plan in the case of the following individuals:

(A) In the case of an individual described in subsection (a)(1)(B) of this section, the State shall seek adjustment or recovery from the individual's estate or upon sale of the property subject to a lien imposed on account of medical assistance paid on behalf of the individual.

(B) In the case of an individual who was 55 years of age or older when the individual received such medical assistance, the State shall seek adjustment or recovery from the individual's estate, but only for medical assistance consisting of—

    (i) nursing facility services, home and community-based services, and related hospital and prescription drug services, or

    (ii) at the option of the State, any items or services under the State plan (but not including medical assistance for medicare cost-sharing or for benefits described in section 1396a (a)(10)(E) of this title).

…

(2) Any adjustment or recovery under paragraph (1) may be made only after the death of the individual's surviving spouse, if any, and only at a time—

(A) when he has no surviving child who is under age 21, or (with respect to States eligible to participate in the State program established under subchapter XVI of this chapter) is blind or permanently and totally disabled, or (with respect to States which are not eligible to participate in such program) is blind or disabled as defined in section 1382c of this title; and

(B) in the case of a lien on an individual's home under subsection (a)(1)(B) of this section, when—

    (i) no sibling of the individual (who was residing in the individual's home for a period of at least one year immediately before the date of the individual's admission to the medical institution), and

    (ii) no son or daughter of the individual (who was residing in the individual's home for a period of at least two years immediately before the date of the individual's admission to the medical institution, and who establishes to the satisfaction of the State that he or she provided care to such individual which permitted such individual to reside at home rather than in an institution),

is lawfully residing in such home who has lawfully resided in such home on a continuous basis since the date of the individual's admission to the medical institution.

…

(c) **Taking into account certain transfers of assets**

(1)

(A) In order to meet the requirements of this subsection for purposes of section 1396a (a)(18) of this title, the State plan must provide that if an institutionalized individual or the spouse of such an individual (or, at the option of a State, a noninstitutionalized individual or the spouse of such an individual) disposes of assets for less than fair market value on or after the look-back date specified in subparagraph (B)(i), the individual is ineligible for medical assistance for services described in subparagraph (C)(i) (or, in the case of a noninstitutionalized individual, for the services described in subparagraph (C)(ii)) during the period beginning on the date specified in subparagraph (D) and equal to the number of months specified in subparagraph (E).

(B)

(i) The look-back date specified in this subparagraph is a date that is 36 months (or, in the case of payments from a trust or portions of a trust that are treated as assets disposed of by the individual pursuant to paragraph (3)(A)(iii) or (3)(B)(ii) of subsection (d) of this section or in the case of any other disposal of assets made on or after February 8, 2006, 60 months) before the date specified in clause (ii).

(ii) The date specified in this clause, with respect to—

(I) an institutionalized individual is the first date as of which the individual both is an institutionalized individual and has applied for medical assistance under the State plan, or

(II) a noninstitutionalized individual is the date on which the individual applies for medical assistance under the State plan or, if later, the date on which the individual disposes of assets for less than fair market value.

(C)

(i) The services described in this subparagraph with respect to an institutionalized individual are the following:

(I) Nursing facility services.

(II) A level of care in any institution equivalent to that of nursing facility services.

(III) Home or community-based services furnished under a waiver granted under subsection (c) or (d) of section 1396n of this title.

(ii) The services described in this subparagraph with respect to a noninstitutionalized individual are services (not including any services described in clause (i)) that are described in paragraph (7), (22), or (24) of section 1396d (a) of this title, and, at the option of a State, other long-term care services for which medical assistance is otherwise available under the State plan to individuals requiring long-term care.

(D)

(i) In the case of a transfer of asset made before February 8, 2006, the date specified in this subparagraph is the first day of the first month during or after which assets have been transferred for less than fair market value and which does not occur in any other periods of ineligibility under this subsection.

(ii) In the case of a transfer of asset made on or after February 8, 2006, the date specified in this subparagraph is the first day of a month during or after which assets have been transferred for less than fair market value, or the date on which the individual is eligible for medical assistance under the State plan and would otherwise be receiving institutional level care described in subparagraph (C) based on an approved application for such care but for the application of the penalty period, whichever is later, and which does not occur during any other period of ineligibility under this subsection.

(E)

(i) With respect to an institutionalized individual, the number of months of ineligibility under this subparagraph for an individual shall be equal to—

(I) the total, cumulative uncompensated value of all assets transferred by the individual (or individual's spouse) on or after the look-back date specified in subparagraph (B)(i), divided by

(II) the average monthly cost to a private patient of nursing facility services in the State (or, at the option of the State, in the community in which the individual is institutionalized) at the time of application.

(ii) With respect to a noninstitutionalized individual, the number of months of ineligibility under this subparagraph for an individual shall not be greater than a number equal to—

(I) the total, cumulative uncompensated value of all assets transferred by the individual (or individual's spouse) on or after the look-back date specified in subparagraph (B)(i), divided by

(II) the average monthly cost to a private patient of nursing facility services in the State (or, at the option of the State, in the community in which the individual is institutionalized) at the time of application.

(iii) The number of months of ineligibility otherwise determined under clause (i) or (ii) with respect to the disposal of an asset shall be reduced—

(I) in the case of periods of ineligibility determined under clause (i), by the number of months of ineligibility applicable to the individual under clause (ii) as a result of such disposal, and

(II) in the case of periods of ineligibility determined under clause (ii), by the number of months of ineligibility applicable to the individual under clause (i) as a result of such disposal.

(iv) A State shall not round down, or otherwise disregard any fractional period of ineligibility determined under clause (i) or (ii) with respect to the disposal of assets.

...

(d) Treatment of trust amounts

(1) For purposes of determining an individual's eligibility for, or amount of, benefits under a State plan under this subchapter, subject to paragraph (4), the rules specified in paragraph (3) shall apply to a trust established by such individual.

(2)

(A) For purposes of this subsection, an individual shall be considered to have established a trust if assets of the individual were used to form all or part of the corpus of the trust and if any of the following individuals established such trust other than by will:

(i) The individual.

(ii) The individual's spouse.

(iii) A person, including a court or administrative body, with legal authority to act in place of or on behalf of the individual or the individual's spouse.

(iv) A person, including any court or administrative body, acting at the direction or upon the request of the individual or the individual's spouse.

(B) In the case of a trust the corpus of which includes assets of an individual (as determined under subparagraph (A)) and assets of any other person or persons, the provisions of this subsection shall apply to the portion of the trust attributable to the assets of the individual.

(C) Subject to paragraph (4), this subsection shall apply without regard to—

(i) the purposes for which a trust is established,

(ii) whether the trustees have or exercise any discretion under the trust,

(iii) any restrictions on when or whether distributions may be made from the trust, or

(iv) any restrictions on the use of distributions from the trust.

(3)

(A) In the case of a revocable trust—

(i) the corpus of the trust shall be considered resources available to the individual,

(ii) payments from the trust to or for the benefit of the individual shall be considered income of the individual, and

(iii) any other payments from the trust shall be considered assets disposed of by the individual for purposes of subsection (c) of this section.

(B) In the case of an irrevocable trust—

(i) if there are any circumstances under which payment from the trust could be made to or for the benefit of the individual, the portion of the corpus from which, or the income on the corpus from which, payment to the individual could be made shall be considered resources available to the individual, and payments from that portion of the corpus or income—

(I) to or for the benefit of the individual, shall be considered income of the individual, and

(II) for any other purpose, shall be considered a transfer of assets by the individual subject to subsection (c) of this section; and

(ii) any portion of the trust from which, or any income on the corpus from which, no payment could under any circumstances be made to the individual shall be considered, as of the date of establishment of the trust (or, if later, the date on which payment to the individual was foreclosed) to be assets disposed by the individual for purposes of subsection (c) of this section, and the value of the trust shall be determined for purposes of such subsection by including the amount of any payments made from such portion of the trust after such date.

(4) This subsection shall not apply to any of the following trusts:

(A) A trust containing the assets of an individual under age 65 who is disabled (as defined in section 1382c (a)(3) of this title) and which is established for the benefit of such individual by a parent, grandparent, legal guardian of the individual, or a court if the State will receive all amounts remaining in the trust upon the death of such individual up to an amount equal to the total medical assistance paid on behalf of the individual under a State plan under this subchapter.

(B) A trust established in a State for the benefit of an individual if—

(i) the trust is composed only of pension, Social Security, and other income to the individual (and accumulated income in the trust),

(ii) the State will receive all amounts remaining in the trust upon the death of such individual up to an amount equal to the total medical assistance paid on behalf of the individual under a State plan under this subchapter; and

(iii) the State makes medical assistance available to individuals described in section 1396a (a)(10)(A)(ii)(V) of this title, but does not make such assistance available to individuals for nursing facility services under section 1396a (a)(10)(C) of this title.

(C) A trust containing the assets of an individual who is disabled (as defined in section 1382c (a)(3) of this title) that meets the following conditions:

(i) The trust is established and managed by a non-profit association.

(ii) A separate account is maintained for each beneficiary of the trust, but, for purposes of investment and management of funds, the trust pools these accounts.

(iii) Accounts in the trust are established solely for the benefit of individuals who are disabled (as defined in section 1382c (a)(3) of this title) by the parent, grandparent, or legal guardian of such individuals, by such individuals, or by a court.

(iv) To the extent that amounts remaining in the beneficiary's account upon the death of the beneficiary are not retained by the trust, the trust pays to the State from such remaining amounts in the account an amount equal to the total amount of medical assistance paid on behalf of the beneficiary under the State plan under this subchapter.

(5) The State agency shall establish procedures (in accordance with standards specified by the Secretary) under which the agency waives the application of this subsection with respect to an individual if the individual establishes that such application would work an undue hardship on the individual as determined on the basis of criteria established by the Secretary.

(6) The term "trust" includes any legal instrument or device that is similar to a trust but includes an annuity only to such extent and in such manner as the Secretary specifies.

...

(f) **Disqualification for long-term care assistance for individuals with substantial home equity**

(1)

(A) Notwithstanding any other provision of this subchapter, subject to subparagraphs (B) and (C) of this paragraph and paragraph (2), in determining eligibility of an individual for medical assistance with respect to nursing facility services or other long-term care services, the individual shall not be eligible for such assistance if the individual's equity interest in the individual's home exceeds $500,000.

(B) A State may elect, without regard to the requirements of section 1396a (a)(1) of this title (relating to statewideness) and section 1396a (a)(10)(B) of this title (relating to comparability), to apply subparagraph (A) by substituting for "$500,000", an amount that exceeds such amount, but does not exceed $750,000.

(C) The dollar amounts specified in this paragraph shall be increased, beginning with 2011, from year to year based on the percentage increase in the consumer price index for all urban consumers (all items; United States city average), rounded to the nearest $1,000.

(2) Paragraph (1) shall not apply with respect to an individual if—

(A) the spouse of such individual, or

(B) such individual's child who is under age 21, or (with respect to States eligible to participate in the State program established under subchapter XVI) is blind or permanently and totally disabled, or (with respect to States which are not eligible to participate in such program) is blind or disabled as defined in section 1382c of this title, is lawfully residing in the individual's home.

(3) Nothing in this subsection shall be construed as preventing an individual from using a reverse mortgage or home equity loan to reduce the individual's total equity interest in the home.

(4) The Secretary shall establish a process whereby paragraph (1) is waived in the case of a demonstrated hardship.

...

INDEX